WEST WYANDOTTE
KANSAS CITY KANSAS
PUBLIC LIBRARY
DATE:

MAR 9 2009
KIA

D0024986

The Ottoman Empire

Recent Titles in
Greenwood Guides to Historic Events, 1500–1900

The Second Great Awakening and the Transcendentalists
Barry Hankins

The Age of Napoleon
Susan P. Conner

The American Civil War
Cole C. Kingseed

The Scientific Revolution and the Foundations of Modern Science
Wilbur Applebaum

The Mexican War
David S. Heidler and Jeanne T. Heidler

The Abolitionist Movement
Claudine L. Ferrell

Maritime Exploration in the Age of Discovery, 1415–1800
Ronald S. Love

The Trail of Tears and Indian Removal
Amy H. Sturgis

Darwin's *The Origin of Species*
Keith Francis

The Age of Romanticism
Joanne Schneider

The Reformation Era
Robert D. Linder

Slave Revolts
Johannes Postma

The Ottoman Empire

MEHRDAD KIA

Greenwood Guides to Historic Events, 1500–1900
Linda S. Frey and Marsha L. Frey, Series Editors

GREENWOOD PRESS
Westport, Connecticut • London

Library of Congress Cataloging-in-Publication Data

Kia, Mehrdad.
  The Ottoman Empire / Mehrdad Kia.
    p. cm.—(Greenwood guides to historic events, 1500–1900, ISSN 1538-442X)
  Includes bibliographical references and index.
  ISBN 978-0-313-34440-4 (alk. paper)
  1. Turkey—History—Ottoman Empire, 1288–1918. I. Title.
DR485.K53   2008
956'.015—dc22   2008024123

British Library Cataloguing in Publication Data is available.

Copyright © 2008 by Mehrdad Kia

All rights reserved. No portion of this book may be
reproduced, by any process or technique, without the
express written consent of the publisher.

Library of Congress Catalog Card Number: 2008024123
ISBN: 978-0-313-34440-4
ISSN: 1538-442X

First published in 2008

Greenwood Press, 88 Post Road West, Westport, CT 06881
An imprint of Greenwood Publishing Group, Inc.
www.greenwood.com

Printed in the United States of America

The paper used in this book complies with the
Permanent Paper Standard issued by the National
Information Standards Organization (Z39.48–1984).

10 9 8 7 6 5 4 3 2 1

Every reasonable effort has been made to trace the owners of copyrighted materials in this book,
but in some instances this has proven impossible. The author and publisher will be glad to
receive information leading to more complete acknowledgments in subsequent printings of the
book and in the meantime extend their apologies for any omissions.

This book is dedicated to my father, Dr. Sadeq Kia, my mother, Kiadokht Kia, my brother, Dr. Ardeshir Kia, and my best friend, Cameron Kia Weix for their unlimited love and support

CONTENTS

Photographs follow page 154.

SERIES FOREWORD

American statesman Adlai Stevenson stated, "We can chart our future clearly and wisely only when we know the path which has led to the present." This series, Greenwood Guides to Historic Events, 1500–1900, is designed to illuminate that path by focusing on events from 1500 to 1900 that have shaped the world. The years 1500 to 1900 include what historians call the early modern period (1500 to 1789, the onset of the French Revolution) and part of the modern period (1789 to 1900).

In 1500, an acceleration of key trends marked the beginnings of an interdependent world and the posing of seminal questions that changed the nature and terms of intellectual debate. The series closes with 1900, the inauguration of the twentieth century. This period witnessed profound economic, social, political, cultural, religious, and military changes. An industrial and technological revolution transformed the modes of production, marked the transition from a rural to an urban economy, and ultimately raised the standard of living. Social classes and distinctions shifted. The emergence of the territorial and later the national state altered man's relations with and view of political authority. The shattering of the religious unity of the Roman Catholic world in Europe marked the rise of a new pluralism. Military revolutions changed the nature of warfare. The books in this series emphasize the complexity and diversity of the human tapestry and include political, economic, social, intellectual, military, and cultural topics. Some of the authors focus on events in U.S. history such as the Salem witchcraft trials, the American Revolution, the abolitionist movement, and the Civil War. Others analyze European topics, such as the Reformation and Counter-Reformation and the French Revolution. Still others bridge cultures and continents by examining the voyages of discovery, the Atlantic slave trade, and the Age of Imperialism. Some focus on intellectual questions that have shaped the modern world, such as Charles Darwin's *Origin of Species*, or on turning points such as the Age of Romanticism. Others examine defining economic, religious, or legal events or issues such as the building of the railroads, the Second Great Awakening, and abolitionism. Heroes (e.g., Meriwether Lewis and William Clark), scientists (e.g., Darwin), military leaders (e.g., Napoleon Bonaparte), poets (e.g., Lord Byron) stride across the pages. Many of these events were seminal in that they marked profound changes or turning points. The Scientific Revolution, for example, changed the way individuals viewed themselves and their world.

The authors, acknowledged experts in their fields, synthesize key events, set developments within the larger historical context, and, most important, present well-balanced, well-written accounts that integrate the most recent scholarship in the field.

The topics were chosen by an advisory board composed of historians, high school history teachers, and school librarians to support the curriculum and meet student research needs. The volumes are designed to serve as resources for student research and to provide clearly written interpretations of topics central to the secondary school and lower-level undergraduate history curriculum. Each author outlines a basic chronology to guide the reader through often-confusing events and presents a historical overview to set those events within a narrative framework. Three to five topical chapters underscore critical aspects of the event. In the final chapter the author examines the impact and consequences of the event. Biographical sketches furnish background on the lives and contributions of the players who strut across the stage. Ten to fifteen primary documents, ranging from letters to diary entries, song lyrics, proclamations, and posters, cast light on the event, provide material for student essays, and stimulate critical engagement with the sources. Introductions identify the authors of the documents and the main issues. In some cases a glossary of selected terms is provided as a guide to the reader. Each work contains an annotated bibliography of recommended books, articles, CD-ROMs, Internet sites, videos, and films that set the materials within the historical debate.

Reading these works can lead to a more sophisticated understanding of the events and debates that have shaped the modern world and can stimulate a more active engagement with the issues that still affect us. It has been a particularly enriching experience to work closely with such dedicated professionals. We have come to know and value even more highly the authors in this series and our editors at Greenwood, particularly Kevin Ohe and Michael Hermann. In many cases they have become more than colleagues; they have become friends. To them and to future historians we dedicate this series.

Linda S. Frey
University of Montana

Marsha L. Frey
Kansas State University

PREFACE

This book is intended as an introductory survey of the political history of the Ottoman state from the last decade of the thirteenth century to the proclamation of the Republic of Turkey in 1923. The Ottoman state expanded from its original home in the district of Söğüt in western Anatolia to incorporate vast territories and to rule other peoples. Each territorial acquisition resulted in the absorption and incorporation of native communities who contributed to the empire's economic power and cultural richness. Indeed, throughout much of its history, the Ottoman Empire remained a mosaic of ethnic, linguistic, and religious groups. Each group possessed its own history, culture, language, religious customs, and traditions. Aside from the Turks, there were Hungarians, Serbs, Bosnians, Montenegrins, Albanians, Greeks, Bulgarians, Romanians, Tatars, Jews, Kurds, Arabs, Armenians, and many others who were allowed to preserve their unique religious beliefs and cultural practices. No account of the Ottoman Empire can, therefore, claim to be comprehensive unless it covers the history of all the peoples and communities, who contributed to the growth and prosperity of this world power and its rich and diverse civilization.

Grasping and appreciating the complexities of this powerful empire also requires looking at the Ottoman world through Ottoman eyes. Such an approach necessitates a careful and in-depth study of Ottoman archives. The Ottomans were diligent record keepers who left a treasure house of documents behind. Non-Ottoman sources also exist, such as diplomatic and consular reports, as well as numerous books, essays, and articles by statesmen, diplomats, travelers, missionaries, and casual observers who wrote in many different languages on various aspects of the Ottoman state and society. These sources are valuable and indeed essential in studying the Ottoman Empire, although they frequently approach their subject with bias and prejudice, trying to denigrate and dismiss the accomplishments of a Muslim enemy, which at the height of its power ruled a vast empire from the gates of Vienna to the mouth of the Persian Gulf. The present narrative, however, is a far more humble enterprise; it makes no pretense of using original documents or offering bold new interpretations. It is designed as an introduction, providing the reader who does not have any prior knowledge or expertise on the subject with a brief and general overview of the political history of the Ottoman Empire.

Aside from the first chapter, which focuses on the institutions of the empire, the remaining seven chapters follow a chronological order. I have divided the history of the Ottoman Empire into several distinct periods. The first begins at the formation of the Ottoman state by the founder of the dynasty, Osman, in the last decade of the thirteenth century, and extends to the defeat of the fourth Ottoman sultan, Bayezid I, at the hands of the Central Asian world conqueror Timur in 1402, and the civil war that followed among the sons of the vanquished sultan. The second period begins with the resurgence of the Ottoman state in 1413 under Mehmed I and ends with the reign of Süleyman the Magnificent in 1566, which signaled the golden age of Ottoman power and civilization. The third period, which marked the beginning of the decline of Ottoman power, starts with the reign of Selim II (1566–1574) and ends with the reign of Murad IV (1623–1640). The fourth period, which witnessed the defeat of Ottoman armies at the hands of European states, focuses on a century and a half that began with the accession of Murad IV in 1623 and ended with the signing of the humiliating Treaty of Küçük Kaynarca with Russia in 1774. The fifth period, which begins with the reign of Selim III in 1789 and ends with the death of Mahmud II in 1839, witnessed the introduction of governmental reforms by the Ottoman state and the rise of the first nationalist movements among the empire's Christian European subjects. The sixth period, or the age of modern reforms, began with the reign of Sultan Abdülmecid in 1839 and culminated with the Young Turk revolution in 1908. The final chapter covers the period between 1908 and 1922, which ended with the collapse and dissolution of the Ottoman Empire after its defeat in the First World War.

ACKNOWLEDGMENTS

The idea for this book came from my friend and colleague, Professor Linda Frey of The University of Montana, who read the entire monograph several times and offered mountains of incisive suggestions and revisions. Without the patience, encouragement, and unlimited support from the general editors, Professor Linda Frey and Professor Marsha Frey, I would not have been able to complete this project. For generosity of time and spirit I owe a special debt of gratitude to Ardi Kia, Andrea Olsen, and Thomas Goltz, who provided me with assistance in the preparation of this book. I also thank Khaled Huthaily, Amal Huthaily, Adnan Misbahi, and Brian Lofink of the Central and Southwest Asia Program at The University of Montana for the many forms of technical assistance they provided toward putting the manuscript into final form. Finally, I thank my friends and colleagues, Rick and Susie Graetz of The University of Montana, for allowing me to use their beautiful photographs in this book. Needless to say, none of these colleagues bears responsibility for what I have written, but all of them have contributed significantly to the completion of this book. What I owe to my family for their love, patience, and support cannot be adequately expressed. This book is dedicated to them.

NOTE ON PRONUNCIATION, TRANSLITERATION, AND SPELLING

The multiplicity of languages used in the Ottoman Empire and the varieties of spelling that were adopted throughout centuries present a number of problems, making complete consistency impossible. With a few exceptions, I have used the modern Turkish spelling system. I have not, however, applied Turkish spellings and pronunciations to non-Turkish words. Thus, Sharif (Arabic) has not been spelled as Şerif (Turkish); likewise, Shah (Persian) has not been spelled as Şah (Turkish).

c (Turkish)   j (English)
ç (Turkish)   ch (English)
ö (Turkish)   ö (German)
ş (Turkish)   sh (English)
ü (Turkish)   ü (German)

CHRONOLOGY OF OTTOMAN HISTORY

1040	The Seljuk Empire is established in Iran.
1071	At the battle of Manzikert (Malazgird), the Seljuks defeat the Byzantine army.
1075–1308	Seljuk Sultanate of Anatolia.
1243	Mongols defeat the Seljuks of Rum at the battle of Kösedağ.
1258	Mongols sack the city of Baghdad, the seat of the Abbasid caliphate.
1290–1326	Osman, the founder of the Ottoman dynasty.
1326	Orhan, the son of Osman and the second Ottoman ruler, captures the Byzantine town of Bursa, declaring it the new Ottoman capital.
1329	Orhan's army defeats a Byzantine force under the leadership of the Emperor Andronicus III at the Battle of Pelekanon (Pelecanum) near Eskişehir.
1331	Orhan captures the town of Nicaea (Iznik).
1335	The end of the Mongol Il Khanid rule in Iran.
1337	Orhan captures the town of Nicomedia (Izmit).
1354	Orhan occupies Ankara and Gallipoli, thus establishing a foothold in Europe.
1361	Prince Murad captures the important Byzantine city of Adrianople (Edirne), declaring it the new Ottoman capital.

1362	With the death of Orhan, his son ascends the throne as Murad I.
1363–1365	Ottomans conquer Thrace and southern Bulgaria.
1371	Ottomans are victorious over Serbian forces at Chermanon.
1385	Sofia is captured. The Bulgarian king accepts Ottoman suzerainty.
1386	Niş (Nish) is captured.
1387	Thessaloniki (Salonica) is captured.
1388	A coalition of Bosnians, Serbs, and Bulgarians defeat the Ottomans at Plošnik (Ploshnik).
1389	At the Battle of Kosovo Polje (Field of Blackbirds), Ottoman forces defeat the combined forces of Serbia, Bosnia, and Albania led by the Serbian king, Lazar. Although Murad I is killed during the battle, the Ottoman victory brings Serbia under Ottoman rule. Bayezid I, known by his title *Yildirim* (Thunderbolt), son of Murad I, is declared sultan.
1390	Bayezid I expands Ottoman territory in Anatolia by defeating the Karamanids.
1395	Bayezid expands Ottoman territory into Wallachia (present day Romania).
1396	At the Battle of Nicopolis, Ottoman forces inflict a humiliating defeat on a European crusading army.
1402	At the Battle of Ankara, the Central Asian conqueror Timur defeats the Ottoman army and captures Sultan Bayezid, who dies in 1403.
1402–1413	Interregnum. The sons of Bayezid fight over the remains of their father's empire.
1413	Mehmed I ascends the Ottoman throne after defeating his brothers.
1421–1444	Murad II consolidates the territorial gains of Mehmed I.
1423–1430	Ottoman forces fight Venice for control of Thessaloniki (Salonica).

1425	Ottomans recapture the Turcoman Principalities of Menteşe and Teke in western Anatolia.
1439	Ottomans annex Serbia.
1443	Hungary invades the Balkans.
1444	At the Battle of Varna, Ottoman forces score an impressive victory against the Hungarians and their allies. Murad II abdicates after the battle, and his son, Mehmed II, replaces his father for two years. Murad returns to power in 1446.
1451	Mehmed II becomes the sultan for the second time.
1453	Mehmed II captures Constantinople and receives the title of *Fatih* (The Conqueror).
1456	Ottomans fail to capture Belgrade.
1459	Ottomans conquer Serbia.
1460	Conquest of Morea.
1461	Conquest of the Empire of Trebizond, an important commercial center on the Black Sea.
1463	Mehmed II conquers Bosnia.
1463–1479	Ottoman war with Venice.
1466	Mehmed II attacks Albania.
1468	Conquest of Karaman principality in southern Anatolia.
1473	At the Battle of Başkent, Mehmed II defeats Uzun Hasan, the leader of the Ak Koyunlu Turcomans, who ruled a significant part of Iran and eastern Anatolia.
1475	Crimea's Tatar Khan accepts Ottoman suzerainty. Genoese colonies in Crimea are conquered.
1480	Ottoman forces land at Otranto.
1481	Upon the death of Mehmed II, his son Bayezid II ascends the throne.
1484	War with Mamluks of Egypt, which continues until 1491.
1499	Ottomans wage war on Venice, which continues until 1503, conquering Lepanto, Coron, and Modon.
1512	Selim I succeeds his father, Bayezid II.

1514	Ottoman armies defeat the Iranian Safavid monarch, Ismail I, in the battle of Chaldiran northeast of Lake Van. Tabriz is occupied before Selim I is forced by his *janissary* corps to withdraw.
1516–1517	Ottoman forces capture Diyarbakir and incorporate the Dulkadir/Dulgadir principality in eastern Anatolia before defeating the Mamluk armies of Egypt at Marc Dâbik/Marj Dâbiq. Selim I captures Syria and Egypt. Mecca, Medina, and Jerusalem fall under Ottoman rule, and the sultan claims the title of the protector of the holy sites of Islam.
1520–1566	The reign of Süleyman, known to Europeans as Süleyman the Magnificent and by his subjects as Süleyman *Kânuni* or the Lawgiver, brings the Ottoman state to the zenith of its power.
1521	Süleyman captures the strategic fortress of Belgrade and opens the road to Hungary.
1522	Siege of Rhodes, the last bastion of the European crusades, which surrenders to the Ottomans in January 1523.
1526	Ottoman victory at the battle of Mohács and the death of the Hungarian king makes Hungary a vassal state.
1529	The first siege of Vienna.
1533	Hayreddin Paşa (Barbarossa or Barbaros) captures Tunis in North Africa.
1533–1534	Süleyman invades Iran. Tabriz and Baghdad are captured by Ottoman forces.
1535	Tabriz is recaptured by Süleyman.
1537	War with Venice, which continues until 1540.
1548	Süleyman invades Iran.
1553–1555	War with Iran, Peace Treaty of Amasya between Ottoman Empire and Safavid Iran.
1565	Siege of Malta.
1566	Selim II succeeds his father, Sultan Süleyman.
1567–1570	Conquest of Yemen.

1569	France is granted capitulations. Ottoman siege of Astrakhan.
1570	Ottomans capture Tunis.
1571	The conquest of the island of Cyprus is completed. At the Battle of Lepanto, the Ottoman navy suffers a defeat at the hands of the Holy League, the combined naval forces of Europe's Christian powers led by Don Juan.
1573	Peace with Venice.
1574	Ottomans recapture Tunis. Murad III becomes sultan.
1578	Morocco comes under Ottoman protection. Murad III uses the chaos following the death of the Safavid monarch, Shah Tahmasp, to invade Iran.
1579–1587	Ottoman control over the Caucasus, which was challenged by Safavids and their Georgian allies, is restored.
1580	Capitulations granted to English merchants.
1589	*Janissaries* revolt in Istanbul.
1592–1606	War with the Habsburgs.
1595–1603	Mehmed III.
1596–1609	*Celali* revolts erupt in Anatolia.
1603–1617	Ahmed I.
1603	War with Iran begins and continues until 1618.
1606	Peace of Zsitvatorok (Zsitva-Torok) with the Habsburgs.
1609	Suppression of the *Celali* revolts in Anatolia.
1617	Ahmed's brother Mustafa I ascends the Ottoman throne.
1618	Mustafa I is deposed. Osman II is declared the new sultan. Ottoman Empire and Iran sign a peace treaty, and Ottoman forces withdraw from Azerbaijan.
1621	Ottoman forces invade Poland.
1622	*Janissaries* revolt. Osman II is dethroned and later murdered. Mustafa I is restored to the throne.

1623	Abaza Mehmed Paşa's revolt begins in Anatolia. Mustafa I is dethroned and replaced by Murad IV.
1624	The Iranian Safavid monarch, Shah Abbas, invades Iraq. Abaza Mehmed Paşa's rebel army is defeated.
1626	The second revolt of Abaza Mehmed in Anatolia.
1628	Surrender of Abaza Mehmed Paşa.
1629	Ottoman campaign to recapture Baghdad from Iran.
1630	Ottoman victory in Iran. The Ottomans fail to capture Baghdad.
1633	Repulsion of Iranian forces attacking Van in eastern Anatolia.
1635	Murad IV invades Iran and captures Erivan and occupies Tabriz.
1636	Erivan is taken by Iran.
1638	Murad IV captures Baghdad.
1639	Treaty of Qasr-i Shirin with Iran.
1640	Death of Murad IV and enthronement of Ibrahim I.
1642	Azov is recaptured.
1645	Campaign against the island of Crete.
1648	Sultan Ibrahim is deposed and strangled. Mehmed IV ascends the throne.
1651	The powerful Kösem Sultan who dominated the imperial *harem* is executed.
1656	Venetians invade and occupy Lemnos and Tenedos. Mehmed Köprülü becomes the grand vezir. Abaza Hasan Paşa revolts.
1657	Ottomans recapture Lemnos and Tenedos from the Venetians.
1658	Ottoman control over Transylvania is reestablished.
1661	With the death of the grand vezir Mehmed Köprülü, his son, Fazil Ahmed Köprülü, replaces his father.
1663	War with the Habsburgs.
1664	Ottomans are defeated by Habsburgs at the Battle of St. Gotthard. Peace of Vasvar.

1669	Fall of Crete. Peace with Venice.
1672	War with Poland, which continues until the Treaty of Zuravno (Zorawno) of 1676.
1676	With the death of Fazil Ahmed Köprülü, his brother-in-law, Merzifonlu Kara Mustafa Paşa, becomes the grand vezir.
1683	Second siege of Vienna by the Ottomans fails. Ottoman forces are routed by Jan Sobieski.
1684	A Holy League comprising the Habsburgs, Venice, Poland, the Pope, Malta, and Tuscany is organized against the Ottoman Empire.
1686	Fall of Buda. Russia joins the Holy League. Venice captures Morea.
1687	Second Battle of Mohács. The Habsburgs defeat the Ottoman Empire. The army revolts. Mehmed IV is deposed. Süleyman II ascends the throne.
1688	Habsburgs take Belgrade.
1689	Habsburgs invade Kosovo. Russia invades Crimea.
1690	Belgrade is recaptured by Ottoman forces.
1691	Ahmed II ascends the throne and rules until 1695. Battle of Slankamen during which the grand vezir Fazil Mustafa Köprülü is killed.
1695	Mustafa II ascends the Ottoman throne.
1697	Habsburgs defeat the Ottomans at the Battle of Zenta.
1699	Treaty of Karlowitz.
1700	Peace with Russia.
1703	Mustafa II is deposed and Ahmed III ascends the throne.
1711	Defeat of the Russian army under Peter the Great at the Battle of Pruth.
1712	Peace treaty with Russia. Azov is recovered.
1714	War with Venice over Morea.
1715	Ottomans recapture Morea.
1716	War with the Habsburgs.
1717	Habsburgs capture Belgrade.

1718–1730	Nevşehirli Damad Ibrahim Paşa serves as grand vezir (The Tulip Period).
1718	Treaty of Passarowitz.
1723	Ottomans invade and occupy Georgia, Azerbaijan, and large parts of western Iran until 1727.
1730	Rebellion of Patrona Halil in Istanbul. Sultan Ahmed III is deposed, and the Tulip Period comes to an end.
1730–1754	Mahmud I rules.
1736–1739	War with the Habsburgs and Russia.
1739	Ottomans recapture Belgrade. Treaty of Belgrade with the Habsburgs and Russia.
1740	Ottomans grant capitulations to France.
1743	War with Iran continues until 1746 when peace is concluded and the boundaries that were established by the Treaty of Qasr-i Shirin are restored.
1754–1757	Osman III rules.
1757	Mustafa III ascends the Ottoman throne.
1768	Ottoman Empire declares war on Russia.
1771	Russia invades and occupies Crimea.
1774	War with Russia ends in the Treaty of Küçük Kaynarca. Crimea and the northern coast of the Black Sea fall under Russian domination.
1774–1789	Abdülhamid I rules. The sultan introduces reforms in the government and army.
1776	Iran captures Basra.
1783	Crimea is annexed to the Russian Empire.
1787–1792	War with Russia.
1788–1791	War with the Habsburgs.
1789	Selim III ascends the Ottoman throne and initiates a new era of governmental and military reforms, which continue until 1807.
1791	Treaty of Sistova with the Habsburgs.
1792	Treaty of Jassy (Yassy) with Russia.

1798	Napoleon Bonaparte invades Egypt, forcing the Ottoman Empire to ally with Russia and Great Britain
1803–1849	Muhammad Ali Paşa (Mehmed Ali) rules Egypt.
1804	Serbia revolts.
1807	Selim III is deposed after *janissaries* lead a revolt against his new army, *Nizâm-i Cedîd*. Mustafa IV ascends the Ottoman throne.
1808	Selim III is assassinated before Bayrakdâr Mustafa Paşa can restore him. Mustafa is deposed and Mahmud II ascends the Ottoman throne. The new sultan signs *Sened-i İttifak*. Janissaries kill Bayrakdâr Mustafa Paşa. Execution of Mustafa IV.
1811	Muhammad Ali puts an end to the Mamluks in Egypt.
1812	Treaty of Bucharest with Russia.
1820	War with the Qajar dynasty in Iran, which continues until 1823.
1821	Greek movement for independence begins.
1822	The Ottomans kill Tepedelenli Ali Paşa (Ali Paşa of Janina).
1823	Treaty of Erzurum with Iran.
1826	Mahmud II destroys the *janissaries*.
1828–1829	War with Russia.
1830	France occupies Algeria.
1831	Syria is conquered by Muhammad Ali's Egyptian army.
1832	At the battle of Konya, Muhammad Ali's forces defeat the Ottoman army and reach Kütahya.
1833	Treaty of Hünkâr-Iskelesi with Russia.
1838	Anglo-Ottoman Trade Agreement.
1839	Abdülmecid ascends the throne and issues the *Hatt-i Şerif-i Gülhane* (The Noble Edict of the Rose Garden), which inaugurates the *Tanzimat* (Reform) era.
1840	Muhammad Ali's dynasty is established in Egypt.
1853–1856	Crimean War.

1856	*Hatt-i Hümâyun* (Imperial Reform Edict). The Treaty of Paris.
1861	Abdülaziz ascends the Ottoman throne.
1865	Formation of Young Ottomans.
1866–1868	Greek nationalist revolt in Crete.
1869	Suez Canal opens.
1876	Abdülaziz is deposed and Murad V ascends the Ottoman throne. Murad V is deposed and replaced by Abdülhamid II. The first Ottoman constitution.
1877	The Ottoman constitution is abolished by Abdülhamid II.
1877–1878	War with Russia.
1878	Treaty of San Stefano. Congress of Berlin. Serbia, Bulgaria, and Romania become independent states.
1881	France occupies Tunisia. Albanian revolt suppressed by Ottoman troops.
1882	The British forces invade and occupy Egypt.
1884	The former grand vezir, Midhat Paşa, is murdered.
1885	Bulgaria annexes East Rumelia.
1889	The Committee of Union and Progress (CUP) is founded.
1890–1896	Attacks by Hamidiye regiments on Armenian communities in Anatolia.
1896–1897	The insurrection in Crete and war with Greece.
1896	Armenian revolutionaries (*Dashnaks*) take over the Imperial Ottoman Bank in Istanbul.
1908	The Young Turk Revolution and the restoration of the constitution.
1909	Abdülhamid II is deposed from the throne and replaced by Mehmed V.
1910	Revolt in Yemen.
1911	War with Italy over Libya. Yemen is granted autonomy.
1912	The First Balkan War.

1913	The Second Balkan War. The Ottoman state is increasingly dominated by the triumvirate of Enver Paşa, Cemal Paşa, and Talat Paşa.
1914	Ottoman Empire enters World War I on the side of Germany and the Austro-Hungarian Empire.
1915	The Constantinople Agreement, which partitions the Ottoman Empire. Husayn-McMahon Correspondence. The British promise an independent Arab state in return for Sharif Husayn of Mecca and his sons leading a revolt against the Ottoman Empire. Forced relocation of the Armenian population. Allied landing at Gallipoli.
1916	Sykes-Picot Agreement. The British and the French partition the Ottoman Empire into spheres of influence.
1917	Balfour Declaration. The British government expresses its support for the establishment of a national homeland for the Jews.
1918	Faisal's army enters Damascus. Mehmed VI ascends the Ottoman throne. Mudros armistice. Allied occupation of Istanbul.
1919	Mustafa Kemal lands in Samsun.
1920	Treaty of Sèvres.
1922	Turkish army defeats Greek forces in western Anatolia. The Grand National Assembly abolishes the Ottoman sultanate. Prince Abdülmecid is declared caliph.
1923	Treaty of Lausanne. Republic of Turkey is established with Mustafa Kemal (Atatürk) as its first president.
1924	The end of the caliphate in Turkey.

SULTANS OF THE OTTOMAN EMPIRE

Osman	1290–1326
Orhan	1326–1362
Murad I	1362–1389
Bayezid I	1389–1402
Interregnum	1402–1413
Mehmed I	1413–1421
Murad II	1421–1444
Mehmed II	1444–1446
Murad II	1446–1451
Mehmed II	1451–1481
Bayezid II	1481–1512
Selim I	1512–1520
Süleyman I	1520–1566
Selim II	1566–1574
Murad III	1574–1595
Mehmed III	1595–1603
Ahmed I	1603–1617
Mustafa I	1617–1618
Osman II	1618–1622
Mustafa I	1622–1623
Murad IV	1623–1640
Ibrahim	1640–1648
Mehmed IV	1648–1687
Süleyman II	1687–1691
Ahmed II	1691–1695
Mustafa II	1695–1703
Ahmed III	1703–1730
Mahmud I	1730–1754
Osman III	1754–1757
Mustafa III	1757–1774

Abdülhamid I	1774–1789
Selim III	1789–1807
Mustafa IV	1807–1808
Mahmud II	1808–1839
Abdülmecid	1839–1861
Abdülaziz	1861–1876
Murad V	1876
Abdülhamid II	1876–1909
Mehmed V (Reşad)	1909–1918
Mehmed VI (Vahideddin)	1918–1922
Abdülmecid II*	1922–1924

* Served only as Caliph

CHAPTER 1

HISTORICAL OVERVIEW

The emergence of the Ottoman Empire as a world power is one of the most important events in the history of southeast Europe, the Middle East, North Africa, and indeed the world. For more than five centuries, the Ottomans ruled a large and powerful empire that held vast territories in Europe, Asia, and Africa. How did the Ottoman state expand from a small principality in western Anatolia in 1290 to one of the largest and most powerful empires the world had ever seen? The Ottoman Empire was not only vast, but it also contained a mosaic of religious, ethnic, and linguistic communities, including: Greeks, Serbs, Bosnians, Hungarians, Albanians, Bulgarians, Romanians, Arabs, Turks, Armenians, Kurds, and Jews. Each group possessed its own history, culture, language, religious values, and traditions. To maintain the unity and integrity of such a vast and internally diverse empire, the Ottomans could not rule as a Muslim Turkish elite imposing its political will over a much larger and diverse non-Turkic population. The ethnic and religious heterogeneity of the empire as well as the geographical vastness and diversity of its land mass required governmental institutions that would ensure the cohesion and the unity of the state.

The Ottoman society was divided in accordance with two distinct categories. The first division of the population organized the subjects of the sultan into religious communities or *millets*. The second divided the population according to their relationship with political power, separating those who worked for the government and military from those who did not.[1] Ottoman society was divided into two distinct classes, namely the *askeri* (the military or the ruling class) and the *reâyâ* (the flock or the subject class).[2] The *askeri* was comprised of several strata. The first were the Turcoman families who had fought with the first Ottoman sultan and had played an important role in transforming the state from a principality to a full-fledged empire. The second were the ruling classes who had been conquered and then incorporated into the Ottoman system. The third were those Christian subjects of the sultan who were recruited into the system through *devşirme*. The *devşirme* was the system of acquiring young Christian children who were educated and trained to assume positions of power in the imperial palace, the administration, or the *kapi kulu* (slaves of the sultan). The fourth were the *ulema*, who were responsible for managing the Islamic legal and educational institutions of the empire.[3] Regardless of their ethnic and religious origins, each member of the Ottoman ruling class had to be a Muslim. He also had to demonstrate his loyalty to the sultan and be familiar with the customs, mannerisms, and language that distinguished a member of the Ottoman ruling class from the members of the subject class. As with the ruling class, the subject class or the *reâyâ* also consisted of several strata, which included peasant farmers, manufacturers, and merchants who produced the goods and paid taxes that sustained the state and the ruling dynasty.[4]

Jews, Christians, and Muslims lived side by side under the Ottoman sultan, a Sunni Muslim Turk, who acted as the protector of all religious communities of the empire. Each community enjoyed religious, cultural, and legal autonomy and managed its own internal affairs under the leadership of its own religious hierarchy.[5] The heads of the religious communities were appointed by the sultan.[6] The system allowed the religious communities in the empire to coexist in relative peace and harmony. It also provided the Ottoman sultan the opportunity to claim that he treated all his subjects with generosity and benevolence regardless of their cultural and religious identity. At a time when Europe was burning with the fervor of religious warfare between Catholics and Protestants, a Muslim monarch could contend that under his rule, Muslims, Jews, and Christians could practice their religions free of persecution. The tolerance displayed by the Ottoman sultans did not mean that the Jews and Christians were viewed and treated as equal to Muslims, however. In accordance with Islamic law or *Şeriat* (Arabic: *Sharia*), Jews and Christians were "people of the book" and considered *zimmi* (Arabic: *dhimmi*) or protected religious communities, which lived under the authority of a Muslim sovereign. The sultan was required to protect the lives and property of his Jewish and Christian subjects. In return, his Jewish and Christian subjects were obligated to remain loyal to him and pay the Ottoman government a poll tax or *cizye* in return for not serving in the military. In all legal matters, the Islamic law had precedence and Islamic courts were open to all subjects of the sultan.[7]

The Christian population of the Ottoman Empire was heterogeneous. The Ottoman government recognized two principal Christian *millets*, namely, the Greek Orthodox and the Armenian Gregorian. Other Christian communities such as the Maronites, Nestorians, and Syrian Orthodox were not recognized as *millets*, although for all practical purposes they functioned as autonomous religious communities under their own leaders.[8] The Muslim population of the empire was equally heterogeneous, but because Islam was the official religion of the Ottoman Empire, the Muslims could not be considered a separate *millet*. However, the Muslim community was organized in the same manner as the Christian communities.[9] The sultan appointed the *şeyhülislâm* as the head of the *ulema*, who were the experts and interpreters of the Islamic law. The *muftis*, who were the official interpreters of Islamic law and issued legal opinions (*fetvas*), also came from the ranks of the *ulema*, and they were assigned by the *şeyhülislâm* to the provinces of the empire. The *kâdis* or judges, who enforced the Islamic law and the *kânun* (the laws issued by the sultan) and administered the courts throughout the empire, were also appointed by the *şeyhülislâm*.[10]

As the Ottoman state was transformed from a small principality in western Anatolia into a full-fledged imperial power, the institutions that had given rise to the early Ottoman fiefdom underwent a profound transformation. The early Ottoman principality was based on the active participation of charismatic Ottoman rulers who carried the title of *khan* or *han* and acted as the chief *gâzi*, a warrior who fights in the name of Islam. Ottoman power and authority derived from Turkish nomadic military units organized and led by the *gâzis* who fought with the Ottoman ruler. The Ottoman army was not only the backbone of the state, but was the state itself. The seat of power was on the saddle of the sultan, who organized and led the raids. His leadership required him to visit and inspect the territory under his rule. As for the religious orientation of the early Ottoman state, the Islam of the *gâzis* lacked the theological sophistication of the Muslim *ulema*, who dominated the mosques and seminaries of Anatolia's urban centers, such as Konya. The Islam of the early Ottoman sultans was simple, personal, unorthodox, eclectic, and mystical.[11] Not surprisingly, the *tekkes* (lodges) of *derviş* (mystical) orders dominated the religious and spiritual life of the frontier *gâzis* who were fighting with Osman, the founder of the Ottoman dynasty, and his son Orhan. One of the earliest accounts of Osman's rise to power describes how he received a blessing from a prominent mystical leader, Şeyh Edebali, who handed him the sword of a *gâzi* and prophesized that his descendants would rule the world.[12] When Osman died in 1326, the ceremony that decided the succession of his son to the throne took place at a *zâviye*, a hospice run and managed by *dervişes* for travelers.[13] Orhan was the first Ottoman ruler to assume the title of sultan, and his son Murad was the first to use the title of *Hüdâvendigâr*, lord or emperor.[14] In 1395, Sultan Bayezid added the title of *Sultan al-Rum* or the Sultan of Byzantine lands.[15] As the power and the territorial possessions of the empire expanded, the Ottoman sultans added new titles, such as *pâdişah* (sovereign), but never abandoned the title of *gâzi*. With the creation of the empire and the establishment of Ottoman power in the urban centers where Sunni Islam dominated the social and cultural life of the Muslim community, the state became increasingly identified with the official Islam of the *ulema*, although the mystical traditions and practices were never abandoned.

The succession to the Ottoman throne did not follow an established procedure.[16] In theory, the rise of a prince to the throne could only be determined by the will of God.[17] When a prince managed to defeat the other contenders for the throne and gain the support of the *ulema*, the army, and palace officials, he could ascend the throne and seize the central treasury.[18] The result of this power struggle was justified as a manifestation of divine support. The reigning sultan appointed each of his sons to the governorship of a province. Each son was accompanied by a tutor who advised him on the art of statecraft. As provincial governors ruling from old Anatolian towns, the sons built their own palaces and established their own courts, replicating the royal palace and the imperial court in the capital.[19] The tutors and administrators who joined each prince were carefully selected from among the loyal servants of the sultan and were expected to provide their royal masters with information on the development and activities of the prince to whom they were assigned.[20] After the death of a sultan, open warfare was a natural and expected phenomenon. After a new sultan ascended the throne, he was expected to execute his brothers and other male contenders to the throne.[21] When there was only one member of the royal family alive, all members of the government remained loyal to him.

As the early Ottoman state expanded, acquired urban centers, and established a court, Turkish nomadic practices were modified by incorporating long established ancient Iranian, Islamic, and Greek imperial traditions. This did not mean that the Ottomans abandoned and concealed their nomadic origins. The sultans continued to carry the title of *han* or *khan*, which they had brought with them from their original home in Central Asia.[22] However, these traditions gradually gave way to the more elaborate customs and practices of kingship borrowed from pre-Islamic Sassanian Iran and the Byzantine Greeks. Indeed, the genius of the early Ottoman rulers and their ministers was a pragmatic approach that allowed them to borrow selectively and eclectically from pre-Ottoman traditions and utilize what served their political, social, and economic needs. As the state expanded its territory, the Ottomans recognized the need to establish an administration that could reliably collect taxes and send them to the central treasury, which used the revenue generated from agricultural production and trade to pay the expenditures of the sultan and the palace.

Under the Ottoman political system, the sultan stood at the top of the power pyramid. He was both the "temporal and spiritual leader," who drew his authority from the *Şeriat* (Islamic law) and *kânun* (the imperial law) and was obligated to preserve the peace, security, and stability of the empire he ruled.[23] The government itself was an extension of the sultan's private household; government officials were the personal servants of their royal master, who were appointed and dismissed in accordance with the sultan's decision or momentary whim. The ancient Iranian theory of the state provided the theoretical foundations of the empire. According to this theory, to rule his domain, a king needed an army. The creation and maintenance of an army, however, demanded the creation of wealth that could only be produced by the labor of the people. For people to produce wealth there had to be prosperity and peace. Peace and prosperity were, however, impossible without justice and law, which required the presence of a ruler and a strong army. This circular theory had been elaborated during the reign of the pre-Islamic Iranian Sassanian monarchs and later modified and adjusted according to Islamic traditions. It was further modified after the arrival of Turkic nomadic groups from Central Asia in the eleventh century and the establishment of Mongol rule in the thirteenth century.[24]

The Ottoman political structure was divided into a central administration and a provincial administration. In accordance with the traditional Iranian–Islamic theory of kingship, the administration of justice constituted the most important duty of a sovereign and his officials. The failure to protect his subjects from injustice could justify the overthrow of the government. The palace was the center of power and served as the residence of the sultan. The Ottoman palace comprised two principal sections: the *enderun* or inner section, and the *birun* or outer section.[25] The two sections were built around two large courtyards, which were joined by the Gate of Felicity where the sultan sat on his throne, received his guests, and attended ceremonies.[26] The sultan lived in the inner section of the palace, which was attached to the royal harem. The *harem* comprised women's apartments and was reserved for the female members of the royal family, such as the mother of the sultan (*vâlide sultan*) and his wives. Since proximity to the sultan determined the power and the status of an individual, the sultan's attendants and servants, particularly the eunuchs who were responsible for the protection of the royal *harem*, exercised a great deal of influence in the government. Much of their power derived from their ability to provide information to various factions in or outside the palace. Until the sixteenth century, the eunuchs were white males recruited from the Caucasus region. Starting in the seventeenth century, they were replaced by black eunuchs from the Sudan.[27] The palace eunuchs were managed and supervised by the *ağa/agha* or the chief of "the Abode of Felicity."[28] Aside from the eunuchs, women of the royal *harem* also played a prominent role in the political life of the palace. As the sultans began to rule from the *harem*, the power of those who surrounded them, particularly their mothers and wives, increased. They enjoyed direct access to the sultan and were in daily contact with him. With the sultan spending less time in the battlefields and delegating his responsibilities to the grand vezir, the mothers and wives began to emerge as the principal source of information and communication between the *harem* and the outside world. They interfered in the internal factional fighting and rivalries within the ruling elite, forming alliances with the grand vezir and army commanders.

The palace constituted the brain center of the empire. The *divan-i hümâyun*, or the imperial council, which constituted the highest deliberative organ of the Ottoman government, met at the palace at fixed times to listen to complaints from the subjects of the sultan. The council comprised the grand vezir and his cabinet, which included the chief of chancellery (*nişânci*), who controlled the *tuğrâ* (the official seal of the Ottoman state) and drew up and certified all official letters and decrees, the chief of the Islamic judicial system (*kâzasker/kâdiasker*), and the treasurers (*defterdârs*) of Anatolia and Rumeli (Ottoman provinces in the Balkans).[29] Until the reign of Mehmed II, the conqueror of Constantinople, the sultan participated in the deliberations of his ministers. As the power and the territory of the empire grew, the sultan became increasingly detached and stopped participating in the meetings of the *divân*. Instead, a square window "overlooking the council chamber" was added so that the sultan could listen to the deliberations of his ministers.[30] Many who managed the empire as governors, provincial administrators, and army commanders received their education and training in the palace. They had been recruited as young slaves and brought to the palace where they were trained as the loyal and obedient servants of the sultan. The sultan and his officials did not recruit the slaves from the native Muslim population. Rather, young Christian boys from the sultan's European provinces provided him with a vast pool from which new slaves could be recruited, converted to Islam, and trained to assume the highest posts in the empire. Known as the *devşirme*, this system also resulted in the creation of the *yeni çeri* or *janissary* corps, who constituted the sultan's elite infantry and were paid directly from the central government's treasury. For centuries before European states modernized their armies, the *janissaries* were Europe's sole standing army, trained and armed with the latest techniques and instruments of warfare, scoring impressive victories.

Even when the territorial expansion of the empire slowed down, the idea of recruiting young Christian boys as soldiers and administrators did not stop. As late as the sixteenth century, the sultan issued a *fermân* or a royal decree, ordering his local officials to summon all Christian boys between the ages of eight and twenty in their rural districts.[31] The government officials selected and registered the best qualified boys and sent them in groups of a hundred to a hundred and fifty to Istanbul where they were received by the *ağa* (commander) of the *janissary* corps.[32] The number of boys recruited through this system in the sixteenth century has been estimated to be from a thousand to three thousand a year.[33] As the future members of the ruling elite, they had to learn Turkish and acquire the customs and etiquette of an Ottoman official. The best and most talented were retained as pages (*iç oğlâns*) in the palace where they received further education and training in various palaces in Istanbul and Edirne under the strict supervision of eunuchs and tutors.[34] Once they had completed their education, the pages were either appointed to positions within the palace or served as the *kapi kullâri* (the slaves of the sultan/the Porte) military units. Those who served as pages in the palace were trained by the eunuchs who organized their daily activities and responsibilities. The young boys grew up with little contact with the outside world. As young men who owed their life, status, and special privileges to the sultan, they remained single until they had reached the age of thirty.[35] The system demanded that they devote their loyalty and services to the sultan and not to a wife and children who could demand their time and energy.

Four principal chambers within the palace served the sultan and his needs.[36] The privy chamber served the sultan's most basic needs, such as cleaning, clothing, and personal security. The sultan's sword keeper (*silâhdar ağa*), the royal valet (*çohâdâr ağa*), and his personal secretary (*sir kâtibi*) were the principal officials in charge of the privy chamber.[37] The treasury chamber was responsible for the sultan's personal jewelry and other valuable items. The third chamber, or the larder, was for the preparation of the sultan's meals, and the fourth, or the campaign chamber, comprised bath house attendants, barbers, drum beaters, and entertainers.[38] Pages with exceptional ability and talent would join the privy chamber after they had served in one of the other three chambers.[39] From the time the sultan woke up to the time he went to bed, the pages of the privy chamber accompanied him and organized the many services that their royal master required.

Until the reign of Mehmed II in the middle of the fifteenth century, the Ottomans, like many previous Muslim dynasties, recruited and trained slaves as soldiers. The majority of non-military functions were reserved for government officials who were recruited from the Muslim Turkish elite. The members of this elite class were for the most part educated in traditional bureaucratic and religious institutions where the knowledge of Islamic sciences as well as Arabic grammar and Persian literature and poetry was mandatory. Many who served as the civil administrators within the Ottoman government were recruited from the ranks of the *ulema* or the learned men of religion and doctors of Islamic law. With the reign of Mehmed II, however, the sultan began to appoint slaves to the top administrative positions of the empire.[40] The policy of replacing the traditional Muslim educated elite with slaves ignited a conflict between the old Turkish elite and the newly converted slaves, forcing the sultan to perform a balancing act in order to avoid an all-out war among his officials.

As with the central administration, the provincial administration also played an important role in preserving the unity and territorial integrity of the empire. To maintain an efficient provincial administration and a strong and highly trained army, the Ottomans had to create a financial organization that would collect taxes and generate revenue. Under Ottoman rule, land constituted the most important source of wealth and government revenue. As in other Islamic states, there were several distinct categories of land ownership. By far the largest category was *miri* (crown land), or land owned and controlled by the state.[41] Theoretically, all lands used for agricultural production in the empire belonged to the sultan. The central government also recognized *vakif* (Arabic: *vaqf*), or land controlled and supervised as a religious endowment, with its revenue providing support for charitable objectives.[42] The state also recognized *mülk*, or privately owned land.[43] The *vakif* and *mülk* could be transferred to crown lands by the order of the sultan. Ottoman sultans were always desperate to increase their revenue base by confiscating *vakif* and *mülk* lands, converting them to *miri* so their revenue could finance their military campaigns. An increase in crown lands also allowed the sultan to increase the number of cavalrymen recruited for the army. Under the Ottoman land tenure system, the peasant enjoyed the hereditary right to cultivate the land but could not sell it or transfer the title without permission from the central government.[44] The hereditary right to cultivate the land passed from father to son.[45]

The Ottoman Empire frequently suffered from a scarcity of silver coinage, which posed a fundamental challenge to the central government.[46] How could the government collect taxes from peasant farmers who could not pay their taxes in cash? And how could the sultan pay his officials and troops their salaries? In response to these challenges, the empire was divided into numerous fiefs or *timars* (literally meaning labor). To each *timar*, the sultan assigned a *sipâhi* or a cavalryman. The *sipâhi* did not exercise the right of ownership over the *timar* he held, but was responsible for collecting taxes and maintaining security in the area under his control, making sure that the cultivation of land would not be disrupted.[47] He provided troops to the army during the time of campaigns, thereby contributing to the central government's cavalry force. Unlike the *janissary*, who used firearms, however, the *sipâhi* and the men he recruited and organized were armed with medieval weaponry.[48] Thus, the cavalryman was simultaneously the tax collector, the local policeman, and the army recruiter. The revenue generated by his *timar* paid for his military services. At the time of the conquest of each new territory, the Ottoman government sent agents to the newly acquired districts to identify and quantify taxable sources, such as crops, and assess the amount of tax that particular community was to pay. These calculations were then entered into government registries. Every twenty to thirty years these tax assessments were revisited and, if necessary, revised. Instead of paying the salaries of military personnel from the sultan's treasury, the troops were thus allowed to directly collect the revenue from agricultural production in lieu of their salary. The *sipâhi*, who lived in a village among peasant farmers, collected the taxes in kind, and it was his duty to convert it to cash.[49] Through the *sipâhis*, the central government penetrated the rural communities of the empire and established direct control over the process of agricultural production and collection of taxes from the peasantry.

The *timar* holders were grouped together under *sancaks* or military-administrative units, which were run by a military governor (*sancak bey*).[50] The military governor was called a *sancak bey* because he had received a *sancak* or a standard/banner from the sultan as the sign and symbol of power and authority.[51] As the Ottoman state expanded and the number of *sancak beys* increased, the central government created a new position, the *beylerbey* or *bey* of the *beys*, responsible for the *sancak beys* in his province (*eyâlet*).[52] Each *beylerbey* ruled from a provincial capital, which had its own *janissary* garrison, religious judge (*kâdi*), and administrators in charge of assessing taxes.[53] This system did not prevail in all provinces and territories controlled by the sultan, however. In several Kurdish and Arab-populated regions, tribal chiefs were appointed as hereditary *sancak beys*. They were responsible for collecting taxes (much of which they retained) and sending troops to Istanbul at a time of war with foreign powers. There were also vassal Christian states such as Moldavia and Wallachia, which were ruled by their princes, and Muslim principalities such as Crimea, which were administered by their *khans*. Aside from the *beylerbeys* and the *sancak beys*, who acted as the direct representatives of their royal master and were recruited from the military class, in all legal matters the sultan was represented by a *kâdi* (judge) who came from the ranks of the *ulema*. The governors could not carry out justice without receiving a legal judgment from the *kâdi*, but the *kâdi* did not have the executive authority to carry out any of his religious rulings.[54] Until the second half of the sixteenth century, *kâdis* were appointed for life, but as the number of prospective judges increased, term limits were imposed by the central government.[55]

The decline of the Ottoman Empire began in the last three decades of the sixteenth century, but it did not happen overnight. What were the principal causes for the decline of the Ottoman state? Did the decline begin internally and at the top of the power pyramid, with the sultan and the palace, or were there social and economic causes at the base that played a significant role? How much of the decline was caused by overextending the territory of the empire? And how far did the wars with European powers and Iran contribute to the military and financial exhaustion that eventually undermined the capability of the central government to maintain effective control over its provinces?

The process of decline was already under way during the reign of Süleyman the Magnificent, but it did not manifest itself to outsiders, particularly to the Christian states of Europe, until a century later. Several factors contributed to the growing decline of the Ottoman state. The rise of Ottoman power to world prominence was related directly to a series of wise, capable, and courageous sultans who were actively engaged in administering their empire. Characteristic of the long period of decline was the growing detachment of successive Ottoman sultans from active participation in decision-making. As the role of the sultan in administering the empire diminished, the power of the grand vezir and his cabinet increased and the influence of the "slaves" recruited through *devşirme* was enhanced. The early Ottoman sultans had been trained to rule by serving their fathers as governors and commanders. They had to participate in administering the affairs of the state and often fought on battlefields against external foes. During the long period of decline, the practice of training the princes was abandoned.[56] The death of Süleyman the Magnificent in 1566 was followed by a series of weak and incompetent sultans who were dominated by their mothers, wives, and chief eunuchs inside the *harem* and by the *janissary* corps outside the palace. They were born and raised in the seclusion of the royal *harem*, detached from the realities of ruling a vast and complex empire. Surrounded by slave girls, who were brought to the *harem* from various parts of the empire, the sultans were converted into sexual machines, sleeping with an unlimited number of women and producing a large number of children who imposed a significant financial burden on the state treasury. With the increase in the number of wives and children, the Topkapi Palace was expanded to accommodate the new members of the royal family. For the next century, as Europe began the long process of modernization and industrialization, the Ottoman state, confident of its power and superiority, fell into a deep sleep from which it awakened only after it was defeated in battles against European armies in the last two decades of the seventeenth century.

Beginning with the reign of Selim II in 1566, the majority of Ottoman monarchs began to disengage from participating in government, delegating much of their executive power to their grand vezirs and the cabinet of ministers. By marrying a daughter or a sister of the reigning sultan, grand vezirs often converted themselves into members of the royal family and increased their influence and power over their royal master. Surrounded by slaves and servants, sex and pleasure, the Ottoman sultans became increasingly isolated, ignorant, ineffective, and dependent on their officials to rule the empire. Without direct contact with reality, the sultans received reports on the state of affairs through the mediation of the grand vezir and the slaves who surrounded them. Royal mothers and wives also began to assume a greater role and more power. Enjoying direct access to the sovereign, they could exercise enormous influence on appointments to the highest governmental posts. The growing power of the women and the competition among them for influence in the *harem* perpetuated a culture of conspiracy and intrigue, which reduced the sultans to hapless observers who could be manipulated to serve the interests and agenda of an individual or faction who had established a close alliance with their mother or wives.

The period of decline was also characterized by the Ottomans abandoning the practice of killing the brothers of a new sultan (fratricide) to avoid internal strife and dynastic warfare.[57] As an increasing number of male offspring of the sultan survived, government expenditure increased. Each prince of the royal family required his own retinue of mother, wives, children, eunuchs, servants, and teachers, who were supported by the central treasury. Aside from the financial burden on the state treasury, the presence of male members of the royal family generated *harem* intrigues and internal instability. Factions were created around each prince with his mother leading the effort to ensure the survival and ascendancy of her son to the Ottoman throne.

Contacts were established, bribes were paid, and promises of power and promotion were made to key palace officials and army commanders to secure their support for a contender.

Aside from palace intrigue, the decline of the empire was caused by a financial crisis triggered from afar. The so-called "age of discovery" in the fifteenth and the sixteenth centuries, which provided European maritime powers such as Spain with access to enormous reserves of silver from South America, flooded the European markets and gave rise to massive inflation.[58] The introduction of silver coinage improved Europe's purchasing power at the time when capitalism was replacing feudalism as the dominant mode of economic production. The rise of capitalism in Europe corresponded with a massive migration of cheap labor from rural communities to the emerging urban centers. As European urban centers grew in size, the demand for raw materials and foodstuff increased, forcing European merchants to tap into the Ottoman market. Raw materials and food stuff from the Ottoman Empire fed Europe's urban centers and the emerging industries on the continent. The introduction of considerable silver coinage into the Ottoman economy introduced massive inflation, forcing the Ottoman government to debase the coinage, further draining basic agricultural goods that were exported to European markets in return for cash. The change, however, benefited the former *timar* holders turned landowners, who used their access to European markets as a means of building a strong economic base, particularly in the regions adjacent to Europe. The debasement of the Ottoman coinage undermined the financial power and security of the ruling elite, who received a fixed salary from the state treasury. To compensate for their financial loss, the government officials began to search for ways to turn their positions into a means of generating financial gain.

The economic and financial decline of the empire was exacerbated by the significant diversion of trade from traditional land routes to new sea routes. Historically, the vast region extending from Central Asia to the Middle East served as a land bridge between China and Europe.[59] The taxes and the custom charges collected by the Ottoman government constituted an important component of the revenue generated by the state and contributed significantly to the financial power and economic prosperity of the empire.[60] The Portuguese rounding of the Cape of Good Hope and subsequent establishment of a direct sea route to Iran, India, and beyond, however, allowed European states and merchants to bypass Ottoman-held territory and export European goods and import various products from Asia without paying taxes and custom dues to Ottoman authorities.[61] The sea routes were faster and cheaper. They also undermined the Ottoman Empire's central role in world commerce and trade. Taking their cue from the Christian states of Europe, the Iranians did everything in their power to avoid exporting their precious goods, such as silk, to Europe via Ottoman transit routes.[62] By building a navy and removing the Portuguese from the area, the Safavid monarchs of Iran inaugurated a policy of exporting their silk through the newly built ports of the Persian Gulf and refused to provide the Ottomans with any share from this lucrative trade.[63]

Another important factor in the long period of decline was the demographic explosion. By all indications, between 1500 and 1700, the population of the empire grew at a rapid rate, which corresponded with the end of territorial expansion. After the death of Süleyman the Magnificent, Ottoman conquests came to a gradual halt. Although Ottoman armies attacked and occupied the island of Cyprus during the reign of Selim II in 1570, the empire did not gain significant territory in eastern Europe. Historically, Ottoman territorial expansion had allowed a large number of Turkish tribesmen from Anatolia to cross the water and settle on the European continent, colonizing Christian European countries in the name of spreading the domain of Islam. This colonization provided Turkish nomads with access to pasture lands for their animals and Turkish peasants with arable land for agriculture. With the end of territorial expansion in Europe, however, access to new territory ceased, and with the rapid growth in population, the empire began to experience the new phenomenon of landlessness and unemployment. It is thus not surprising that the sixteenth and seventeenth centuries witnessed the spread of mass rebellions and uprisings against the central government that quickly attracted wide popular support.

While the Ottoman Empire declined from within, the European states that had been defeated and humiliated by the Ottomans for several centuries began their rise to power and prosperity. The rise of absolutist states in central and western Europe capable of maintaining well-trained and well-equipped professional armies on the battlefield was a major development. These armies no longer comprised peasant farmers, who had been forced to join a battle and were anxious to return home for the harvest. Europe now had the equivalent of what the Ottomans had enjoyed for centuries through the *janissary* corps, namely, a permanent killing machine that owed its existence and financial survival to the will of a monarch. Triumphant in most battles they had fought against Christian Europe, the Ottomans showed little interest in studying and observing the fundamental political, technological, social, and economic transformations that Europe was undergoing.

Notes

1. Peter F. Sugar, *Southeastern Europe under Ottoman Rule: 1354–1804* (Seattle: University of Washington Press, 1996), 33.

2. Ibid. Virginia H. Aksan, *An Ottoman Statesman in War and Peace: Ahmed Resmi Efendi, 1700–1783* (Leiden: E.J. Brill, 1995), x–xi.

3. Ibid. Aksan, *An Ottoman Statesman*, x–xi.

4. Ibid., 33–4. Aksan, *An Ottoman Statesman*, x–xi.

5. Colin Imber, *The Ottoman Empire* (New York: Palgrave Macmillan, 2002), 216. See Benjamin Braude and Bernard Lewis, eds. *Christians and Jews in the Ottoman Empire*, 2 vols. (New York: Holmes & Meier Publishers,1982).

6. Ibid., 216–17.

7. Ibid., 217.

8. Justin McCarthy, *The Ottoman Turks: An Introductory History to 1923* (London: Addison Wesley Longman Limited, 1997), 130.

9. Ibid., 128.

10. Ibid., 121–22. Halil Inalcik, *The Ottoman Empire: The Classical Age 1300-1600*, trans. Norman Itzkowitz and Colin Imber (New York: Praeger Publishers, 1973), 169–72.

11. Halil Inalcik, "The Rise of the Ottoman Empire" in *A History of the Ottoman Empire to 1730*, ed. M.A. Cook (Cambridge: Cambridge University Press, 1976), 17.

12. Inalcik, *Ottoman Empire*, 55. Sugar, *Southeastern Europe under Ottoman Rule*, 8.

13. Ibid., 55, 226.

14. Ibid., 56.

15. Ibid., 55–6.

16. Ibid., 59. See, A.D. Alderson, *The Structure of the Ottoman Dynasty* (Westport, Connecticut: Greenwood Press, 1982), 4–16.

17. Ibid.

18. Ibid.

19. Ibid.

20. Ibid., 60.

21. Alderson, *The Structure of the Ottoman Dynasty*, 5.

22. Inalcik, *Ottoman Empire*, 56.

23. Aksan, *An Ottoman Statesman*, xi.

24. Inalcik, *Ottoman Empire*, 65.

25. See Sabahattin Türkoğlu, *The Topkapi Palace* (Istanbul: 1989). Sugar, *Southeastern Europe under Ottoman Rule*, 34–5.

26. Ibid.

27. Stanford J. Shaw, *History of the Ottoman Empire and Modern Turkey*, 2 vols. (Cambridge: Cambridge University Press, 1977), 1:115.

28. Ibid.

29. André Clot, *Suleiman the Magnificent* (London: Saqi Books, 2005), 344. Selcuk Aksin Somel, *Historical Dictionary of the Ottoman Empire* (Lanham: Scarecrow Press, 2003), 72–3, 145, 215–16, 311.

30. Inalcik, *Ottoman Empire*, 90.

31. Ibid., 78.

32. Ibid.

33. Ibid.

34. Ibid., 78–9.

35. Ibid., 79.

36. Ibid., 80.

37. Shaw, *History of the Ottoman Empire*, 1:115.

38. Ibid., 1:117. Inalcik, *Ottoman Empire*, 80.

39. Ibid. Inalcik, *Ottoman Empire*, 80.

40. McCarthy, *The Ottoman Turks*, 55.

41. Inalcik, *Ottoman Empire*, 109.

42. McCarthy, *The Ottoman Turks*, 116–18.

43. Ibid., 118–19.

44. Inalcik, *Ottoman Empire*, 109.

45. Ibid.

46. Ibid., 107.

47. Shaw, *History of the Ottoman Empire*, 1:26.

48. Inalcik, *Ottoman Empire*, 108.

49. Ibid., 107.

50. Shaw, *History of the Ottoman Empire*, 1:26. Gustav Bayerle, *Pashas, Begs and Effendis: A Historical Dictionary of Titles and Terms in the Ottoman Empire* (Istanbul: Isis Press, 1997), 140.

51. Inalcik, *Ottoman Empire*, 104.

52. Ibid., 104–6. Shaw, *History of the Ottoman Empire*, 1:26.

53. McCarthy, *The Ottoman Turks*, 121.

54. Inalcik, *Ottoman Empire*, 104.

55. Bayerle, *Pashas, Begs and Effendis*, 97.

56. Shaw, *History of the Ottoman Empire*, 1:170.

57. Ibid.

58. McCarthy, *The Ottoman Turks*, 152.

59. Ibid., 151.

60. Ibid.

61. Ibid.

62. Sir Percy Sykes, *A History of Persia*, 2 vols. (London: Mcmillan and Co., 1951), 2:189.

63. Ibid., 2:191–7.

CHAPTER 2

FOUNDERS OF THE EMPIRE

The origins of the Ottoman state are shrouded in mystery. The story of its rise begins with the migration of Turkic-speaking nomadic groups from the harsh environment of Central Asia and Outer Mongolia to Transoxiana, the Iranian plateau, and Asia Minor. Scarcity, limited pasture, and pressure from neighboring tribes and governments forced the nomads to move in order to seek new pasturage and trade opportunities. Starting in the tenth century, various Turkic tribes made numerous attempts to cross the Oxus (Amu Darya) and enter northeastern Iran. A major incursion of Turkic nomadic groups into the Iranian plateau took place when a confederation of Oghuz/Ghuzz Turkic tribes and their allies, under the leadership of the Seljuks/Seljuqs, entered Transoxiana in the tenth century, seeking land and pasturage for their animals.[1] After several clashes with the ruling Ghaznavid dynasty, the Seljuks inflicted a humiliating defeat on a large Ghaznavid force at the fortress of Dandanqan between Sarakhs (in northeastern Iran) and Marv (in present-day Turkmenistan) in May 1040.[2] The defeat of the Ghaznavid army made the Seljuks the masters of northeastern Iran with the Seljuk chief, Tuğril, ascending the throne and proclaiming himself the ruler (*Amir/Emir*) of Khorasan.[3] Tuğril then moved the main Seljuk army to northern Iran, capturing Ray (south of present-day Tehran) and proclaiming it his capital.[4] In 1055, he entered Baghdad with pomp and ceremony.[5] The Abbasid caliph bestowed upon the Seljuk ruler the title of sultan, while Tuğril accepted the supremacy of the caliph as Islam's supreme religious commander and committed the Seljuk state to the defense, protection, and expansion of Sunni Islam against internal and external threats.[6]

The death of Tuğril in 1063 triggered an eruption of dynastic wars between the contenders to the Seljuk throne. In 1064, after defeating his rivals, Tuğril's twenty-two-year-old nephew, Alp Arsalan (1064–1072) emerged as the new sultan. He completed his uncle's conquest of Iran and then moved his army northward toward Azerbaijan and Armenia to consolidate Seljuk rule in the southern Caucasus. As the

Seljuk army moved west and crossed into the Greek Byzantine territory, a military confrontation became unavoidable. The decisive battle
was fought on August 12, 1071 in Manzikert (Malazgird) north of Lake
Van, where the Seljuk army, led by Alp Arsalan, routed a much larger
Byzantine force led by Emperor Romanus Diogenes (Romanus IV) who
was captured by Seljuk forces. For the first time in history, a Byzantine
emperor was presented to a Muslim ruler as a prisoner of war. The Seljuk sultan treated his prisoner with courtesy and released him after a
week in return for a ransom.[7] The defeat proved to be a devastating
blow to the political and military might of the Byzantine state, from
which it would never fully recover.

In Constantinople, the news of the defeat threw the panic-
stricken Byzantine court into disarray, and internal quarrels ensued.
Neither the humiliated Byzantine army nor the demoralized Byzantine
bureaucracy mustered the discipline or the organization to prevent the
flood of Turcoman nomads from entering Anatolia, plundering urban
and rural communities, and seizing pasture land for their flocks. Such
was the level of anxiety gripping Constantinople that the Byzantine
court appealed to its principal religious rival, the Pope, for urgent assistance to counter the Turkish onslaught. The invasion of Anatolia by
the Seljuks, the collapse of Byzantine defenses, and the subsequent fall
of Jerusalem to the Turks provided sufficient justification for Pope
Urban II to call on Christian Europe in 1096 to join a crusade to liberate the Christian holy lands from the Muslim Turkish occupiers.

The Christian crusades against the Turks could not, however,
save the Byzantine state, which shrank in territory, power, and influence until it collapsed four centuries later in May 1453. The defeat of
the Byzantine army at Manzikert opened the gates of Anatolia to Turkic
nomads who settled in Asia Minor and in the process transformed the
ethnic, linguistic, and religious composition of the region. In the areas
where the population was non-Greek, the natives adjusted to the new
political reality by collaborating with the Seljuk Turks. In eastern Anatolia, the Armenian population survived by entering into an alliance
with the newly arriving Turkish conquerors. The same was true in
southeastern Anatolia, where Kurdish tribal chiefs joined the Seljuk
army and played an important role in its military campaigns. The
brunt of colonization must have been felt by the Greek population,
particularly in central and western Anatolia, where the majority of
Turks settled. An increasing number of Greek city dwellers and peasant
farmers, who had lost their political, cultural, and religious ties to the
Byzantine state, converted to Islam. Their conversion served as the first
major step toward acculturation and co-option into the ever growing
Muslim and Turkish-speaking population of Anatolia.[8]

In 1075, Alp Arsalan's successor, Malik Shah (1072–1092), sent a member of the Seljuk dynasty, Süleyman, to establish the Seljuk state in Anatolia, which would soon proclaim its independence from the Seljuk Empire of Iran.[9] After decades of fighting with the Byzantine state, the European crusades, and various Turkish chieftains, this branch of the Seljuk dynasty established itself in Anatolia, ruling a vast region from its capital, the city of Konya. Muslim writers referred to this branch of the Seljuk dynasty as the Seljuks of Rum (Salajeqa-yi Rum or Seljuks of Byzantine lands). In the two hundred years that lie between the Seljuk victory in Manzikert and the rise of the Ottoman state in western Anatolia, the Seljuks of Rum served as the instrument for the Turkification and Islamization of Anatolia.

The Islamization and Turkification of Anatolia intensified when the Mongols, under the command of their leader Chengiz Khan, invaded Central Asia and the Middle East in 1220. The armies of Kharazm Shah, who ruled Central Asia and Khorasan, were defeated. The Mongols devastated urban and rural life in a vast region extending from Samarqand (Afrasiyab) in the east to Nishapur and Ray in the west.[10] In almost every city, the civilian population was systematically exterminated, and those who survived "were led away into slavery and captivity, or died of epidemics or hunger."[11] Many were forced to eat "human flesh, dogs, and cats for a whole year, because the warriors of Chengiz Khan had burned down all the granaries."[12] One native historian and geographer observed that "even if for a thousand years to come no evil befalls the country, it would not be possible to repair the damage, and bring back the land to the state in which it was" before the destruction and massacres carried out by Mongols.[13]

As the Mongol armies swept through Central Asia and Khorasan, tens of thousands of refugees began to flee their homes for Anatolia. Mystics, poets, scholars, merchants, artisans, and nomads fled westward as the Mongols devastated urban and rural life in Central Asia and Iran. By defeating the Kharazm Shah, the Mongols made themselves the eastern neighbor of Rum Seljuks, raiding Anatolia as far west as Sivas.[14] In 1243, a Mongol army invaded Anatolia and defeated the Seljuk ruler, Qiyassudin Kay Khosrow II (1237–1246), in the battle of Kösedağ near Sivas. This victory established the Mongols as the overlords of Anatolia and forced the Seljuks of Rum to accept Mongol suzerainty and pay tribute to the Mongol Khans of Iran who had established the Il Khanid dynasty.

The complete collapse of the Seljuk dynasty in 1308 was followed by the growing weakness and disintegration of the Il Khanid state in Iran. As the Seljuk state disappeared and Mongol power waned, the small Turcoman Principalities in Anatolia began to assume more authority and independence. By 1335, when the reign of the Il Khanid dynasty came to an end, the Turcoman Principalities in Anatolia had emerged as independent states. They were still too small to be called kingdoms, but they were free to expand their territories westward at the expense of the Byzantine state. One of these Turcoman Principalities in western Anatolia was the small fiefdom established by a Turkish frontier commander (*bey*) named Osman.

The ancestors of Osman, the founder of the Ottoman dynasty, had arrived as nomadic Oghuz Turkish horsemen from Central Asia. A myth was constructed later, tracing the origins of the family to a certain Süleyman, leader of the Kayi (Qayi) tribe, who lived in northeastern Iran but had been forced to flee his home at the time of the Mongol invasion.[15] Süleyman is said to have drowned as he crossed the river Euphrates, but one of his sons, Ertuğril, moved his tribe into Anatolia, where he entered the service of the Seljuks of Rum, who rewarded him with a small fiefdom around the district of Söğüt. His son, Osman, emerged as the actual founder of the Ottoman state.

With the Mongol invasion of Asia Minor and the defeat of the Seljuk army, more refugees, including merchants, manufacturers, scholars, and *sufi* leaders sought refuge in the western regions of Anatolia, bringing with them their knowledge and talents. As the Seljuk state of Rum lost its legitimacy and began to disintegrate, the military commanders of marches established small principalities that attracted a diverse population. These *gâzis* waged religious war against infidels, expanding the domain of Islam. As long as the Seljuk state remained the dominant political and military power in Anatolia, they paid a tribute to the sultan who ruled from Konya. With the defeat of the Seljuks at the hands of the Mongols, they preserved the relative autonomy of their principalities by recognizing the Mongol Il Khan as their new master and sending him the customary tribute. As long as the Mongols left them alone, they could continue with their push westward at the expense of the beleaguered Byzantine state.

The rise and expansion of the Ottoman state was greatly aided by the weakness and internal fragmentation of European states—particularly in southeast Europe—and by the dynamism and charismatic leadership of wise and competent sultans who expanded their territory into the heart of the Balkans by forming alliances and manipulating the internal conflicts and jealousies among various Christian states in the region.[16] The political flexibility of the early Ottoman rulers was best demonstrated in their approach to conquest, which was based on coopting and controlling rather than uprooting and destroying the newly conquered lands and their inhabitants. In many instances, the Ottomans allowed the reigning Christian monarchs of southeast

Europe to retain their power as vassals of the sultan while paying tribute and providing the Ottoman armies with military and logistical support.[17] In the process, the early Ottomans demonstrated a remarkable tolerance toward the existing cultures and religious traditions, allowing the Christian orthodox churches of southeast Europe to survive as long as taxes were paid to the Ottoman central authority and the rule of the sultan was not challenged.

It is generally believed that the founder of the Ottoman state, Osman (1290–1326), was a *gâzi* or a frontier commander (*bey*) who first established himself in the district of Söğüt around 1290.[18] Waging *gazâ/ghaza* or holy war against infidels allowed him to establish a reputation for himself as a devout and dedicated Muslim ruler who sought to expand the domain of Islam (*Dar ul-Islam*) at the expense of the Byzantine Empire and other Christian rulers of Europe who belonged to the domain of war (*Dar ul-Harb*). While this claim may have provided a convenient ideological legitimization for Ottoman westward expansion, it is very clear that a religious war against the infidels was not sufficient to rally fighters around the Ottoman banner.[19] The war against infidels could only succeed if it provided material incentives and promised profitable gains for those who participated. Some may have justified their actions under the banner of religious holy war, but in reality the promise of material gain and upward social mobility motivated them.[20] Thus, the *gâzis* not only waged *gazâ* but also launched raids (*akin*) against non-Muslims, allowing the *akincis* to plunder rural and urban communities and amass booty and slaves.[21] They also acted as the front line shock troops plundering enemy territory, spreading fear in the hearts and minds of the population who were about to be invaded and conquered.

The principal objective of Osman was to avoid moving against neighboring Turcoman Principalities to the south and east and focus on expanding west and northwest against the Byzantine state and the Christian states of southeastern Europe.[22] The Ottomans were well aware that such a policy could be easily justified under the banner of holy war against nonbelievers. They also knew that the politically fragmented and internally divided southeast Europe was a far easier target than the neighboring Muslim states. In their expansion into the Balkans, the Ottomans tried to maintain the status quo by forming alliances with the leaders and elites who enjoyed legitimacy among the native population. As long as the ruling dynast and his government cooperated with the sultan and did not challenge his suzerainty, the Ottomans did not remove him.

Osman expanded his territory from the region of Eskişehir northward, encountering local feudal lords who functioned as representatives of the Byzantine state. Some of these local notables were defeated on the battlefield, while others were co-opted through marriages and alliances.[23] Soon, he attacked and occupied the important town of Yenişehir, which was proclaimed the Ottoman capital.[24] On July 27, 1301, Osman defeated a Byzantine army outside Nicomedia (Izmit). The victory brought recognition and prestige for Osman Gâzi and allowed the *beys* fighting under his command to push toward the Sea of Marmara and the Aegean. Determined to capture vulnerable Byzantine towns, which were not receiving adequate support from Constantinople, Osman cut the communication lines between Nicaea (Iznik) and Nicomedia (Izmit). Before his death in 1326, Osman had extended his territory all the way to the port of Mudanya and had cut the communication line between Constantinople and the important Byzantine city of Bursa.[25]

Throughout his reign, Osman focused much of his attention on capturing Bursa, an achievement that could significantly enhance his prestige and power. His dream became a reality when, after a seven-year siege, Bursa surrendered in 1326 to his son Orhan, who proclaimed it not only his new capital but also a model of Ottoman generosity, patronage, and support for urban growth and development.[26] The North African traveler and chronicler, Ibn Battuta, who visited Bursa during the reign of Orhan, described the town as "a great and important city with fine bazaars and wide streets, surrounded on all sides by gardens and running springs."[27] He also presented Orhan as "the greatest of the kings of the Turkmens and the richest in wealth, lands, and military forces," who possesses nearly a hundred fortresses, and "for most of his time he is continually engaged in making the round of them, staying in each fortress for some days to put it into good order and examine its conditions."[28] Referring to his role as a *gâzi*, Ibn Battuta wrote that Orhan "fights with the infidels continually and keeps them under siege."[29]

With Bursa as their center of political power and military operations, the Ottoman conquests picked up pace, defeating a Byzantine army of four thousand men under the leadership of the Emperor Andronicus III at the Battle of Pelekanon (Pelecanum) near Eskişehir in 1329, "the first personal encounter between a Byzantine emperor and an Ottoman Emir."[30] Orhan then captured Nicaea (Iznik) in 1331, thus incorporating the entire northwest Anatolia into Ottoman lands.[31] But the Ottomans were not the only power to pose a serious threat to the security and very survival of the Byzantine state. To the west, an alliance between the Serbs and the Bulgarians was concluded in 1332 after the Serbian ruler Stephan Dušan married the sister of the Bulgarian monarch. The Serbian and the Bulgarian monarchs shared the objective of destroying the Byzantine state and replacing it with a Slav empire ruled from Constantinople. By the summer of 1333, the growing threat from Serbia and Bulgaria and the increasing pressure from the Ottomans had forced Andronicus to secretly negotiate a promise of tribute in return for Orhan's stopping the attacks on Byzantine possessions in Asia.[32] Four years later, in 1337, however, the important city of Nicomedia (Izmit) surrendered after the Ottomans allowed the native population who wished to leave for Constantinople to abandon the city before they entered it. With the fall of Nicomedia, the Ottomans established their rule on the southern shore of the Black Sea, making the Ottoman *beylik* the most important and influential neighbor of the Byzantine state.

This newly acquired power and confidence was demonstrated in Orhan's decision to mint silver coins proclaiming himself sultan. His eldest son Süleyman used the newly acquired Ottoman territories to raid the southern shores of the Sea of Marmara and the important strategic region of Gallipoli. By 1354, the Ottomans had occupied Gallipoli, establishing a foothold on the European continent for the first time.[33] Using Gallipoli as the base for their military operations, they intensified their attacks against southern Thrace, which they had raided since 1352. Thrace would hereafter emerge as the territorial base for Ottoman raids and the eventual conquest of southeast Europe.[34]

Their newly gained territory and influence allowed the Ottomans to intervene in fractious Byzantine power politics, dominated by the Cantacuzenus and Palaeologus families, and making an alliance with the former that was strengthened in 1346 when the Byzantine leader offered the second of his three daughters, Theodora, to Orhan as the sultan's new bride.[35] The following year, when Cantacuzenus returned to Constantinople and was proclaimed joint emperor with John V Palaeologus, Ottoman influence within the Byzantine court grew significantly. In 1347, the city was struck by the Black Death. The epidemic killed a large segment of the population, disrupting life and commerce in the Balkans and depopulating towns and villages.[36] The Black Death, the aggressive and expansionist policy of Ottoman Turks from the east, the emergence of Serbian power under Stephan Dušan to the west, and the continuing rivalry between Venice and Genoa over controlling the shipping routes that connected the Black Sea to the Aegean and the Mediterranean, put the very existence of the Byzantine state in extreme jeopardy. The ultimate cause for the rapid decline of the Byzantine state, however, was financial. The empire, which in its heyday ruled a vast territory from the eastern shores of the Italian peninsula to the western borders of Iran, was now reduced to a few isolated enclaves in Anatolia, a number of islands in the Aegean, and the cities of Adrianople and Thessaloniki (Salonica/Salonika) in Thrace.[37] With the sharp decrease in state revenue, it was impossible to reorganize the Byzantine army. What the state collected in revenue was spent on bribing foreign enemies or hiring mercenary armies to fight on behalf of the beleaguered ruling elite.[38]

In his desperate attempt to revive the state and confront the threat posed by Stephan Dušan, Cantacuzenus turned to Orhan for military support. The anti-Serbian alliance allowed the sultan's eldest son, Süleyman, to confront and neutralize the Serbian army as it advanced against Thrace in 1352, bringing Ottoman troops to the European side of the Straits, who were soon followed by Turkish settlers. Thus, in confronting the Serbian threat, Cantacuzenus had unwittingly enhanced the power and influence of the Ottoman state, providing it with a bridgehead to Europe. Cantacuzenus tried unsuccessfully to bribe the Ottomans to abandon their new territory but Süleyman was determined to hold on. He expanded his possessions after an earthquake destroyed hundreds of towns and villages on the Gallipoli Peninsula in March 1354, thus allowing Ottoman forces to occupy the ruins and to transport new settlers to rebuild and repair the homes and farms evacuated by their Greek inhabitants. In response to the Byzantine demand for restitution, Süleyman replied that the devastated villages and towns had fallen into his hands not by conquest but by the will of God, and that returning them "would be an act of impious ingratitude."[39]

The establishment of Turkish settlements on the European continent and the growing Ottoman influence in the Byzantine court created a movement against Cantacuzenus, who was forced to abandon the throne. With Cantacuzenus out of power, the Emperor John V Palaeologus appealed to Pope Innocent VI for assistance, hoping that a new crusader army from Catholic Europe would rescue him from the tightening Turkish noose. But a new crusade was unlikely. France and England were absorbed with the Hundred Years War, which had started in 1337. The Church in Rome was torn by internal conflicts, while the Venetians and Genovese were engaged in "mutually destructive" warfare.[40] In the east, the small and feeble feudal states of the Balkans were divided by old rivalries and lacked the political and military organization to mount a formidable defense against the Ottomans.[41]

But if Christian Europe could not mobilize a strong crusade, events of a different kind helped the beleaguered Byzantine elite to recover momentarily from its panic-stricken state. In the summer of 1357, Orhan received the news of the death of his eldest son and designated successor, Süleyman.[42] At almost the same time, Orhan's twelve-year-old son Halil was captured by pirates in the Gulf of Iznik.[43] In his attempt to win Halil's freedom Orhan was forced to appeal to the Byzantine emperor for assistance. The Byzantine ruler agreed, but demanded that the Ottomans halt their territorial advances against the Byzantine state and stop their interference in the empire's internal affairs, including the withdrawal of their support to the new pretender to the Byzantine throne, Cantacuzenus's son Matheos. Furthermore, the Ottomans would forgive the emperor's remaining debt and assume the cost of rescuing Halil. Orhan agreed to the terms, and for the next two years Ottoman troops did not launch any attacks on Byzantine territory. True to his word, the Byzantine emperor dispatched a rescue mission to free Halil, who was brought to Constantinople in 1359. With Halil in the Byzantine capital, the emperor arranged for a marriage between his daughter Irene and the young Ottoman prince, requesting Orhan to designate Halil as crown prince and the next sultan.[44]

But the agreement reached between the Byzantines and Ottomans did not stop Constantinople from pursuing its double-pronged strategy. The Byzantine emperor was painfully aware that peace with Orhan would be short-lived and that the Ottomans would revive their expansionist policy in southeast Europe as soon as they had secured the release of Halil. During the next several years, Emperor John V traveled to several European courts in order to organize an anti-Ottoman alliance. His efforts, however, were in vain. In addition to the English–French rivalry, the major European naval power, Venice, was engaged in its own conflict with a major European land power, Hungary, over the control of Dalmatia. And the Ottomans were not idle. With Halil's freedom, the Ottomans resumed their expansionist policy toward the Byzantine state, besieging Constantinople by land from Asia and Europe. Shortly after the death of Süleyman, Orhan had designated his second son Murad as the commander of all Ottoman forces in the west.[45] When his brother Halil was rescued in 1359, Murad reassumed the leadership of holy war in southeast Europe, focusing his military campaign on consolidating Ottoman territorial gains in Thrace and capturing the important Byzantine city of Adrianople (Edirne). Under the direct command of Prince Murad, the Ottoman forces stormed the city in 1361 and immediately proclaimed it the new capital of the Ottoman state. The fall of Edirne allowed the Ottoman forces to push into southern Bulgaria and Macedonia and confront the threat posed by the Serbian state, which had declined significantly since the death of its leader, Stephan Dušan, in 1355. With the accession of Murad to the throne in 1362, the new capital began to serve as the residence of the Ottoman sultan. In tightening the noose around Constantinople and consolidating the newly conquered Ottoman possessions in Thrace,

Murad began to organize a campaign into the heart of the Balkans. Before moving against southeast Europe, however, he was forced to deal with a threat posed by the powerful Turkish principality of Karaman in Anatolia. Murad's quick and impressive victory against Karaman allowed the Ottomans to expand their territory eastward and served as a warning to other Turcoman Principalities not to take advantage of the Ottoman preoccupation with Europe. Once the threat from Karaman was neutralized, Murad returned to Edirne to prepare his army for the conquest of the entire Balkan Peninsula.

The expansion of Ottoman rule into southern Bulgaria and Macedonia alarmed Serbia, which had dreamt of carving a Serbo-Greek empire. In their first major military campaign against Serbia, the Ottomans defeated a Serbian army at Chermanon (Chernomen) on the bank of the river Maritsa on September 26, 1371, bringing Bulgaria, Macedonia, and southern Serbia under their control. Sofia was then occupied in 1385, followed by Niş (Nish) in 1386, and Thessaloniki (Salonica) in 1387.[46] Despite these setbacks, the Serbs continued their efforts to establish a united Christian front against the Ottoman state. Initially, their effort was viewed by other rulers in the region as an attempt to impose Serbian hegemony. However, the successful Ottoman military campaign against northern Greece and the conquest of Bulgaria convinced the Christian states of southeast Europe that the time had arrived for a concerted effort to block further Ottoman expansion.[47] Prince Lazar of Serbia, King Tvrto of Bosnia, and John Stratsimir of Vidin agreed to join a Christian alliance, which defeated an Ottoman army in August 1388 at Plocnik (Ploshnik) west of Niş.[48]

Recognizing the threat posed by the alliance, Murad rushed back from Anatolia where he had defeated the Turcoman Principalities of Germiyan, Hamid, and Karaman, forcing them to accept Ottoman suzerainty.[49] The sultan then moved his forces to southern Serbia. The decisive battle took place on June 15, 1389 at the Kosovo Polje (Field of the Blackbirds) near Pristina. Although Murad was killed during the battle, the Ottomans managed to pull a victory out of the jaws of defeat. Prince Lazar was killed at the end of the battle, and the devastating defeat forced Serbia to accept Ottoman suzerainty. Many centuries later, the memory of the battle of Kosovo Polje was celebrated by Serbian nationalists as the last desperate, heroic attempt to save the independence of Serbia and the rest of Orthodox Christian Europe.

Murad was succeeded by his son Bayezid I (1389–1402), known by his title *Yildrim* (Thunderbolt), who replaced his father on the battlefield of Kosovo Polje and proved himself to be a dynamic and charismatic leader, expanding and consolidating newly gained Ottoman domains in the Balkans and Anatolia. The new sultan also intended to conquer Constantinople, transform "the Lower Danube into a safe maritime border," and seize "Christian and Islamic strategic centers on the western and southern littoral of the Black Sea."[50] Shortly after ascending the throne, Bayezid attacked and conquered the Turcoman Principalities of Menteşe, Aydin, Saruhan, Hamid, and Germiyan in Anatolia in 1390. After Ottoman armies annexed northern Bulgaria in 1393, the ruler of Wallachia, Mircea the Old, was forced to accept the suzerainty of the Ottoman sultan in 1395. In 1396, Christian Europe finally mustered sufficient will to organize an anti-Ottoman crusade. At the behest of Pope Boniface IX (1389–1404), the ruler of Hungary, King Sigismund (1387–1437), assumed the leadership of the crusade, which was joined by Christian knights from "England, Scotland, Poland, Bohemia, Austria, Italy, and Switzerland as well as from the lands of southeastern Europe more directly threatened by the Ottomans."[51] The crusading army crossed the Danube at Nicopolis in summer 1396, capturing the towns of Orsova and Vidin and putting the Muslim population to the sword. But Bayezid, who had rushed to the shores of the Danube from Anatolia, routed the Christian army on September 25, killing thousands.

While the *gâzi* core of his forces was determined to push farther into southeast Europe, Bayezid turned his attention from Europe to Anatolia. The sultan viewed the expansion of Ottoman territories in Asia Minor as the first stage of an invasion of the Arab Middle East and Egypt, which were ruled by the Mamluks. By turning away from further expansion in southeast Europe, Bayezid alienated many of his fighters, who believed in the continuation of holy war against the Christian powers of the Balkans. These soldiers, officers, and commanders, who were raised in the *gâzi* tradition, despised the idea of waging war against fellow Muslims. Moreover, military campaigns in Anatolia did not produce "the kind of booty and estates found in Europe."[52] Finally, Bayezid's reliance on European vassals, who had preserved much of their independence, undermined the cohesion and unity of the Ottoman army.

Greatly alarmed by Bayezid's territorial ambitions, the Mamluks of Egypt and the Turcoman Principalities in Anatolia, particularly the Karaman who had lost significant territory to the sultan, began to search for a powerful ally and protector who would be willing to counter the Ottoman power. They thought they found him in Timur the Lame (Teymur-i Lang or Tamirlane). Since 1380, Timur had expanded his territory from the heart of Central Asia into Afghanistan, India, Iran, the Arab world, and the south Caucasus. As early as 1393/4, his forces had approached Anatolia from the south after capturing Baghdad, Takrit, Mosul, Kirkuk, Mardin, and Diyarbakir.[53] After several quick victories, however, Timur was distracted by the events in Iran,

Central Asia, and India and left the region. In 1399, Timur shifted his attention westward yet again, attacking and occupying the southern Caucasus. He also sent a letter to Bayezid, reminding him of his recently acquired power and glory and warning the Ottoman sultan against further military operations against the Turcoman Principalities (*beyliks*) in Anatolia.[54] The response from Bayezid to the insulting and condescending message was a volcanic eruption of abuse and counter threats.[55] Meanwhile, Timur's army entered eastern Anatolia through Erzurum, capturing Sivas and Kayseri before arriving in Ankara in July 1402.[56] The decisive battle was fought on July 28 with the Ottoman army routed and Bayezid captured. Surprisingly, Timur did not order the execution of Bayezid, treating the defeated sultan with the utmost respect and extending his magnanimity to the sultan's sons who pleaded for mercy.

The humiliation of living as a captive came to an end for Bayezid when he died on March 8, 1403 in Akşehir.[57] Meanwhile, Timur pushed his conquests all the way to the shores of the Mediterranean Sea, capturing Smyrna (Izmir) in December 1402, before returning to Central Asia, where he died in 1405 just as he was preparing for the invasion of China. As for Anatolia, his goal seemed to consist of strengthening the Turkish *beyliks* of Karaman, Germiyan, and Hamid against a possible Ottoman restoration by redistribution of Bayezid's empire. Mehmed, the prince of Karaman, was particularly favored by Timur, who viewed him as the principal obstacle to the restoration of Ottoman power and was thus rewarded with significant territory and an impressive army. As a further deterrent, Bayezid's sons, Süleyman, Isa, Musa, and Mehmed, were all kept alive by Timur, who gave each a small fiefdom, knowing that they would have to fight amongst themselves before one could emerge as the successor to their father.[58] Thus began a period of eleven years of war among Bayezid's sons, which came to be known as the Interregnum or "*Fetret*" in Turkish.[59]

Initially, the war for succession to Bayezid's throne centered on Süleyman in Edirne, Isa in Bursa and Balikesir, and Mehmed in Amasya. Having established himself in Edirne and using his father's *gâzis* and cavalry forces, which had remained intact, Süleyman was the most powerful of all contenders to the Ottoman throne. He consolidated his position further when he signed several peace treaties with the Christian states of Europe. Through territorial concessions, such as the return of Salonica to the Byzantine emperor in October 1403, Süleyman tried to gain the political and financial support of Serbia and the Byzantine state. His strategy was to consolidate his rule in southeast Europe and use it as a base to attack Anatolia with the support of his newly found Christian allies. Süleyman's brothers, Mehmed and

Isa, viewed Süleyman as the principal threat to their rule, although all three Ottoman princes accepted the suzerainty of Timur. Curiously, perhaps, it was neither Musa, Isa, nor Süleyman (who Timur recognized as his father's successor because the Ottoman prince was centered in southeast Europe and did not pose any threat to Timur's empire in the Middle East and Central Asia) who emerged victorious after eleven years of civil war, but Prince Mehmed of Amasya. Interesting too that the Christian states of Europe failed to take advantage of post-Timurid Ottoman disunity and internal strife to prevent the re-emergence of Ottoman power and hegemony under a single ruler. Instead, they allied themselves with one Ottoman prince against the other in the hope that the sons of Bayezid would remain dependent on European states for their survival. Thus, they ensured the restoration of Ottoman power, which ultimately established itself as the hegemon in the region after conquering Serbia, Constantinople, and eventually Hungary.

As the new Ottoman sultan ruling a unified empire, Mehmed removed the controversial religious leader Bedreddin and dismissed the *gâzi* leaders who had supported his brother Musa, sending them into exile in Anatolia. To appease the Byzantine emperor, Manuel, Mehmed returned Salonica and all Byzantine territory around Constantinople. He also signed a peace treaty with Genoa and Venice. Mehmed's strategy was clear. He intended to restore the power of notable Ottoman families and religious leaders at home and rebuild the army before engaging it in another military adventure. He soon realized, however, that his peace strategy could be misinterpreted as a sign of weakness, particularly among the leaders of various Turkish *beyliks* in Anatolia who had gained a great deal from the defeat of Bayezid in 1402. Thus, Mehmed attacked the Turcoman Principalities of western and southwestern Anatolia, recapturing most possessions that Murad and Bayezid had taken from Karaman and that Timur had restored to them after his victory at Ankara.[60] The Ottoman sultan could not, however, continue his military campaigns in Anatolia because of several internal revolts that challenged Ottoman authority in Europe. The first of these was led by the followers of Şeyh Bedreddin, who had been sent into exile by Mehmed. The controversial religious leader did not curtail his activities while in exile. Worse, he fled Ottoman territory and soon landed in Wallachia, where he was received with pomp and ceremony and sufficient support to mobilize his followers in Europe, many of whom were recruited from among the Turkish nomads who had recently moved from Anatolia. Inspired by his popularity, the Şeyh's followers in Anatolia began to organize local revolts to challenge the Ottoman state. While the revolts in Anatolia were suppressed, the situation in Rumeli (the European provinces of the Ottoman Empire) deteriorated when Şeyh Bedreddin raised the flag of open rebellion in Dobrudja. To make matters worse, a man claiming to be Prince Mustafa, the lost son of Sultan Bayezid who had been held in prison by Timur, surfaced and immediately staged a rebellion with the support of the Byzantine state and Wallachia.[61] Encouraged by these rebellions, the Venetians attacked and destroyed the Ottoman fleet at Gallipoli on May 29, 1416.[62] Mehmed sent one army against Düzme Mustafa (the False Mustafa) and another against Bedreddin, scoring a quick victory against the former who was defeated and forced to flee to Constantinople. In the autumn of 1416, Ottoman forces crushed Şeyh Bedreddin's revolt.[63] Bedreddin himself was captured and shortly after executed on December 18, 1416.[64] With the challenge from False Mustafa neutralized, Mehmed turned east and completed his conquest of western and southwestern Anatolia. He had already annexed Hamid in 1414, Aydin in 1415, and Menteşe in 1416. Teke and Antalya were now added to Ottoman domains.[65] Though determined to pursue his victories in Anatolia, Mehmed was forced to return to Europe where he carried out a series of raids against Wallachia, forcing Prince Mircea to accept Ottoman suzerainty and capturing the important strategic town of Giurgiu (Yergögü) in 1419.[66]

With the death of Mehmed in 1421, his son ascended the Ottoman throne as Murad II. His reign may be described as the most intriguing of all periods in Ottoman history. Perhaps the most fascinating aspect of this period was the sultan himself, a man of science and learning who despised wars and bloodshed and preferred poetry and mysticism. He abdicated in favor of his son, Mehmed II, in 1444 but was forced to return to the throne in 1446 after his grand vezir, Çandarli Halil, pleaded with him to assume the reins of power.

During the first three years of his reign, Murad focused his efforts on eliminating the threat posed by the return of the False Mustafa, who took Edirne with support from the Byzantine state.[67] Mustafa raised an army against the new sultan and Murad had to defend Bursa and the rest of Ottoman territory against the pretender, who was confronted and defeated at Ulubat in January 1422. Panicked by the defeat, Mustafa escaped but was captured and killed in Edirne.[68] The elimination of the False Mustafa allowed Murad to attack the Byzantine state, which had supported his uncle.[69] His siege of Constantinople, however, allowed Turcoman principalities in Anatolia to revolt, encouraging the sultan's younger brother, Mustafa, to attack Bursa.[70] Murad was forced to raise the siege of the Byzantine capital and lead his troops against Turcoman Principalities in Anatolia, which were suppressed with ease.[71] While Menteşe and Teke were recaptured in

1425, the sultan could not annex the Karaman and the Candar. The Ottomans feared that an invasion of the Karaman would be used as a justification by Shahrokh, the Timurid ruler of Iran, to invade Anatolia.[72] They could not have forgotten the bitter defeat of Bayezid at the battle of Ankara in 1402, and they were determined not to commit the mistake of providing an excuse for a son of Timur to invade Ottoman territory.

The Ottomans confronted two principal obstacles in their attempt to establish total hegemony in southeast Europe. On the land, Hungary possessed the political and military power to organize a unified Christian resistance against Ottoman domination. On the sea, the power capable of creating serious obstacles to Ottoman hegemony was Venice, which took Salonica from the Byzantine state in the summer of 1423.[73] The Venetians were determined to maintain their hegemony over the trade and commerce of the Aegean and at the same time prevent the establishment of Ottoman control in Macedonia and Albania.[74] Thus, war between the two powers became inevitable. The Ottoman–Venetian war continued until 1430, when Ottoman forces captured Salonica. [75]

In their attempt to prevent the Ottoman Empire from establishing its control over southeast Europe, it was crucial for Hungarians to maintain their influence over Serbia, Transylvania, and Wallachia, which served as buffer states against northward Ottoman expansion. Throughout Murad's reign, the Ottomans fought to establish and preserve the sultan's suzerainty over Serbia and use it as a territorial base to carry out raids against Hungary. In response, Hungarians pressured Serbia and Wallachia to throw off Ottoman vassalage and join a unified anti-Ottoman Christian alliance under their leadership. Meanwhile, Serbia and Wallachia tried to maintain their independence by playing one power against the other. When Ottoman armies were fighting in distant Anatolia, Serbia and Wallachia carried out raids across the Danube with the encouragement and support of Hungary, but when the sultan returned to Rumeli and carried out raids against their territory, as Murad did in 1424, they retreated and eventually accepted Ottoman suzerainty in return for a promise that the raids against their territory would be stopped.[76] This game of cat and mouse continued until 1427 when Djordje (George) Branković emerged as the ruler of Serbia. A year later, the king of Hungary and the Ottoman sultan agreed to sign a peace treaty, recognizing Branković as the prince of Serbia. For the next three years, Serbia acted as a buffer state between the Hungarians and the Ottomans.[77] With the termination of the treaty in 1431, however, the conflict resurfaced. The sultan returned to the policy of attacking Hungary, while the Hungarians tried to use their influence in Bosnia, Serbia, and Wallachia to organize an anti-Ottoman coalition.

The Ottomans could not respond immediately to the situation in the Balkans. Anatolia had been invaded by the armies of Shahrokh, the ruler of Iran, in 1435.[78] By reassuring the Timurid monarch that he did not intend to undermine and destroy the independence of the principality of Karaman and by supporting Shahrokh against the Mamluks of Egypt, Murad avoided open warfare and expanded Ottoman power and influence in Anatolia. With the Timurid threat neutralized, Murad turned his attention to southeast Europe, where the death of the Hungarian monarch, Sigismund, in 1437, had resulted in internal anarchy and chaos. That confusion allowed the Ottoman forces to carry out attacks against Bosnia, Serbia, and Transylvania from 1438 to 1439, capturing the important fortresses of Semendria that had been built by the Serbian king Djordje Branković, and forcing the Serbs and the Bosnians to pay annual tribute to the Ottoman sultan. A year later, they attacked Belgrade but failed to capture it.[79]

The Hungarian reaction to Ottoman raids was swift. The new king of Poland and Hungary, Vladislav (Ladislas), appointed the Romanian János (John) Hunyadi the governor of Transylvania. Under the charismatic leadership of the new governor, the Hungarian forces scored several impressive victories against Ottoman armies in 1441 and 1442, "killing tens of thousands of Ottoman soldiers at the battles of Hermanstadt and Vazağ (Jalomitcha)."[80] They recaptured the fortress of Semendria and pushed Ottoman forces out of Transylvania, reviving the hope of Christian Europe that it was still possible to confront the Ottoman threat. With the active support from King Vladislav and Djordje Branković, and the participation of crusaders who had been mobilized from various European countries, Hunyadi pushed through Ottoman defenses in southern Serbia capturing the town of Niş, encouraging the Albanians under George Castriotes (Skanderbeg) to rise against Ottoman authority and join the victorious Christian crusade. With the momentum on his side and the main Ottoman army bogged down in a campaign in Anatolia, Hunyadi led his forces through the Balkan Mountains, entering western Bulgaria in 1443.[81]

With the winter of 1444 approaching, the Ottomans confronted a multifaceted challenge. But then Hunyadi halted his southward push from Bulgaria toward Edirne, allowing Murad sufficient time to devise a diplomatic solution. It must have been clear to the sultan and his advisors that they needed time to reorganize their forces. With encouragement from his grand vezir and his Serbian wife Mora, Murad began to negotiate for a cessation of hostilities.[82] The Treaty of Edirne signed with Hungary and its allies on June 12, 1444 can, therefore, be viewed as an attempt by the Ottomans to buy time and neutralize the formidable alliance organized against them. Hunyadi demanded and received the promise that Ottoman forces would return to Anatolia.[83] The Ottomans maintained their rule over Bulgaria.[84] The true winner, however, was Djordje Branković, who restored the autonomy of the Serbian state.[85] Back in Anatolia in the summer of 1444, Murad signed the Treaty of Yenişehir with the Karaman, ceding some of the territory of Hamid that he had occupied.[86] The sultan then abdicated in favor of his twelve-year-old son, who ascended the Ottoman throne as Mehmed II.[87]

Murad's abdication caused "a power struggle" within the Ottoman government between the grand vezir, Çandarli Halil, and the new sultan's personal tutor, Zaganos, and the *beylerbey* of Rumeli, Şihâbeddin.[88] Meanwhile, a new campaign was being organized and led by Hungary. The Hungarians enjoyed the support of the Pope, the Byzantine state, Venice, and George Castriotes in Albania.[89] Alarmed by the prospect of another attack by Hunyadi, the factions within the government decided that the young Mehmed II would be incapable of leading the empire at a time of such serious crisis and appealed to Murad to assume the command of the Ottoman army.[90] The Christian army, organized in Buda under the leadership of the king of Hungary and Poland, had already pushed south toward Bulgaria with the goal of attacking the Ottoman capital at Edirne. Despite several early successes, however, the Christian army suffered a devastating defeat at Varna on November 10, 1444, after King Vladislav was killed on the battlefield.[91] The last concerted effort to halt the Ottoman conquest of the Balkans had failed, and the Ottoman Empire regained the prestige and power lost to Hunyadi. The Ottoman victory at Varna also sealed the fate of the Byzantine state.[92] Less than ten years after Varna, the Ottomans would sack the city of Constantinople and bring to an end the reign of Byzantine emperors. Following his victory at Varna, Murad withdrew from politics again, but his retirement lasted only two years. Soon the internal conflict within the Ottoman government erupted again. The grand vezir, Çandarli Halil, defended Murad's policy of peace with the Christian states, while the advisers of the young Mehmed, Zaganos and Şihâbeddin, blamed the Byzantine state for organizing the anti-Ottoman alliance and advocated a "final assault" on Constantinople.[93] An uprising by the *janissaries* organized by the wily Çandarli Halil forced Mehmed to abdicate in favor of his father, who ascended the throne for a second time. Once on the throne, Murad carried out a series of aggressive campaigns against former vassals.[94] The sultan was clearly convinced that some, if not all, of the southeastern European provinces had to be brought under the direct rule of the Ottoman state. Thus, after forcing the Byzantine ruler of Morea to accept Ottoman suzerainty, Murad began to impose direct rule in much of mainland Greece.[95] The same policy was applied to Bulgaria, where local princes who had betrayed their allegiance to the sultan were dismissed and replaced by Ottoman administrators.[96] When the Hungarians led by Hunyadi attacked Ottoman territory again, Murad inflicted another devastating defeat on their army at the second battle of Kosovo in October 1448. With Ottoman rule firmly established south of the Danube, Murad sent his forces to Wallachia in 1449, punishing the country for lending its support to Hunyadi and forcing it to accept Ottoman suzerainty.[97] He also attacked Skanderbeg in Albania in 1450. By the time Murad died in February 1451, he had reestablished Ottoman rule within the territory controlled by Bayezid before his defeat at the hands of Timur in 1402. In the process, the Ottomans had recognized that creating an empire based on a system of vassals was inherently unstable and, therefore, untenable. To maintain a strong and unified empire, there was no other alternative but to impose direct Ottoman rule.

Notes

1. Muhammad ibn Ali ibn Sulayman Ar-Rawandi, *Rahat us-Sudur wa Ayat us-Surur*, ed. Muhammad Iqbal (Leiden: E.J. Brill, 1921), 86–7.

2. Ibid., 100–1. Muhammad ibn Hussein Bayhaqi, *Tarikh-i Bayhaqi* (Tehran: 1945), 602–27.

3. Bayhaqi, *Tarikh-i Bayhaqi*, 796. Claude Cahen, *The Formation of Turkey: The Seljukid Sultanate of Rūm: Eleventh to Fourteenth Century*, trans. P.M. Holt (Essex: Pearson Education Limited, 2001), 1.

4. Rawandi, *Rahat us-Sudur*, 104.

5. Ibid., 105–6.

6. Cahen, *The Formation of Turkey*, 2.

7. John Julius Norwich, *A Short History of Byzantium* (New York: Alfred A. Knopf, 1997), 240–1.

8. See Cahen, *The Formation of Turkey*, 7–14, 75–85.

9. M. Fuad Köprülü, *The Origins of the Ottoman Empire*, trans. Gary Leiser (Albany: State University of New York Press, 1992), 43.

10. See Ata Malik Juwaini, *Tarikh-i Jahangosha* (Tehran: 1984).

11. I.P. Petrushevsky, "The Socio-Economic Condition of Iran Under the Il-Khans" in *The Cambridge History of Iran*, ed. J.A. Boyle (Cambridge: Cambridge University Press, 1968), 5:486.

12. Ibid.

13. Hamdullah Mostowfi, *Nuzhat ul-Qulub*, ed. G.L.E. Strange (Leiden: E.J. Brill, 1915), 27.

14. Ibn Bibi, *Akhbar-e Salajeqe-ye Rum* (Tehran: 1971), 182–83.

15. For an excellent discussion of the tribal origins of Osman, see Köprülü, *The Origins of the Ottoman Empire*, 72–7.

16. Barbara Jelavich, *History of the Balkans Eighteenth and Nineteenth Centuries* (Cambridge: Cambridge University Press, 1995), 30–1.

17. Ibid., 31.

18. Several sources maintain that Osman began his reign as early as 1280 or 1281.

19. See Heath W. Lowry, *The Nature of the Early Ottoman State* (Albany: State University of New York Press, 2003).

20. Ibid., 45–6.

21. Ibid., 46.

22. Shaw, *History of the Ottoman Empire*, 1:13–14.

23. Ibid., 1:14.

24. Ibid.

25. Ibid.

26. McCarthy, *The Ottoman Turks*, 43. Köprülü, *The Origins of the Ottoman Empire*, 109.

27. *The Travels of Ibn Battuta A.D. 1325–1354*, trans. H.A.R. Gibb (Cambridge: Cambridge University Press, 1962), 2:449–50.

28. Ibid., 2:451–52.

29. Ibid., 2:452.

30. Norwich, *A Short History of Byzantium*, 339.

31. Ibid.

32. Ibid., 340.

33. Shaw, *History of the Ottoman Empire*, 1:16.

34. Ibid.

35. Ibid.

36. Norwich, *A Short History of Byzantium*, 345.

37. Ibid., 345–46.

38. Ibid., 346.

39. Ibid., 348.

40. Jelavich, *History of the Balkans*, 30.

41. Ibid., 31.

42. Caroline Finkel, *Osman's Dream: The Story of the Ottoman Empire 1300–1923* (New York: Basic Books, 2005), 17.

43. Ibid.

44. Ibid.

45. Ibid.

46. Jelavich, *History of the Balkans*, 31.

47. Sugar, *Southeastern Europe under Ottoman Rule*, 21.

48. Ibid.

49. Inalcik, *Ottoman Empire*, 14–15.

50. Nagy Pienaru, "The Black Sea and the Ottomans: the Pontic Policy of Bayezid the Thunderbolt" in *Ottoman Borderlands: Issues, Personalities,*

and Political Changes, ed. Kemal H. Karpat with Robert W. Zens (Madison: The University of Wisconsin Press, 2003), 33.

51. Shaw, *History of the Ottoman Empire*, 1:33.

52. Ibid., 1:35.

53. Khand Mir, *Habib us-Siyyar*, 4 vols. (Tehran, 1984), 3:455–59.

54. Ibid., 3:490.

55. Ibid.

56. Ibid., 3:506–7.

57. Ibid., 3:513.

58. Alderson, *The Structure of the Ottoman Dynasty*, 6.

59. Ibid.

60. Shaw, *History of the Ottoman Empire*, 1:42.

61. Ibid., 1:43.

62. Inalcik, *Ottoman Empire*, 18.

63. Ibid.

64. Somel, *Historical Dictionary of the Ottoman Empire*, xxi. Finkel, *Osman's Dream*, 34–5.

65. Shaw, *History of the Ottoman Empire*, 1:44.

66. Inalcik, *Ottoman Empire*, 18. Sugar, *Southeastern Europe under Ottoman Rule*, 28.

67. McCarthy, *The Ottoman Turks*, 59.

68. Somel, *Historical Dictionary of the Ottoman Empire*, xxi.

69. Inalcik, *Ottoman Empire*, 19.

70. Ibid.

71. Ibid.

72. Shaw, *History of the Ottoman Empire*, 1:45.

73. Inalcik, *Ottoman Empire*, 19. McCarthy, *The Ottoman Turks*, 60. Shaw, *History of the Ottoman Empire*, 1:46–7.

74. Shaw, *History of the Ottoman Empire*, 1:47.

75. Ibid., 1:48. Inalcik, *Ottoman Empire*, 19.

76. Ibid., 1:47.

77. Inalcik, *Ottoman Empire*, 19.

78. Ibid., 60.

79. Sugar, *Southeastern Europe under Ottoman Rule*, 28–9. Shaw, *History of the Ottoman Empire*, 1:50.

80. McCarthy, *The Ottoman Turks*, 60–1.

81. Ibid., 61.

82. Shaw, *History of the Ottoman Empire*, 1:52.

83. Ibid.

84. Ibid.

85. Ibid.

86. Inalcik, *Ottoman Empire*, 20.

87. Shaw, *History of the Ottoman Empire*, 1:52.

88. Inalcik, *Ottoman Empire*, 20.

89. Sugar, *Southeastern Europe under Ottoman Rule*, 29.

90. Tursun Beg, *The History of Mehmed the Conqueror*, trans. Halil Inalcik and Rhoads Murphey (Minneapolis: Bibliotheca Islamic, 1978), 32.

91. Shaw, *History of the Ottoman Empire*, 1:53.

92. Sugar, *Southeastern Europe under Ottoman Rule*, 29. Inalcik, *Ottoman Empire*, 21.

93. Inalcik, *Ottoman Empire*, 20–1.

94. Ibid., 21.

95. Shaw, *History of the Ottoman Empire*, 1:53.

96. Ibid.

97. Ibid., 1:54.

CHAPTER 3

ZENITH OF OTTOMAN POWER

Many Muslim rulers had dreamed of capturing Constantinople. As early as AD 674, the Umayyad caliphs, who ruled a vast Islamic empire from their capital in Damascus, Syria, had attacked the city. They tried for the second time in 717–718, but failed again.[1] Although the Byzantine state was now devoid of its ancient glory and power, Constantinople held significant strategic, financial, and symbolic value. The city connected the Black Sea to the Aegean and provided the shortest and easiest land route from Anatolia to the Balkans.[2] It also separated the Anatolian possessions of the Ottoman state from its southeast European provinces.[3] As long as it remained in the hands of the Byzantine state, the city could be used as a base for attacks against Ottoman armies and to blockade shipping from the Black Sea to the Aegean. Economically, Constantinople was an important center of commerce and trade, the most important stop for the traders and merchants who carried goods from Central Asia, Iran, and Anatolia to Europe. The city was also home to important merchant communities, such as the Venetians and the Genovese, who functioned as middlemen between the economies of Asia and Europe. Finally, the symbolic aspect of conquest was as important as its strategic and economic value. The city was known as the Rome of the east, and the Greek rulers of the Byzantine state carried the title of Caesar.[4] For the Ottoman rulers, who lacked the noble blood of the Abbasid caliphs of Baghdad and the imperial lineage of the Byzantine emperors, the conquest of Constantinople would add a great deal of prestige and legitimacy.[5] Indeed, it would promote them from the status of a prominent regional player to that of a superpower, while at the same time filling the coffers of the state treasury and providing more fuel to the Ottoman military machine. From the very beginning of their empire, the Ottoman sultans had viewed Constantinople as the greatest prize they could acquire. The symbolic significance of the city was reflected in the concept of *Kizil Elma* (Red Apple), an expression the Ottomans used to speak of Constantinople as the most important prize in their drive to create a world empire.[6] By plucking the red apple, the sultan could end the reign of Byzantine emperors who had offered protection to numerous pretenders to the Ottoman throne, stirring up internal conflicts and civil wars that had undermined the security and stability of the Ottoman state.[7] It should not come as a surprise, then, that upon ascending to the throne in February 1451, Mehmed II ordered his army to prepare for the siege and assault of the city.

Despite all these potential benefits, some powerful Ottoman officials opposed the attack. The most prominent among them was the grand vezir Çandarli Halil. Mehmed disliked the aging statesman for the role he had played during his father's abdication when the young Mehmed had temporarily ruled as the sultan, only to be deposed with the encouragement and support from the *janissaries* and Çandarli Halil.[8] Confident of his power and influence inside the government, Çandarli Halil now opposed the dream that the young sultan had cherished since childhood. Mehmed enjoyed the grand vezir's vehement opposition to the project, for it had already tarnished his reputation by allowing opponents at the court to label him as the agent of the Greek emperor and the alleged recipient of bribes from the Byzantine court.

In preparing for the final assault on Constantinople, Mehmed constructed an Ottoman navy to impose a blockade on the city. A fortress called Rumeli Hissar (European Fortress), armed with siege cannons, was built on the Bosphorus to destroy any ships that might try to run the blockade and supply the city's starving population with fighting men, weaponry, and provisions from Black Sea colonies.[9] Meanwhile, by the spring of 1453, the Ottomans had assembled one of the largest and most formidable land forces the ancient empire had ever seen. By then, the population of the city had decreased significantly, as many of its residents had fled before the assault began. Those who remained behind fought heroically and repulsed several Ottoman assaults, but they were fighting a losing battle against one of the world's best armies. On May 29, the Ottoman troops broke through the city's walls and defenses. The last Byzantine Emperor, Constantine XI, who was fighting with the city's defenders, was killed during the battle. In accordance with the established practice of the day, a city conquered by assault was subjected to plunder by the conquering army.[10] As the Ottoman troops swept through the city, the sultan walked into the Hagia Sophia (Aya Sofya or St. Sophia), the church built by the emperor Justinian in the sixth century AD, and declared it a mosque for

Islam, proclaiming "Hereafter my capital is Istanbul."[11] After allowing his army to pillage the city for three days, the sultan ordered the reconstruction of his new capital.[12] To establish himself as the new caesar and *padişah* who had inherited the Byzantine Empire, Mehmed had to create a government that could serve as the exclusive instrument of his will. For the Ottoman state to be recognized as a world power, its capital had to represent not only power and prosperity but also openness and tolerance. Thus, the Greek population, which had been decimated, was invited to return, and the Greek Orthodox Church, under the leadership of its Patriarch, was allowed to remain and prosper under the protection of the sultan.[13] The sultan also invited the Armenian Patriarch to settle in his new capital.[14] In order to attract Muslim religious leaders and scholars, Mehmed ordered the construction of the Fatih Mosque overlooking the Bosphorus.[15] By the end of his reign, the construction of new mosques, *medresas*, and bazaars had restored much of Istanbul's past glory and prosperity.

With the conquest of Constantinople, Mehmed received the title of *Fatih* (the Conqueror). The capture of the city made the young sultan the most powerful and popular sovereign in the entire Islamic world. Confident of his ability, Mehmed introduced an absolutist rule. To ensure the loyalty of the officials and commanders who surrounded him and to remind all those at the court who was in charge of the empire's affairs, he ordered the execution of Çandarli Halil and the expropriation of his wealth. The message was loud and clear. The sultan was the sole master of his empire and did not tolerate any opposition or criticism of his decisions, even if it came from such a prominent and powerful individual. The government officials were servants of the sultan; they obeyed and executed his orders and did not enjoy the right to interfere and undermine the royal decrees and decisions.

Mehmed also ordered the construction of a new palace to represent the new style of leadership. Built on land overlooking the Bosphorus, the new palace, which was named Topkapi (Cannon Gate), allowed the sultan to live in privacy and seclusion.[16] Before Mehmed, Ottoman sultans intermingled with their officials, army commanders, and even soldiers. The design of Topkapi, however, made the Ottoman sultan less accessible to his government, the army, and the populace. Several buildings and many layers of palace hierarchy stood between a visiting dignitary or ambassador and the sultan. The eunuchs and the *divan*, or the council chamber, where the grand vezir and his ministers met four times a week, were some of the layers that blocked direct access to the sultan.

Having established himself as the most powerful Muslim sovereign, Mehmed had to confront those European powers posing the most serious threat to Ottoman hegemony in southeastern Europe, namely Hungary to the north and Venice to the west. The Hungarians intended to use their influence on Serbia, which had been resurrected in 1444, to maintain and expand their power in the Balkans. For the Ottomans, there was no other alternative but to confront Hungary by bringing Serbia under their direct control. In two campaigns, the first in 1454 and the second in 1455, Mehmed tried to impose Ottoman rule on Serbia, but he failed to capture Belgrade in 1456. When Djordje Branković died, the conflict between the Ottoman state and Hungary resurfaced. After another series of campaigns in 1459, Mehmed finally occupied much of Serbia, but the problem of Hungarian involvement in Serbian internal affairs persisted until the reign of Süleyman the Magnificent, when the Ottomans finally occupied Belgrade and used it as a land bridge to attack and defeat the Hungarians.

As for Venice, Mehmed moved his forces to the Morea in 1459, establishing Ottoman control over the region by 1460.[17] The Ottoman position in the region, however, remained tenuous since Venice continued to hold such important strategic fortresses as Modon and Coron, which were supported from the sea by the Venetian maritime forces. Taking advantage of the collapse of Byzantine power, Venice also established itself on the Isthmus of Corinth, using it as a land bridge to push northward and threaten the Ottoman forces from the rear. The result was the renewal of wars with Venice which would continue until 1479, undermining Mehmed's attempts to establish Ottoman control over mainland Greece.

In 1463, Ottoman forces invaded and occupied Bosnia.[18] In sharp contrast to other Christian areas of southeastern Europe, in Bosnia there were massive conversions to Islam following the Ottoman conquest.[19] As mosques and religious schools transformed the urban landscape, Islam gradually penetrated the Bosnian countryside. The newly converted Bosnian nobility retained its Slavic language and culture and gradually emerged as a close ally of the Ottoman state, which rewarded it with enormous political and economic power.[20]

The invasion and occupation of Bosnia reignited the war with the Hungarians, who sought an alliance with Venice. In searching for formidable allies who could strengthen their united front against the Ottomans, Hungary and Venice sought and received the support of the Albanian rebel, Skanderbeg. Their most important ally was not, however, a Christian prince, but a new Muslim ruler by the name of Hasan Beyk also known as Uzun Hasan (Tall Hasan), who was determined to resurrect the empire of Timur. Venetian ambassadors arrived at the court of Uzun Hasan, the chief of the Ak Koyunlu (White Sheep) Turcomans, to negotiate an alliance that would allow Venice and the Ak

Koyunlu forces to coordinate a joint military campaign against the Ottoman Empire.

Since the early 1460s, the Ottomans had watched anxiously the rise of Uzun Hasan as the ruler of a new and powerful state in eastern and southeastern Anatolia. In November 1467, Uzun Hasan defeated Jahan Shah, the leader of the rival Kara Koyunlu (Black Sheep). Two years later, he routed the armies of the Timurid prince, Abu Said, and Jahan Shah's son, Hasan Ali, who committed suicide.[21] With these impressive victories, Uzun Hasan emerged as the master of Iran, and the tone of his letters to Mehmed shifted from a humble and obedient ally to a proud and confident monarch who viewed himself as an equal to the conqueror of Constantinople, a change that could not have gone unnoticed by Mehmed.[22]

The Ak Koyunlu leader was well aware that he needed allies in his confrontation with the Ottoman state. To the south, the Mamluks, who ruled Egypt and Syria, constituted the most powerful state in the region. Uzun Hasan maintained a close relationship with the Mamluks as demonstrated by the correspondence between the rulers of the two states. He hoped that the Ak Koyunlu and the Mamluks would form an alliance against the Ottomans. Between the Ottomans and the Ak Koyunlu in Anatolia stood the last two remaining Turcoman Principalities, the Dulkadir/Dulgadir and the Karaman, the latter having been defeated and conquered by Mehmed between 1468 and 1470.[23] Despite their defeat and loss of independence, the chiefs of Karaman had not given up on the dream of regaining their principality by using the Ak Koyunlu as an ally against the Ottomans. Since the annexation of their principality, they had sought refuge in the Taurus Mountains, appealing persistently to Uzun Hasan for an alliance against the Ottomans.[24] The powers willing and committed to wage an attack on the Ottoman state were the Venetians and the Knights of Rhodes, who had sent emissaries to court the Turcoman chief, forming an alliance in 1464 and providing him with financial support and weaponry.[25] As a formidable maritime power, Venice could attack the Ottomans from the west while the Ak Koyunlu waged a land assault from the east. In 1472, after he had received an urgent request from the Karaman for support against a major Ottoman force led by the sultan, Uzun Hasan mobilized his army for a major campaign and attacked eastern Anatolia.[26]

An Ottoman army of nearly one hundred thousand was mobilized to face the Ak Koyunlu threat. The decisive battle took place near the village of Başkent in northeastern Anatolia on August 11, 1473.[27] The Ottoman forces, which included ten thousand *janissaries*, inflicted a crushing defeat on the Ak Koyunlu army, killing one of Uzun Hasan's sons and forcing the Turcoman chief to flee the battlefield.[28] As part of the victory celebration over Uzun Hasan, in one day alone, three thousand members of the Ak Koyunlu were executed. At each stop on their way back to Istanbul, the Ottomans beheaded four hundred Ak Koyunlu men, leaving their bodies on the road as a warning to those who were contemplating a revolt against the authority of the sultan.[29] With the defeat of Ak Koyunlu, the Karaman as well as Kastamonu and Trebizond were fully incorporated into the Ottoman state.

Genoa and Venice had instigated the conflict between the Ottomans and Uzun Hasan by financing and arming the Ak Koyunlu ruler. The attack on Genoa was primarily focused on the Genovese colonies of Amasra, Sinop, Trebizond, Kaffa, and Sudak on the Black Sea, which the Ottomans forced to pay annual tribute before occupying them between 1459 and 1475.[30] On the other hand, the assault on Venice began by Ottoman forces laying siege to the Venetian-held district of Shkodër (Işkodra) in Albania. After four years of war, the two parties reached a peace agreement.[31] According to this agreement, Shkodër, Akçahisar, Lemnos, and the islands of Euboia were ceded to the Ottoman Empire, while Venice retained its control of Lepanto, Coron, and Modon in the Morea as well as the right to trade in the sultan's domains. Venice also agreed to pay the sultan ten thousand gold coins annually.[32]

With Venice and Genoa neutralized for a time, Mehmed pursued his strategy of establishing a complete Ottoman hegemony on the Black Sea basin by bringing the Crimean Tatars under Ottoman protection. In return for Ottoman protection against the empire of the Golden Horde, the Khanate of Crimea accepted Ottoman suzerainty in 1475. Thus, the northern shores of the Black Sea were incorporated into the Ottoman state, which came to dominate maritime trade in the region.[33]

With the establishment of Ottoman rule in the Black Sea region, Mehmed turned his attention once again to Venice and concentrated his energy and forces on an ambitious plan to conquer Italy. He also intended to capture Rhodes from the Knights of Hospitallers, but the army he sent against them was defeated. However, the Ottoman forces attacking Italy landed at Otranto in the summer of 1480, establishing a land base from which they planned to pursue their conquest the following spring. The Italian city states as well as the Pope in Rome were preparing themselves for the worst when the news of Mehmed's death arrived. The sultan died at forty-nine years of age in May 1481, before his dream of conquering Italy could become a reality.[34]

Upon Mehmed's death, a war of succession erupted between the sultan's older son, Prince Cem, and his younger son, Prince Bayezid. During his life, the Conqueror and his grand vezir Karamani Mehmed Paşa had favored Cem. However, powerful forces within the state, particularly the *janissaries* stationed in Istanbul, and influential army commanders, such as Gedik Ahmed Paşa and his father-in-law Işak Paşa, who despised the grand vezir, supported Prince Bayezid.[35] As soon as Mehmed died, the army commanders went into action, encouraging *janissary* units stationed in the capital to riot and storm the palace, where they killed the grand vezir. Meanwhile, Işak Paşa blocked Prince Cem and his supporters from reaching Istanbul. This allowed Prince Bayezid to rush to Istanbul and declare himself the sultan. Cem did not, however, accept defeat. Although he had failed to reach the Ottoman capital in time to declare himself the new sultan, Cem rallied his supporters, who assembled in Bursa. With his supporters rallying to his cause, Cem declared himself the sultan of Anatolia in May 1481 and proposed to divide the empire, taking Anatolia for himself and allowing Bayezid to rule as the sultan of Rumeli.[36]

After rejecting Cem's offer to divide the empire, Bayezid led his troops against his brother, who was defeated at Yenişehir in June 1481. Cem and his supporters fled the battlefield and eventually sought refuge in Mamluk territory. To undermine the internal stability of their powerful neighbor to the north, the Mamluks provided Cem with sufficient support to organize an army. The "practice of offering political asylum to Ottoman princes was a longstanding method used by Mamluk sultans to divide and weaken the Ottoman house."[37] Cem was also joined by dispossessed Turkish princes, notables, and feudal lords, such as the former ruler of Karaman. In the spring of 1482, Cem marched his forces from Syria into central Anatolia, but the rebellion by the Turkish aristocracy that he had hoped for did not materialize. His attempt to capture Konya also failed when his army was defeated by Bayezid's eldest son, Abdullah.[38] By July, when his army reached Ankara, Cem recognized that neither the *janissaries* nor the Turkish aristocracy would rally around his banner.[39] The collapse of Cem's last campaign convinced the prince of Karaman to renounce his claims and join the Ottoman ruling elite as a governor. Other Turcoman notables followed suit, setting aside their differences with the sultan and joining Ottoman service. With the disappearance of Karaman, which had served as a buffer between the Ottoman Empire and the Mamluks of Egypt, a confrontation between the two powerful Muslim states became inevitable. Starting in 1484, the two sides waged a series of campaigns over the fate of Dulkadir, the last remaining Turkish principality in southern Anatolia.[40] Despite their initial success against the Ottomans, the Mamluks decided to sue for peace in 1491. The peace between the Ottomans and the Mamluks lasted until 1516 when Bayezid's son and successor, Sultan Selim (The Grim), attacked and conquered Syria and Egypt and put an end to Mamluk rule.

In southeast Europe, Bayezid organized a series of campaigns against Moldavia, capturing the fortresses of Kilia and Akkerman and occupying the entire western and northwestern shores of the Black Sea by the summer of 1484, thus blocking Hungary, Moldavia, and Wallachia from enjoying access to the mouth of the Danube.[41] The sultan's conquest of Moldavian territory made Poland the new northern neighbor of the Ottoman Empire. Convinced that they would be the next target of the sultan, the Poles attacked in 1497, but they were defeated by an Ottoman army in Bukovina and forced to sue for peace in 1499. The Poles had recognized that the war with the Ottoman Empire had benefited the Crimean Tatars, who expanded their territory northward at the expense of the Polish state and Muscovy.

During this tumultuous period, as he fought the Mamluks in the south and conquered Moldavian territory to the north, the sultan consolidated his authority within the central government. The conflict between Cem and Bayezid had partially reflected the tension within the Ottoman system between the old Turkish aristocracy and the *kapi kullari* (the Christian boys who were trained as slaves of the sultan) who had been recruited through the *devşirme* system. Bayezid had seized the Ottoman throne with the active support of *devşirme*, who exercised a great deal of power over him. To free himself from their influence, Bayezid ordered the execution of Gedik Ahmed Paşa and dismissed his father-in-law, the grand vezir Işak Paşa, in 1482 and replaced them with men who owed their new position and power to him.[42] Many of the new appointees were recruited from the ranks of Turkish aristocracy and *ulema* who had initially supported Prince Cem. By allowing them to occupy the positions of power, the sultan tried to check the influence of *devşirme* on the throne and diminish the power and influence of Cem, who had remained popular among many segments of Ottoman society.

After the collapse of his campaigns in central Anatolia, Cem fled to Rhodes, where he sought the protection and support of the Christian knights who ruled the island. To neutralize Cem, Bayezid paid the knights forty-five thousand gold pieces, requesting that his brother be transported as far away from the Ottoman territory as possible.[43] With support and encouragement from the Knights of Rhodes, Cem traveled to France and from there to Italy where he met Pope Innocent VIII in 1486.[44] His popularity among the Ottoman ruling class and populace made Cem even more attractive to Europe and dangerous to the sultan. After Rome was attacked and occupied by the French monarch Charles VIII in 1495, Cem was detained and dispatched to France. Before reaching France, however, he died suddenly in Naples in February 1495.[45] The news of Cem's death must have come as a relief to the sultan in Istanbul. As long as Cem was alive, Bayezid had maintained a cautious and conciliatory approach toward the Christian states of Europe.[46] With Cem out of the picture, the Ottomans built a strong fleet to challenge Venetian naval hegemony in the eastern Mediterranean and dislodge their trading outposts and bases in Greece and the eastern Adriatic coast. Thus, during a four-year campaign that began in 1499 and ended in 1503, the Ottoman forces attacked and occupied the Venetian fortresses of Modon, Navarino, Coron, and Lepanto.[47] The peace agreement signed in 1503 allowed Venice to retain some of its ports in Morea and Albania, but it also confirmed the emergence of the Ottoman Empire as a major naval and economic power with firm control over shipping and trade routes that connected the Black Sea to the Aegean and the Mediterranean.

After the conclusion of peace with Venice, Bayezid began to withdraw from active participation in the day-to-day affairs of the empire, delegating much of his power to the grand vezir. The sultan had always been a great champion of learning and arts. He preferred spending time with scholars, historians, poets, musicians, and *sufi* mystics. He supported Kemal Paşazade in writing his *Tevârih-i Âl-i Osman* (Histories of the Ottoman Dynasty) and Idris Bitlisi in completing his *Heşt Behişt* (Eight Heavens) or the history of the Ottoman Empire under the first eight sultans in verse.

The reign of Bayezid II (1481–1512) witnessed the consolidation of Mehmed's conquests. The sultan also reversed some of the harsh policies of his father. In his zeal to expand his empire, Mehmed II had increased custom duties as well as taxes on the peasantry.[48] Aside from debasing the silver coinage, he had also tried to increase the state revenue by confiscating thousands of villages that had been held either as religious endowments (*vakif*) or privately owned farms (*emlak*, plural of *mülk*) and distributing them as *timars*.[49] These measures had generated strong opposition from notable families, the *ulema*, *şeyhs*, and *dervişes*.[50] Furthermore, Mehmed's unceasing drive to expand his empire had exhausted the *janissary* corps, who rebelled shortly after the news of the sultan's death. Bayezid reduced the taxes on custom duties and the peasantry. He also restored respect for Islamic law and returned the villages that had been confiscated by his father to their rightful owners, thereby winning the hearts and minds of the religious classes. To win the support of the *janissary* corps, he significantly reduced the number of military campaigns.

The conciliatory policies of Bayezid worked until 1501, when a new threat from the east began to loom on the horizon. The rise of the Shia Safavid dynasty in Iran reenergized the Turcoman tribes in southern and eastern Anatolia, who opposed the centralizing tendencies of the Ottoman government and were drawn toward heterodox religious movements. The arrival of pro-Safavid Shia preachers from Iran, who heralded the arrival of a new *Imam* and savior, ignited a popular movement that threatened the power and the prestige of the Ottoman state. The Safavids conquered Baghdad in 1504. Three years later, they attacked the principality of Dulkadir, "which lay in the Ottoman sphere of influence," and occupied Kharput and Diyarbakir in southeastern Anatolia.[51] Meanwhile, their agents continued to fan the flames of discontent in Anatolia where a pro-Safavid revolt erupted in 1511. With the sultan failing to suppress the uprising, the time had come for a change in direction and leadership of the empire.

As Bayezid began to display the signs of aging and illness, the contest for succession to the Ottoman throne intensified. The sultan had five sons, two of whom had died, leaving the contest to the three remaining adult princes, Ahmed, Korkud, and Selim. The eldest and the favorite of the sultan was Ahmed, who had been appointed by his father as the governor of Amasya. The second son, Korkud was the most learned, having been educated at the court of his grandfather Mehmed II in Islamic sciences, music, and poetry. The shrewdest son, however, was Selim, who had consolidated his position among the *janissaries*, where apprehension about the Safavid Shia threat from Iran was the greatest. By the spring of 1512, Bayezid's policy of appeasement toward Safavid Iran could no longer be tolerated. Thus, the *janissary* divisions stationed in Istanbul forced Bayezid to abdicate. While Selim rushed to the capital to assume the reins of power, Bayezid departed Istanbul to avoid conflict with his son and to live the remaining years of his life in peaceful seclusion. The retiring sultan, however, died before arriving at his destination.

Selim ascended the Ottoman throne with the goal of reversing his father's conciliatory approach to neighboring powers and reintroducing the aggressive and expansionist policies of his grandfather Mehmed II, which had aimed at the creation of a world empire. The principal instrument in Selim's drive to world supremacy was the *janissary* corps, whose power, size, salary, and prestige were greatly enhanced during his reign. Aware of the anarchy and chaos that the succession process introduced to the Ottoman body politic, Selim eliminated all of his brothers and nephews, leaving only one of his own sons alive in order to guarantee the peaceful transition of power and the preservation and continuation of the dynasty. He then embarked on an ambitious campaign to neutralize the threat posed by two formidable powers in the Islamic world. In the process, he halted the spread of Shia Islam in Anatolia and established Ottoman rule in the heart of the Arab world. The first challenge came from the

Safavid dynasty in Iran, which had reunified the Iranian state under the charismatic leadership of Shah Ismail (1487–1524). Although the Safavid family claimed descent from Musa Kazim, the seventh Shia *Imam*, their actual origins have been traced to the great scholar and *sufi* leader, Sheikh Safi ud-Din of Ardebil (1252–1334). Ismail enjoyed enormous power and prestige among the Turcoman tribal groups who had settled in northern Syria and southern as well as eastern Anatolia. Having converted to Shia Islam, they emerged as the military backbone of the Safavid state. As they wore a distinct red headgear, which comprised twelve triangles representing the twelve *Imams* of Shia Islam, they came to be known as the *Kizilbaş* or *Qizilbaş* (Red Heads). With the support and participation of the *Kizilbaş* tribesmen, who considered him a direct descendant of the Prophet Muhammad and their religious and spiritual leader, Shah Ismail dreamt of recreating the Persian empire of pre-Islamic Iran, which extended from the plains of Central Asia to the eastern shores of the Mediterranean Sea.

For Selim, the Ottoman invasion of eastern Anatolia could not confine itself to a military confrontation with Shah Ismail's army. Aside from destroying the *Kizilbaş* forces, Selim had to uproot the social base of support and the rural and urban networks that the Safavids and their supporters had established. Thus, as the Ottoman army pushed into central and eastern Anatolia, tens of thousands of men and women who were suspected of sympathizing with the Safavid cause were massacred and their bodies displayed on the roads as a reminder to those who dreamt of joining the Shia Iranians. The confrontation between the Ottoman and Safavid armies took place on the plain of Châldiran (Châlduran) northeast of Lake Van on August 23, 1514.[52] The Iranians were defeated and forced to retreat after the Ottoman artillery and muskets destroyed the Safavid cavalry, which was armed with swords, spears, and bows. The Ottoman forces pushed into the heart of Azerbaijan, capturing Tabriz, the political, administrative, and military heart of Safavid Iran.

The arrival of an early and harsh winter, the incessant surprise attacks by Safavid irregulars who harassed and cut off the Ottoman army's limited food supplies, and the increasing pressure from the *janissary* units on the sultan to return, however, forced Selim to withdraw his army back to eastern Anatolia. The two powers did not negotiate a peace treaty, and frontier raids and skirmishes continued for the next four decades. Although the Ottomans withdrew their forces from Azerbaijan, the victory at Châldiran neutralized the immediate threat posed by the Shia Safavids, allowing Selim to impose Ottoman rule over eastern Anatolia and much of Kurdistan.

The second campaign in the east centered on Egypt and Syria, which had been ruled since the thirteenth century by the Mamluks. The Mamluks had always been a source of great irritation to the Ottomans. They frequently provided pretenders to the Ottoman throne and dissatisfied and rebellious Turkish princes with a safe base of operation. They also laid claim to territories in southern Anatolia, particularly in the region of Cilicia, which blocked Ottoman access to the Arab world. Finally, by holding claim to the holiest sites in Islam, Mecca and Medina, the Mamluks challenged the claim of the Ottoman sultan to act as the principal defender of Islam. Regardless, Selim used the imaginary alliance between the Mamluks and the Safavids as his principal justification to attack Syria. Unlike the heretical Shia Iranians, the Mamluks were Sunni Muslims, but they had supported the Shia heretics and could therefore be attacked.[53]

Having annexed the Dulkadir principality that served as a buffer between the Ottomans and the Mamluks, the sultan's forces entered Syria and inflicted a crushing defeat on the main Mamluk army at Marc Dâbik (Marj Dâbiq) north of Aleppo on August 24, 1516, killing the Mamluk sultan, Qansu al-Ghawri, on the battlefield.[54] The cities of Aleppo, Damascus, and Jerusalem soon surrendered to the Ottoman sultan. As in the campaign against the Safavids, the Ottoman cannon and muskets proved to be the most important factors in the Ottoman victory over the Mamluks.[55] Despite the Mamluks' best effort to reorganize their forces under Tuman Bey, who had proclaimed himself the new sultan, Selim arrived at the gates of Cairo by January 1517, having defeated the remaining Mamluk forces at Raydaniyya.[56] Tuman Bey tried to organize a guerrilla force, but he was captured and executed by the Ottomans, who established themselves as the new masters of the Arab world. With the defeat of the Mamluks, Egypt, Syria, and Hijaz (western Arabia) were incorporated into the Ottoman state, and the sultan received the title of "Protector of the Two Holy Cities" (Mecca and Medina) from Sharif of Mecca.[57] By the time Selim died in September 1520, the Ottoman Empire spanned three continents, ruling vast possessions in Europe, Asia, and Africa and a population of roughly fifteen million.[58]

Upon the death of Selim, Prince Süleyman, who had been groomed to succeed, ascended the throne at the age of twenty-six. The reign of Süleyman (1520–1566) marked the zenith of Ottoman power and prosperity. From the beginning of his rule, the Ottoman war machine was focused on implementing an ambitious and multi-pronged strategy that would establish the Ottoman state as the most powerful empire in the world. The new sultan was determined to conquer Hungary, through which the Ottomans could establish a bridgehead to central Europe and exert enormous pressure on the Habsburgs. In his attempt to pressure and isolate the Habsburgs, Süleyman was greatly assisted by the king of France, Francis I (1515–1547), who was locked in an intense rivalry with the Habsburg emperor, Charles V (1519–1556). The Ottoman expansion also benefited from the rise of the Reformation among German princes, who had lent their support to Martin Luther, refusing to join another anti-Ottoman Christian crusade that could only benefit Catholic powers and the Pope.[59] The Ottomans attempted to encourage division and internal strife among European states, and it is not surprising, therefore, that they championed the cause of Calvinism throughout Europe, particularly in Hungary.[60]

The Catholic powers of Europe, particularly the Habsburgs, Venetians, Spaniards, and Portuguese, countered Ottoman growing power and influence in Europe by establishing close diplomatic, military, and commercial ties with Safavid Iran, the principal nemesis of the Ottoman state in the east. To neutralize the threat from Iran, the new sultan intended to build on his father's victories and remove Safavid power and influence from Iraq, Azerbaijan, and the south Caucasus region. With encouragement and support from the sultan, the Sunni Uzbeks in Central Asia waged repeated attacks against Safavid territory in Transoxiana and Khorasan, including the northern regions of modern day Afghanistan. The defeat of Shah Ismail and his army in 1514 had boosted Ottoman confidence and intimidated the Safavids. Indeed, until the rise of Shah Abbas in 1587, the Safavids turned their attention toward Afghanistan and Central Asia to check Uzbek power and carve an empire in the east. However, as long as the Safavids remained in control of Azerbaijan, Armenia, Georgia, and southern Iraq, the power and security of the Ottoman Empire could be challenged and undermined by Iranian intervention and meddling on the eastern borders of the empire. The conquest of southern Iraq, particularly the cities of Baghdad and Basra, would allow the Ottomans to reach the Persian Gulf, where Süleyman planned to build a naval force that would counter the Portuguese navy and establish Ottoman hegemony in the Indian Ocean. Finally, the new sultan was determined to weaken the enormous power and influence of Venice and Genoa by building a formidable Ottoman navy, which could dominate the trade and commerce of the Mediterranean.

Süleyman began his reign by planning an invasion of Belgrade, which controlled the road to the southern plains of Hungary. The Ottomans were determined to take advantage of the opportunities that the internally divided Hungarian state offered. They were also fully aware that the developing conflict between France and the Habsburgs would allow them to play an increasingly crucial role in European politics.

In forming an alliance with France, Süleyman increased the pressure on the Habsburgs, forcing them to retreat from Hungary. The Ottoman forces under the leadership of their sultan attacked and captured Belgrade on August 29, 1521.[61] Before pushing farther north, Süleyman turned his attention to the island of Rhodes, where he defeated the Knights Hospitallers of St. John and forced them to withdraw after a prolonged siege on January 21, 1522.[62] By 1525, the rivalry between the Habsburg Charles V and Francis I of France had culminated in open warfare between the two European monarchs. Only six years before, when they were candidates for the crown of the Holy Roman Empire, both had "promised to mobilize all the forces of Europe against the Ottomans."[63] When Charles was elected as the emperor in 1521, however, the two Christian monarchs split the Catholic world into two warring factions and provided Süleyman with a golden opportunity to attack and occupy Belgrade. The conflict between the Holy Roman Emperor and France reached a new height when Francis was captured and imprisoned in 1525, forcing the French to seek Ottoman assistance and support. Exploiting the opportunity that the conflict between France and the Holy Roman Emperor provided, Süleyman struck, pushing his army into a divided Hungary fighting a civil war over the role of the Habsburgs. Lacking unity and cohesion, the Hungarian army under the leadership of King Louis suffered a devastating defeat at the hands of the Ottomans at the Battle of Mohács on August 29, 1526.[64] The death of King Louis and thousands of his men on the battlefield sealed the fate of the Hungarian state. The road was now open to Buda, which was sacked by Süleyman's army on September 10. When the Ottoman army returned in 1529, Süleyman focused his campaign on recapturing Buda and conquering Vienna. The long journey and heavy rain which made the roads impassable and the transportation of men and artillery impossible, and the arrival of winter which deprived the horses of forage and rendered the Ottoman cavalry useless, forced Süleyman to lift the siege on the Habsburg capital after three weeks on October 16.[65]

Süleyman turned his attention to establishing Ottoman supremacy on the Mediterranean Sea, where Venice and Genoa had historically dominated. Having appointed the famed Hayreddin Paşa, also known as Barbarossa or Barbaros, as the grand admiral of Ottoman naval forces (*Kapudan-i deryâ*), Süleyman expanded Ottoman domains into North Africa, capturing Tunis in August 1533 and threatening the Venetian islands of the Ionian Sea.[66] The Ottomans were sending a signal to Venice, Genoa, Spain, and Portugal that their empire was no longer just a land power but now also a giant sea power with which they would have to contend. In 1537, the Ottoman fleet attacked Venetian positions, laying siege to Corfu and threatening Italy. The growing supremacy of the Ottoman navy on the Aegean and the Mediterranean forced Venice to sue for peace in October 1540.

In late summer 1533, the Ottoman forces invaded Iran. The death of the charismatic Shah Ismail at the age of thirty-seven in 1524 had significantly weakened the power of the Iranian throne. It brought to power his ten-year-old son, Tahmasp, who did not enjoy the prestige and authority of his father and who was used as a pawn in the internecine conflicts between rival *Kizilbaş* chiefs and commanders. Aware that Süleyman intended to invade his empire, Tahmasp and his advisors had dispatched several embassies to European courts, seeking an alliance against the Ottoman Empire. Habsburg and Venetian emissaries arrived at the court of Shah Tahmasp to plan a joint attack on Ottoman territory from the east and the west. Learning from their mistakes at Châldiran, the Safavids also adopted a new strategy, which emphasized avoiding open warfare and adopting a scorched earth policy. Thus, as the Ottoman forces under the personal command of Süleyman invaded their territory in 1534, the Safavid troops began to retreat, burning and destroying towns and villages and denying food, harvest, and shelter to the Sunni invaders. The Safavids were convinced that with the arrival of the harsh Iranian winter and increasing shortages of food and supplies, the Ottoman forces would withdraw while the shah's army would follow the invaders in their retreat and recover the lost territory in the process. Despite these calculations, Süleyman's first campaign against the Safavid state proved to be a great success, as Ottoman forces captured Mesopotamia and Azerbaijan. The city of Tabriz fell into Ottoman hands once again in July 1534. To outdo his father, Süleyman pushed his army farther east to Sultaniyya before he turned west, crossing the Zagros mountain range and arriving at the gates of Baghdad, which surrendered to the Ottoman forces after a short siege in November.[67]

With the fall of Baghdad and the earlier conquest of Egypt, the Ottoman Empire established itself as the dominant power in the Middle East, a position it continued to occupy until the end of World War I in 1918. It was becoming clear to both sides, however, that while the Safavids could not defeat the superior Ottoman army in a face to face confrontation, the Ottomans had also failed to destroy the Safavid monarchy. For the Ottomans, the invasion of Iran was difficult and costly, forcing them to travel long distances while maintaining extensive supply lines, which were under constant attacks from the Safavid irregular forces. For the Safavids, the Ottoman invasions and occupations undermined the prestige and power of the shah among his subjects and resulted in a significant reduction of revenue sent to the central government.

Despite the difficulties of waging war against Iran, Süleyman decided to invade Safavid territory again in 1548 after Elqas Mirza, a brother of Shah Tahmasp, fled to Ottoman territory and sought protection and support from the sultan. Convinced that the internal struggle over the Iranian throne could be used to expand Ottoman power and territory, Süleyman dispatched an army with Elqas Mirza, which took Tabriz, but once again failed to establish permanent Ottoman rule. The campaign disintegrated after Elqas Mirza quarreled with his newly found ally, forcing the Ottomans to withdraw their support for the Iranian pretender. After three long, costly, and exhausting campaigns, the Ottomans and Safavids signed the peace Treaty of Amasya on May 29, 1555. Although the Safavids regained some of the territory they had lost to Süleyman, the Ottomans retained their control of southern Iraq, including the city of Baghdad. For the remaining years of Süleyman's reign, both the Ottoman Empire and Iran avoided costly military campaigns.

During the reign of Süleyman the Magnificent, the Ottoman Empire reached the height of its political and military power. From Budapest to Baghdad and from Crimea to Hijaz, the authority and power of the Ottoman sultan reigned supreme. The might of the empire under Süleyman was best manifested not only in its armies but also in the Ottoman arts, architecture, prose, and poetry, which achieved a golden age under the patronage of the sultan. An accomplished artist and poet, Süleyman financed numerous mosques, *medresas*, aqueducts, and architectural complexes (see Document 1). Many of these masterpieces were designed and built by the imperial architect, Sinan (1489–1588). Among his most well known works are the Süleymaniyye mosque complex in Istanbul and his mosque in Edirne, which remain masterpieces of Ottoman architecture.[68] Under the patronage of the sultan, Ottoman poetry flourished. The two greatest poets of the era were Fuzuli and Bâki (Mahmud Abdülbâki), who composed brilliant poetry (*kasidas*) in praise of the sultan. The sultan not only showered them with royal praises and generous gifts but also bestowed upon Bâki the title of *Sultan ul-Şuarâ* (King of Poets).

Toward the end of his reign, Süleyman was called upon to select his successor. His oldest son, Mustafa was popular among the *janissary* corps and their *ağas*. However, the second son, Selim, was the favorite of his father as he was the offspring of Süleyman's love affair with Hürrem Sultan (Roxelana), who enjoyed great influence over her royal husband. Despite serious reservations, the sultan chose Selim over Mustafa, who was strangled as his father watched from behind a curtain in the royal *harem*. Ironically, the decline of the Ottoman state began during the reign of Selim II, who ascended to the Ottoman throne in 1566.

Notes

1. McCarthy, *The Ottoman Turks*, 69.
2. Ibid.
3. Ibid.
4. Ibid.
5. Ibid.
6. Sina Akşin, "The Conquest of Istanbul" in *Essays in Ottoman-Turkish Political History* (Istanbul: Isis Press, 2000), 162. Finkel, *Osman's Dream*, 48.
7. Tursun Beg, *Mehmed the Conqueror*, 33.
8. Ibid., 32.
9. Ibid., 33–4.
10. Inalcik, *Ottoman Empire*, 26.
11. Ibid.
12. Ibid.
13. Shaw, *History of the Ottoman Empire*, 1:58–9.
14. McCarthy, *The Ottoman Turks*, 129.
15. Shaw, *History of the Ottoman Empire*, 1:60.
16. Ibid., 1:59. McCarthy, *The Ottoman Turks*, 70.
17. Tursun Beg, *Mehmed the Conqueror*, 43–4.
18. Ibid., 50–52.
19. Jelavich, *History of the Balkans*, 32.
20. Ibid.
21. Abu Bakr-i Tehrani, *Kitab-i Diyar Bakriyya (Ak Koyunlular Tarihi)*, ed. Faruk Sumer (Ankara: 1964), 421–27 and 457–464. H.R. Roemer, "The Türkmen Dynasties" in *The Cambridge History of Iran*, eds. Peter Jackson and Laurence Lockhart (Cambridge: Cambridge University Press, 1986), 6:173–4.
22. *Asnad va Mukatabat-i Tarikhi-yi Iran*, ed. Abdul Hossein Navai, (Tehran: 1992), 576–77.
23. See Shai Har-El, *Struggle for Domination in the Middle East: The Ottoman-Mamluk War* (Leiden: E.J. Brill, 1995), 80–1, 86–9.
24. Shaw, *History of the Ottoman Empire*, 1:65. Halil Inalcik, "The Rise of the Ottoman Empire" in *The Cambridge History of Islam*, eds. P.M. Holt, Ann K.S. Lambton, Bernard Lewis (Cambridge: Cambridge University Press, 1970), 1:299.
25. Roemer, "The Türkmen Dynasties," 6:176. Shaw, *History of the Ottoman Empire*, 1:66.
26. Tehrani, *Kitab-i Diyar Bakriyya*, 554.
27. Roemer, "The Türkmen Dynasties," 6:179.
28. Tehrani, *Kitab-i Diyar Bakriyya*, 570–584.
29. Ibid., 583.
30. Halil Inalcik and Gunsel Renda, eds., *Ottoman Civilization* (Istanbul: Republic of Turkey, 2003), 1:87.

31. Tursun Beg, *Mehmed the Conqueror*, 55–6.

32. Inalcik and Renda, *Ottoman Civilization*, 1:87.

33. Ibid.

34. Shaw, *History of the Ottoman Empire*, 1:70.

35. Inalcik, *Ottoman Empire*, 30.

36. Alderson, *The Structure of the Ottoman Dynasty*, 7.

37. Har-El, *Struggle for Domination in the Middle East*, 105.

38. Finkel, *Osman's Dream*, 83.

39. Shaw, *History of the Ottoman Empire*, 1:71.

40. Ibid., 1:73.

41. Inalcik, *Ottoman Empire*, 30–1.

42. Ibid., 30.

43. McCarthy, *The Ottoman Turks*, 78.

44. Halil Inalcik, "A Case Study in Renaissance Diplomacy: The Agreement between Innocent VIII and Bayezid II regarding Djem Sultan" in *The Middle East and the Balkans under the Ottoman Empire: Essays on Economy and Society* (Bloomington: Indiana University Turkish Studies, 1993), 342–44.

45. Shaw, *History of the Ottoman Empire*, 1:71.

46. Inalcik, *Ottoman Empire*, 31.

47. Ibid.

48. Ibid., 30.

49. Ibid.

50. Ibid.

51. H.R. Roemer, "The Safavid Period" in *The Cambridge History of Iran*, 6:220. See also V. J. Parry, "The Reign of Bayezid II and Selim I, 1481–1520" in *A History of the Ottoman Empire to 1730*, ed. M.A. Cook (Cambridge: Cambridge University Press, 1976), 65.

52. Finkel, *Osman's Dream*, 106.

53. Ibid., 109.

54. Imber, *The Ottoman Empire*, 47. McCarthy, *The Ottoman Turks*, 85. Shaw, *History of the Ottoman Empire*, 1:84.

55. Finkel, *Osman's Dream*, 109.

56. Ibid., 110.

57. Alderson, *The Structure of the Ottoman Dynasty*, 115.

58. Suraiya Faroqhi, *The Ottoman Empire and the World Around It* (New York: I.B. Tauris, 2004), 100.

59. Jelavich, *History of the Balkans*, 34.

60. Inalcik, *Ottoman Empire*, 37.

61. See Clot, *Suleiman the Magnificent*, 36–39.

62. Ibid., 39–44.

63. Inalcik, *Ottoman Empire*, 35.

64. See Clot, *Suleiman the Magnificent*, 56–61.

65. Finkel, *Osman's Dream*, 124.

66. See Haji Khalife, *History of the Maritime Wars of the Turks*, trans. James Mitchell (London: J. Murray, 1831), 28–80. Ernie Bradford, *The Sultan's Admiral: The Life of Barbarossa* (London: Harcourt Brace and World, 1968).

67. See Clot, *Suleiman the Magnificent*, 89–94.

68. See Godfrey Goodwin, *Sinan: Ottoman Architecture and its Values Today* (London: Saqi Books, 1993).

CHAPTER 4

DECLINE OF THE EMPIRE

Historians of the Ottoman Empire have generally argued that the decline of Ottoman power began during the reign of Selim II, who succeeded his father, Süleyman the Magnificent, in September 1566. Known for his love of women and wine, the new sultan was called *Sarhoş* (Drunkard) in Turkish and Selim the Sot in Europe.[1] Selim spent much of his time in the *Dar üs-Saade* (the House of Felicity) located in the inner section of the Topkapi Palace, leaving the affairs of state to his grand vezir, Sokollu Mehmed Paşa, who had served Süleyman and was married to Selim's daughter, Esmahan. The grand vezir's power and influence grew as the sultan became increasingly more detached from the everyday affairs of state.[2] Selim's favorite wife, Nur Banu Sultan, reputed to be of Jewish origin and mother of the future sultan, Murad III, also played a prominent role in the palace's decision-making. The so-called "reign of women" had begun.[3]

Regardless, the policy of expanding the empire and consolidating the territorial gains of previous sultans continued unabated. In 1568, the armies of the sultan invaded Yemen after a revolt erupted, capturing Aden and Sana a year later, establishing their control over the trade and commerce of the Red Sea.[4] To the extreme north, the Ottomans embarked on an ambitious campaign to capture the key strategic town of Astrakhan on the Caspian, which would allow the sultan to block a Russian advance toward the Caucasus, threaten the Iranian-held regions of south Caucasus and Azerbaijan, establish a direct link with the Uzbeks (the principal ally of the Ottomans in Central Asia), and revive the old caravan routes connecting the east and the west by diverting them from the Iranian and Russian territory and bringing them under the sultan's direct control.[5] Despite the best efforts of Sokullu Mehmed, the project did not materialize and the Ottomans were forced to rely on their allies, the Crimean Tatars, to act as a buffer against Russian ambitions on the northern coast of the Black Sea.

The Ottomans were far more successful in their campaign to capture the island of Cyprus, which was considered a safe haven for pirates who raided Ottoman ships in the eastern Mediterranean.[6] In September 1570, the Ottomans captured Nicosia and went on to conquer Famagusta in August 1571. The fall of Cyprus convinced the Christian powers of Europe to unify their forces in an attempt to regain the island. Under the leadership of Don Juan of Austria, the naval forces of the newly formed Holy League attacked and trapped the Ottoman fleet that had recently returned from the conquest of Cyprus and was anchored at Lepanto on the Greek coast. The Christian fleet destroyed most of the Ottoman ships, killing a large number of sailors.[7] The victory at Lepanto on October 7, 1571 was hailed throughout Europe as the beginning of the end of Ottoman domination in the eastern Mediterranean and was a great boost for European morale. A European Christian force had finally achieved an impressive victory against the hated Turks. To the disappointment of Europe, however, the Ottomans bounced back from the humiliation at Lepanto within a short time. The Ottoman navy was rebuilt within a year and immediately began to challenge the Holy League and its fleet in the waters of the eastern Mediterranean. In 1573, Venice, which constituted the most important naval power within the Holy League, sued for a separate peace with the sultan. In August 1574, the reorganized Ottoman fleet attacked and occupied Tunis, establishing a formidable territorial base for the Ottoman Empire in North Africa.[8]

Upon the death of Selim II, his oldest son, Murad III (1574–1595) ascended to the Ottoman throne and immediately ordered the execution of his five brothers.[9] The new sultan possessed a voracious sexual appetite. During his twenty-one-year reign, the sultan enjoyed the company of numerous concubines who gave birth to nearly 102 sons and "uncounted" daughters.[10] The presence of so many children and their mothers intensified *harem* jealousies, rivalries, and intrigues. The most powerful faction, led by the mother of the sultan, Nur Banu Sultan, was opposed by a second faction, led by the wife of the sultan, Safiye Sultan. The first faction was allied to the powerful Sokullu Mehmed and his wife Esmahan Sultan, the daughter of Selim II. Sokullu Mehmed had served Selim II as grand vezir and continued to hold his position under the new sultan until his assassination in 1579. The second faction was closely allied with the pro-Venetian ministers and officials who despised Sokullu Mehmed and his enormous influence. Aside from personal jealousies and rivalries, one of the most important reasons for the conflict between the two factions was their approach to foreign policy. Sokullu Mehmed seems to have favored a more peaceful and diplomatic approach in resolving the political, economic, and territorial disputes between the Ottoman Empire and its powerful neighbors to the east and the west, whereas his opponents advocated a more aggressive and confrontational attitude, which aimed at attacking and intimidating the Safavid dynasty in Iran and the Habsburgs in central Europe.

Sokullu Mehmed was triumphant in the early years of Murad's reign, renewing peace treaties with Venice (1575), the Habsburgs (1577), and Poland (1577). Farther west in North Africa, the Ottomans took advantage of internal rivalries in Morocco to attack and occupy the country in 1578. The establishment of Ottoman rule in Morocco was aimed at countering Spanish and Portuguese designs on the region and served as a warning that the sultan controlled a territorial base from which he could launch an attack on Spain. To counter the Spanish, Venetian, and French monopoly over the commerce and trade of the Mediterranean Sea, the Ottomans established a close relationship with England, negotiating a trade agreement in 1580, and offering commercial privileges that until then had been reserved for Venice and France.[11] English traders and merchants were granted the right to conduct business in the Ottoman territory without intervention from Ottoman authorities.[12] As the political and economic power of the empire declined and European states became increasingly more aggressive and expansionist in their policies, these capitulations were used as legal justification for intervention in the internal affairs of the Ottoman state.

Despite his successes in international diplomacy, Sokullu Mehmed failed to silence those factions within the royal *harem* who opposed him and encouraged the sultan to adopt a more aggressive policy toward Iran. In the end, the war party outmaneuvered Sokullu Mehmed. With the death of Shah Tahmasp in 1576 and the accession of Ismail II to the Iranian throne, the Safavid state entered a period of decline and internecine conflict within the ruling family.[13] Recognizing the weakness and vulnerability of the Safavid state, the war party began to advocate a massive invasion of Iran with the aim of regaining the territory that had been conquered during the reign of Süleyman the Magnificent. Aside from allowing Ottomans to amass booty and increase the revenue of the central government, the conquest of Azerbaijan and the Caucasus would enable the Ottoman Empire to establish direct political, military, and commercial contact with the Uzbeks, who viewed the Shia Safavids as the principal threat to their domination of Central Asia.

The war party was supported by the *ulema* who viewed the Shia Safavids as heretics deserving of death and destruction. The military campaign in the east, which began in 1578, was also promoted by the pro-Venetian faction inside the sultan's *harem*, who preferred wars against Iran to military actions against Venice in the west. As in the past, the Ottoman army was successful at first. The Iranian forces withdrew into the interior of their territory while the Georgian princes who had accepted the suzerainty of the shah defected to the Ottoman camp. Georgia, Armenia, Karabagh, Daghistan, and Shirvan fell to the sultan's troops. The initial victories against the Safavids in the Caucasus sealed the fate of the grand vezir Sokullu Mehmed, who had opposed another futile and costly campaign in the east. In October 1579, the grand vezir was assassinated by an agent of the sultan.[14]

Meanwhile, the war against the Safavids continued for more than a decade. With support from the Uzbeks who attacked the Iranian province of Khorasan from the northeast, the Ottomans forced the new Safavid monarch Shah Abbas to sue for peace in March 1590. The victory over the Safavids and the conquest of the Caucasus, Azerbaijan, and Kurdistan were celebrated in Istanbul. The size of the empire had expanded, and booty and taxes from the newly conquered territories had revived the treasury. The conquests in the east were, however, short lived. The defeats at the hands of the Ottomans awakened the Iranians to the need for reform and reorganization of their army. For the next decade, Shah Abbas worked tirelessly to reorganize the Safavid forces with the support and assistance of European states. When the two Muslim powers clashed thirteen years later, the Ottomans were shocked by the mobility and efficiency of the new Iranian army, which would defeat them repeatedly and allow Iran to regain the provinces it had lost.

The conclusion of military campaigns against Iran freed the Ottoman armies to confront the looming threat posed by the Habsburgs. As long as the Ottomans were fighting the Safavids, the sultan and his advisers had maintained peace with the Habsburg Empire. But Ottoman raiders carried out attacks into Habsburg territory while Habsburgs attacked Ottoman possessions in Bosnia and Transylvania. The ferocity of Ottoman raids forced the Habsburg emperor to declare war on the sultan in 1592. The Habsburg army invaded Ottoman territory and scored an impressive victory over the sultan's forces at Sissek (Sisak) on June 20, 1593.[15] The war with the Habsburgs lasted for nearly thirteen years and brought the Pope and Venice into an alliance with the emperor. The most important ally of the Habsburgs, however, proved to be Prince Michael of Wallachia, who revolted in protest over the excessive taxation by the sultan in 1594.[16] As the bread basket of the empire, Wallachia and Moldavia supplied Istanbul with meat and grain and commanded the important commercial routes of the Black Sea and the Danube, which were used by the Ottomans to transport their armies against the Habsburgs.[17]

With the death of Murad III, his son Mehmed III (1595–1603) ascended the Ottoman throne.[18] Once again the new sultan unleashed a reign of terror against his own family, ordering the strangulation of his nineteen brothers and twenty sisters, "all innocent and guiltless."[19]

The sultan's mother, Safiye Sultan, continued to exercise enormous power and influence while the grand vezir conducted the ongoing military campaigns against the Habsburgs and the insurgency in Wallachia.[20] The Ottoman forces managed to invade Wallachia and capture Bucharest. However, the Wallachian counter attacks, combined with a very harsh winter, forced the Ottoman army to retreat, while neighboring Moldavia joined the rebellion. With Wallachia and Moldavia in turmoil and chaos, the sultan appealed to his ally, the Crimean khan, to attack the two Principalities from the north. The Ottoman decision to involve Crimean Tatars rang alarm bells in Poland, which responded by sending its armies into the Principalities to stop the Tatars.

The failure of the campaigns in the Balkans finally forced the sultan to leave the palace and assume the leadership of the Ottoman forces in the field.[21] On October 26, 1596, an exhausted Ottoman army defeated the Habsburgs at Mezőkeresztes (Haç Ova).[22] Despite the victory, however, the Ottomans failed to establish and maintain defensible positions. Thus, by 1598, Michael of Wallachia attacked Nicopolis and captured Moldovia and Transylvania a year later. The expansion of Habsburg power and influence caused anxiety not only in Istanbul but also among the Poles, who joined the Ottomans in a campaign to restore the suzerainty of the sultan over the two rebellious Principalities. Transylvania was to be governed by Stefan Bocskai, who had served as an advisor to the king of Poland.[23] Order had finally been restored, but it had come at a high price. The war against the Habsburgs and Wallachia had exposed the weaknesses of the Ottoman army and command structure. Without the support and participation of the Poles and Crimean Tatars, the sultan could not have maintained the territorial integrity of his empire.

The inability of the Ottoman army to sustain its victories against the Habsburgs was partially caused by a series of rebellions known as the *celâli* revolts, which shook the Ottoman Empire to its foundation.[24] The origins of the revolts have been traced back to the decision by the Ottoman grand vezir, Câğalazâde Sinan Paşa, to restore discipline among his troops after the victory over the Habsburgs at Haç Ova. The Ottoman commander had announced that all troops not present in front of his tent after the end of the battle would be viewed as deserters, with the punishment being execution and the confiscation of the deserter's property by the central government.[25] Angry at the government they had served faithfully on the battlefields of Europe, thousands of armed men fled to Anatolia. Their arrival fueled the economic grievances and resentments that had been building for decades.

Mehmed III died of a sudden stroke and was replaced by his son Ahmed I (1603–1617), who was at the time only thirteen years old.[26]

The young sultan, who ruled under the influence of his mother Handan and the eunuch Derviş Mehmed Ağa, was faced with the continuing war against the Habsburgs, the rise of Shah Abbas in Iran, and the continuation of the *celâli* revolts in Anatolia. The *celâli* revolts, combined with a new wave of attacks from Safavid Iran, had convinced the Ottoman Empire of the need to conclude a peace treaty with the Habsburgs so that the main army could focus its men and resources on suppressing the rebels in Anatolia and confront the challenge posed by the charismatic Iranian monarch. The prospect of a peace treaty improved in September 1604 when Ottoman forces captured Pest. By 1605, the Habsburgs had evacuated Transylvania, allowing Bocskai to emerge as its unchallenged prince. The new ruler and the prince of Wallachia agreed that the Principalities would accept the suzerainty of the sultan in Istanbul. The Ottomans signed the peace Treaty of Zsitvatorok (Zsitva-Torok) on November 11, 1606.[27] The Ottoman territories north of the Danube remained intact, but the sultan agreed to treat the Habsburg emperor as an equal and relinquish the claim that he was required to pay tribute.[28] With the cessation of hostilities in Europe, the Ottoman state shifted its focus eastward, where a determined Iranian ruler was wreaking havoc and challenging Ottoman rule over the Caucasus, Azerbaijan, and Kurdistan.

The Iranian monarch, Shah Abbas, had concluded that the *Kizilbaş* cavalry, the backbone of his army, was not adequately armed, trained, and organized to face the challenges posed by the more advanced Ottoman army. Worse, they owed their loyalty to their tribal chiefs rather than to their royal master, the shah. Thus, he signed a peace treaty with the Ottomans in 1590, ceding vast territories in Azerbaijan and the Caucasus to the sultan. The treaty bought the young shah badly needed time and allowed him to reorganize the Safavid army with the help of European governments and weaponry. In creating his new lean and mean war machine, Shah Abbas reduced the number of tribal cavalry and created a ten thousand–man cavalry and twelve thousand–man infantry paid and trained by the royal treasury.[29]

This new infantry corps of *tofangchis* (riflemen) was modeled after the Ottoman *janissaries*, and its members were recruited primarily from young Georgian *ghulâms* (slaves) who had converted to Islam.[30] Armed with cannon and rifles, the new army was trained by Europeans who were recruited and paid by the Safavid monarch.[31] By 1597, Shah Abbas was ready to strike. Having first defeated the Uzbeks in the east, the Safavid monarch turned his attention to the west in 1603, moving his forces against the Ottomans at a blazing speed, catching Ottoman garrisons in the Caucasus and eastern Anatolia by surprise and capturing the city of Tabriz in September and Nakhchivan in October

1603.[32] He then pushed into eastern Anatolia and southern Caucasus in 1604, laying siege to Erivan and Kars, which surrendered in June.[33] Using Armenia as his base, Shah Abbas invaded and occupied the entire eastern Caucasus as far north as Shirvan.[34]

It was now clear to the Ottoman sultan and his advisors that the Safavids had abandoned their defensive posture and after a century of defeat were determined to openly challenge Ottoman hegemony and power. The crisis caused by the campaigns of Shah Abbas coincided with the death of Mehmed III and the accession of Ahmed I.[35] The new Ottoman sultan mobilized a large force of one hundred thousand against an Iranian force of sixty-two thousand. When the two armies clashed near Lake Urumiyya (present day northwestern Iran) on September 9, 1605, however, it was the Iranians who scored an impressive victory against the larger Ottoman force.[36] Some twenty thousand Ottoman fighters lost their lives on the battlefield. The victory liberated Iran and the Safavid monarchy from "the stigma of inferiority" to the Ottomans.[37] In addition to Azerbaijan and the Caucasus, the Safavids captured Kurdistan as far west as Diyarbakir in southeastern Anatolia. The Safavids also added northern Iraq, including the city of Mosul, as well as southern Iraq and the cities of Baghdad, Najaf, and Karbala, to their new territorial conquests. The victory over the Sunni Turks and the conquest of important Shia religious centers in southern Iraq enhanced the prestige and popularity of the Safavid monarch among his people, who had been indoctrinated to view the Ottoman state as their existential enemy. The defeat undermined the Ottoman rule in Anatolia. Kurdish and Turcoman tribal chiefs defected, and a new series of *celâli* revolts erupted, particularly in Syria where the Kurds staged an uprising against the Ottoman state.[38]

The Ottomans could not allow the Shia heretics from Iran to undermine the authority of the sultan in the eyes of his Arab and Kurdish subjects. No other alternative remained for Ahmed but to mobilize a second army that would suppress the *celâli* revolts and crush Shah Abbas and his army. The Ottoman commander assigned to this difficult mission was Kuyucu Murad Paşa, who swept through Anatolia, capturing and massacring *celâli* rebels and their sympathizers. By the summer of 1608, the ruthless and determined Ottoman commander had crushed the *celâlis*. He then moved against the main Safavid army. As the large Ottoman force moved toward eastern Anatolia, Shah Abbas ordered his troops to fill water wells, burn the harvest, and force the evacuation of the local population. As the Safavid army retreated, thousands of villagers, mostly Armenians, were forced out of their homes as they marched eastward to the interior of Iran. Many were never allowed to return to their homes. Instead, the shah ordered them to reside in various provinces of his vast empire. Those who were forced to settle in the Caspian provinces of Gilan and Mazandaran perished en masse from malaria. Those who were moved to the new Safavid capital of Isfahan fared better. The Iranian shah built them a city, named New Julfa, across from his capital on the banks of the river Zâyanderud, where they settled and helped the monarch to implement his policy of diverting Iranian silk exports from Ottoman routes.

Despite his earlier success, Murad Paşa could not dislodge the Safavid forces from eastern Anatolia and Azerbaijan. With his death in 1611, the Ottoman offensive came to a sudden halt. Recognizing the change in the Iranian military capabilities and the determination of the Safavid shah to hold his newly gained territories, the Ottoman Empire agreed to a peace treaty with Iran, which was signed in November 1612. According to the new treaty, the sultan accepted the Iranian conquest of Azerbaijan and Caucasus while the shah agreed to send the sultan "two hundred loads of silk annually" and to support the Ottoman government's efforts to check Russian incursions into the Caucasus.[39] Despite the peace treaty, border skirmishes continued and Shah Abbas reneged on his promise to send the loads of silk. Instead, he organized a campaign against Georgia. The sultan responded in 1616 by dispatching an Ottoman force to lay siege to Erivan. The campaign against Iranian-held Armenia, however, proved to be a disaster. Thousands of Ottoman troops froze to death as they tried to retreat during the harsh winter of the south Caucasus.

Ahmed died in 1617. Despite the many difficulties and challenges he had confronted during his fourteen-year reign, the young sultan left behind a remarkable legacy in his promotion of religion, the arts, and architecture. It was during his reign that the Sultan Ahmed Mosque was designed and constructed. Among one of Istanbul's architectural wonders, the mosque, also known as the Blue Mosque, continues to dazzle visitors to the magnificent city. An accomplished poet, the sultan also sponsored literary and scholarly works and supported the construction of new schools. The death of Ahmed caused panic and anxiety within the royal *harem*, where a struggle ensued over the succession. A faction led by Ahmed's concubine, Mahpeyker, also known as Kösem Sultan, triumphed, and the brother of Ahmed ascended the throne as Mustafa I. The new sultan had been born and raised in the royal *harem* surrounded by women and eunuchs. Weak, incompetent, and wholly dependent on Kösem Sultan, Mustafa remained a pawn in the internecine *harem* intrigues. In February 1618, he was removed from the throne and Osman II was installed as the new sultan. Although he killed his blood brother Mehmed, Osman did not order the assassination of his half brothers, Murad and Ibrahim, and their mother, Kösem Sultan. During his short reign from 1618 to 1622, the Ottomans sent a large force to capture the city of Tabriz, the capital of Iranian Azerbaijan. This army, however, suffered severe losses in September 1618 at Pol-e Shekasteh, but as it continued to push toward the interior of Iran, the shah agreed to renew the peace treaty of 1612. The Safavids received all the Iranian territory lost to Selim I and a reduction of the amount of silk to be sent to the sultan from two hundred loads of silk to one hundred.[40] Osman also led his army against the Poles, who had allied themselves with the Habsburgs and were intervening in the Danubian Principalities of Wallachia and Moldavia. The Ottomans won a victory against the Poles in September 1620 with support from Crimean Tatars. A year later, the Ottoman conquest of the fortress of Khotin forced Poland to sue for peace and promise not to intervene in the Principalities and to respect the sultan's authority over them.

Despite the quick resolution of the conflict with Poland, the sultan's zeal for reforms triggered a fatal confrontation with the *janissary* and *sipâhi* corps recruited through the *devşirme*. Critical of their efforts in the war against the Poles, the sultan had hinted at replacing the *devşirme*-based army with newly trained units from Anatolia. He also tried to centralize power by curbing the influence of *şeyhülislâm* and forbidding him from appointing the members of the *ulema*.[41] Thus, the sultan created a unified opposition, which included the *janissaries*, the *sipâhis*, the *ulema*, and the faction within the royal *harem* led by Kösem Sultan who was anxious to secure the throne for her sons. The pretext for the revolt against the sultan was provided when Osman announced his intention to make a pilgrimage to Mecca. Troops opposed to the idea of a new army gathered at the Sultan Ahmed Mosque where they were joined by the members of *ulema*. With the blessing of the *şeyhülislâm*, who issued a *fetva* against corrupt officials surrounding the sultan, the rebellious troops rampaged through the streets of the capital killing any official they encountered. As the sultan vacillated between resisting and giving in to their demands, the rebels stormed the palace and eliminated his immediate advisors. Osman was deposed and murdered a short time later on May 20, 1622.[42] In place of the reform-minded Osman, the weak and incompetent Mustafa I was restored to the throne with support from the wily Kösem Sultan, the mother of Princes Murad and Ibrahim.

The assassination of Osman and the restoration of Mustafa provoked protests and violence both in Istanbul and Anatolia. Kösem Sultan, who had reemerged as the power behind the throne, tried to maintain order by installing her ally, the Albanian Mere Hüseyin Paşa, as the grand vezir. The incompetence and corruption of the new grand vezir only added fuel to an already volatile situation. *Janissaries* and *sipâhis* who did not have any confidence in the new administration took over the capital, looting and plundering people's homes. In response to the chaotic situation, the governor of Erzurum, Abaza Mehmed Paşa, mobilized a large army and called for the sultan to be replaced by Prince Murad. Meanwhile, the situation in the capital continued to deteriorate, with the *ulema*, the *janissaries*, and the *sipâhis* joining the Anatolian rebels and demanding the removal of the grand vezir. Under intense pressure, the grand vezir stepped down in late August 1623. With many provinces in revolt and most governors refusing to send their taxes to the central treasury, there was no other alternative but for a new sultan to ascend to the Ottoman throne. On September 10, 1623, Mustafa was deposed and Prince Murad declared the new sultan.

Notes

1. Shaw, *History of the Ottoman Empire*, 1:175–6.

2. John Freely, *Istanbul the Imperial City* (London: Penguin Books, 1998), 206.

3. Ibid., 206–7.

4. Imber, *The Ottoman Empire*, 61–2.

5. Ibid.

6. V.J. Parry, "The Successors to Sulaiman" in *A History of the Ottoman Empire to 1730*, 108–10.

7. Ibid., 109.

8. Ibid., 110.

9. Shaw, *History of the Ottoman Empire*, 1:179. Imber, *The Ottoman Empire*, 109.

10. Mustafa Naima (Mustafa Naim), *Annals of the Turkish Empire from 1591 to 1659 of the Christian Era*, trans. Charles Fraser (1832: reprint, New York: Arno Press, 1973), 41. Shaw, *History of the Ottoman Empire*, 1:179. Shaw states that Murad had one hundred thirty sons.

11. Shaw, *History of the Ottoman Empire*, 1:181–2.

12. Ibid., 1:182.

13. See Molla Jalal ud-Din Monnajem, *Tarikh-i Abbasi ya Rouznamehy-i Molla Jalal* (Tehran: 1988), 31–9.

14. Imber, *The Ottoman Empire*, 63. Shaw, *History of the Ottoman Empire*, 1:182.

15. Naima, *Annals of the Turkish Empire*, 14. Shaw, *History of the Ottoman Empire*, 1:184.

16. Ibid., 37–8. Shaw, *History of the Ottoman Empire*, 1:184–5.

17. Shaw, *History of the Ottoman Empire*, 1:184.

18. See Naima, *Annals of the Turkish Empire*, 39–41.

19. Ibid., 41. Shaw, *History of the Ottoman Empire*, 1:184. Imber, *The Ottoman Empire*, 109.

20. Ibid., 48–51, 53–6.

21. Ibid., 71–2. Shaw, *History of the Ottoman Empire*, 1:185.

22. Sugar, *Southeastern Europe under Ottoman Rule*, 158.

23. Shaw, *History of the Ottoman Empire*, 1:185.

24. McCarthy, *The Ottoman Turks*, 167–71.

25. Shaw, *History of the Ottoman Empire*, 1:186.

26. Alderson, *The Structure of the Ottoman Dynasty*, 110.

27. Parry, "The Successors to Sulaiman," 120–1. Sugar, *Southeastern Europe under Ottoman Rule*, 196.

28. Shaw, *History of the Ottoman Empire*, 1:188.

29. Sykes, *A History of Persia*, 2:175.

30. Ibid.

31. Shaw, *History of the Ottoman Empire*, 1:188.

32. Eskandar Beg Monshi, *History of Shah Abbas the Great (Tarikh-e Alamara-ye Abbasi)* trans. Roger M. Savory (Boulder: Westview Press, 1978), 2:830–3. Naima, *Annals of the Turkish Empire*, 243–6, 263–4.

33. Ibid., 833–36. Naima, *Annals of the Turkish Empire*, 248–9. Sykes, *A History of Persia*, 178.

34. See Naima, *Annals of the Turkish Empire*, 264–65.

35. Ibid., 249–51.

36. Sykes, *A History of Persia*, 178. Shaw, *History of the Ottoman Empire*, 1:188.

37. Ibid.

38. Shaw, *History of the Ottoman Empire*, 1:188.

39. Ibid., 1:189. Sykes, *A History of Persia*, 2:179.

40. Halil Inalcik, "The Heyday and Decline of the Ottoman Empire" in *The Cambridge History of Islam*, 1:339.

41. Shaw, *History of the Ottoman Empire*, 1:191.

42. Alderson, *The Structure of the Ottoman Dynasty*, 64.

CHAPTER 5

TRADITIONAL REFORMS AND TERRITORIAL DISMEMBERMENT

With the accession of Murad IV (1623–1640), the Ottoman Empire entered a new period of rejuvenation. During the first few years of his reign the young sultan remained under the influence of his mother, Kösem Sultan, and the officials who had supported his accession to the throne.[1] Once he assumed the reins of the state and established firm control over the army, the chaos and internal rivalries subsided and the sultan restored the authority of the central government. But in the beginning of his reign, the anarchy in the capital and the rebellion of Abaza Mehmed Paşa in eastern Anatolia encouraged the Safavid dynasty of Iran to embark on a plan to expand Iranian territory in the Arab world and regain the provinces it had lost to Selim I and Süleyman the Magnificent. A Safavid army led by Shah Abbas invaded Iraq, occupied Baghdad on January 12, 1624, and massacred the Sunni population of the city. Emboldened by their victory, the Iranians moved north toward southeastern Anatolia.

The brutality displayed by the shah and his troops in Baghdad caused a popular anti-Shia outcry in Istanbul and a demand for action against the Iranian heretics who had dared once again to threaten the territorial and religious integrity of the Ottoman state. Meanwhile, the Iranian advance toward southeastern Anatolia encouraged Abaza Mehmed Paşa to raise the flag of rebellion for a second time. The sultan blamed the fall of Baghdad on the grand vezir Kemankeş Kara Ali Paşa, who was dismissed and replaced by Çerkes Mehmed. The new grand vezir assumed command of the Ottoman army and immediately marched against Abaza Mehmed, who was defeated in September 1624. Despite this, the grand vezir retained Abaza Mehmed as the governor of Erzurum and proceeded with the invasion of Iraq. Ottoman attempts to recapture Baghdad in May 1625 and April 1626, however, failed. Iranian resistance and the arrival of a Safavid force led by Shah Abbas forced the Ottoman troops to withdraw. Encouraged by the Ottoman failure to conquer Iraq, Abaza Mehmed staged a third revolt in July 1627, which was once again crushed by the Ottomans in September 1628. To the shock of many who expected the sultan to order his execution, Murad extended a pardon to Abaza Mehmed and his men and ordered them to join the Ottoman army.

With the death of the energetic and charismatic Shah Abbas in 1629, a new monarch ascended the Safavid throne as Shah Safi. Viewing the death of Abbas as an opportunity, the Ottomans invaded western Iran and captured the city of Hamedan in June 1630. The population of the ancient city was put to the sword by the order of the sultan, who then turned toward Baghdad.[2] As they began their assault, the walls of Baghdad were leveled by Ottoman artillery, but the sultan's forces sustained heavy casualties when they attempted but failed to capture the city. The tactical defeat of the Ottoman army at the gates of Baghdad in November 1630 inspired anti-Ottoman rebellions in the Arab provinces of the empire, including Egypt, Lebanon, and Yemen. Worse, in 1631, the dismissal of the grand vezir Husrev Paşa, who had failed to capture Baghdad, ignited massive rebellion by *janissary* and *sipâhi* corps in Istanbul, which spread to Anatolia.[3] Remarkably, the sultan then invited the rebellious troops to travel to Istanbul so they could express their grievances in person.

Armed, angry, and determined, the rebellious army units returned to disrupt life in the capital and, under pressure from the troops, the sultan executed a number of high officials, including the grand vezir.[4] However, the anarchy did not subside. With the arrival of new army units from Anatolia, the violence in Istanbul intensified as gangs of bandits joined the rebellious troops in looting homes, shops, and businesses. As the anarchy spread, the *janissary* and *sipâhi* corps fought for control of Istanbul, even while the sultan used the situation in the capital and the exhaustion of the warring factions to consolidate his rule. With support from his advisors, Murad demanded that all army units sign an oath of loyalty to his person, promising that they would join forces to suppress the rebellious troops and bandits roaming through the capital and disturbing the peace in Anatolia. Shortly after peace and order were restored, the sultan appealed to his people and loyal troops to eliminate the individuals who were responsible for the recent disturbances. In the name of eliminating banditry, corruption, and bribery, thousands of government officials, officers, and individuals who had played a prominent role in the recent disturbances were removed from their posts and subsequently executed. When on

September 2, 1633, a devastating fire burned thousands of shops in the capital, the sultan interpreted it as a sign of God's wrath and demanded the restoration of the moral order.[5] The usage of coffee and tobacco were prohibited, and coffeehouses that had been used as centers of political and social mobilization were closed.[6] A network of spies and informants organized by the palace identified the troublemakers who had criticized the sultan and his high officials. Members of the *ulema*, elements of the educated class, as well as prominent poets and writers, were also punished with death when they failed to toe the line.

Having established control over the government and the army, Murad began to focus on securing the northern borders of his empire against the raids carried out by the Cossacks, who were supported by Poland. In 1634, the Ottomans organized a powerful army, which failed to neutralize the threat, but they ultimately agreed to a peace offer from Poland. In exchange for an Ottoman promise to prevent the Tatars from attacking Polish territory, the Poles agreed to put an end to Cossack raids. The peace with Poland allowed Murad to return to the Iranian front. Five years after the failure to capture Baghdad, the Ottoman forces struck again. This time, the targets were Erivan and Tabriz, which were occupied without resistance from the Safavid army in August and September 1635. But the Ottoman ruler knew full well that the temporary glory could not be sustained. Following the established pattern, the Safavids followed the Ottoman main army until it left Iranian territory and then laid siege to the cities captured by the Ottoman troops, quickly re-taking Erivan in April 1636. But Murad was not to be denied. In October 1638, Ottoman forces returned to Mesopotamia, stormed Baghdad, and captured the city despite sustaining heavy casualties in December. These included the grand vezir who "was killed leading the assault."[7] The Safavids sued for peace, and on May 17, 1639 the Ottoman Empire and Iran signed a treaty on the plain of Zahab near the town of Qasr-i Shirin/Kasr-i Şirin (in present day western Iran), which ended nearly 140 years of hostility and warfare between the two Islamic states.[8] The Treaty of Qasr-i Shirin established the Ottoman sultan as the master of Iraq while Safavid Iran maintained control over Azerbaijan and the southern Caucasus, including Erivan.[9] The Safavids promised to end their Shia missionary activities and military raids in Ottoman territory. As a symbolic gesture, the Iranians also agreed to cease the practice of publicly cursing the Sunni caliphs, which had become widespread among the Shia population in Iran.[10]

The charismatic Sultan Murad IV died on February 9, 1640, and with his demise, decline resumed. The new Ottoman monarch, Ibrahim (1640–1648), who had lived his entire life in the royal *harem*, did not have any training or experience in ruling an empire. While the sultan became increasingly infatuated with the pleasures of the inner palace, his mother Kösem Sultan, his tutor, the grand vezir, the chief eunuch, and the *janissary* commanders vied for power and influence. The grand vezir, Kemankeş Kara Mustafa Paşa, who had faithfully served Murad, continued with governmental reforms, emphasizing fiscal responsibility, a sustained campaign against corruption, and a refusal to debase the coinage. He "sought to reduce in number the *janissaries* and *sipâhis*" and "introduce a more effective and just assessment of taxation."[11] He also pursued the policy of countering Polish and Russian expansionism on the northern shores of the Black Sea by maintaining a close alliance with the Crimean Tatars, who expelled the Cossacks from Azov in February 1642.[12] After signing a peace treaty with Poland, he also reestablished normal ties with Venice. An intelligent tactician, the grand vezir had recognized that peace and cooperation with Poland and Venice would undermine any effort by the Pope and the Habsburgs to organize a united Christian front against the Ottoman Empire. Despite his best efforts, however, Kara Mustafa Paşa could not silence and neutralize Kösem Sultan, who used his financial reforms to instigate a rebellion against the grand vezir.[13] When attempts to dislodge the grand vezir by organizing provincial revolts failed, Kösem Sultan and other elements within the government used their close alliance with the sultan's tutor to secure the dismissal and execution of Kemankeş Kara Mustafa Paşa in January 1644.[14]

Kösem Sultan and her supporters then encouraged the sultan to embark on a naval campaign against the Venetian-controlled island of Crete. The war for control of the island dragged on for years, and the promised booty never materialized. Meanwhile, the personal excesses of the sultan and his craze for women, silk, and fur, which was imported for him from Russia, reached such a height that the people began to call their monarch *Deli Ibrahim* (Ibrahim the Mad).[15] The sultan's increasing demand for booty and gifts intensified the corruption that undermined the fabric of the body politic, as each official imitated his royal master by demanding bribes from his subordinates. Meanwhile, the Venetians blockaded the Dardanelles, causing panic in the capital. By August 1648, the situation had become intolerable. The *ulema*, the *janissaries*, and the *sipâhis* united and stormed the palace. After a series of negotiations, the rebels gained the support of the sultan's mother, Kösem Sultan.[16] Ibrahim was deposed and replaced with his seven-year-old son, Mehmed IV.[17] A few days later, on August 18 the deposed sultan was executed in accordance with a *fetva* issued by the *şeyhülislâm*.[18] The reign of Ibrahim has been viewed as one of the lowest points in the entire Ottoman history. No other sultan would ever again assume the same name for himself or his children.[19]

The new sultan, Mehmed IV (1648–1687) was merely a pawn in the hands of his grandmother, mother, the grand vezir, army commanders, and *harem* attendants who surrounded him. Initially the grand vezir Sofu Mehmed Paşa allied himself with the *janissaries* who established their monopoly over the political and commercial life of the capital. A short time later, however, the grand vezir broke his alliance with the *janissaries* and began to challenge their growing power by appealing to the *sipâhis* and even the *celâlis* in Anatolia in an attempt to rescue the sultan from the clutches of the arrogant *ağas*. His strategy for maintaining his control over the *sipâhi* and *janissary* corps by playing one against the other failed, however, and he was dismissed from his post and replaced by Kara Murad Ağa (Paşa), the commander of the *janissaries*, who emerged as the most powerful man in the government.[20] As factionalism within the *harem* and the army spread into the provinces, the Venetians lay naval siege to the Dardanelles in March 1650, throwing the capital once again into a mass panic. The presence of a powerful foreign fleet, along with a shortage of food, caused an increase in the price of basic goods in Istanbul, which only intensified the suffering of the sultan's subjects.[21] The revolt that many had anticipated finally erupted on August 21, 1651, after ships that had bypassed the Venetian fleet to supply Ottoman troops in Crete were attacked and destroyed.[22] The popular revolt allowed the mother of the sultan, Turhan Sultan, to stage a coup with the support of palace eunuchs. The powerful and meddling Kösem Sultan was murdered in September, and her ally the grand vezir was dismissed.[23] The young Sultan Mehmed used the opportunity to purge the *janissary ağas*, killing and exiling those commanders who had established their military rule over the government. With the elimination of Kösem Sultan, Turhan Sultan, who was supported by the chief eunuch Süleyman Ağa, now emerged as the power behind the throne.[24]

Unable to break the siege of Dardanelles by the Venetians, however, this victorious faction faced the possibility of another popular uprising. Famine, starvation, and rampant inflation had eroded the confidence of the populace in their government.[25] With all hope lost and the empire poised on the verge of collapse, Turhan Sultan and Süleyman Ağa invited Tarhoncu Ahmed Paşa, the capable administrator and commander who at the time was serving as the Ottoman governor of Egypt, to assume the reins of power and rescue the empire from further disintegration.[26] During his short tenure (1652–1653), the new grand vezir embarked on a series of political and financial reforms.[27] He reorganized the imperial treasury, regained the funds that had been stolen from it by the members of the ruling elite, and clamped down on bribery and nepotism. He also attempted to reform the system of tax farming, confiscating many *timars* and large estates held by highly placed palace officials. New taxes were also imposed on the high officials of the state, and an annual budget was prepared and submitted for the first time prior to the beginning of the fiscal year.[28] These measures significantly increased the revenue of the central government, but they also alienated the palace and the members of the imperial administration. The opposition unified to demand Tarhoncu Ahmed Paşa's dismissal, for while they had been willing to absorb a cut in their income, they could not tolerate the loss of prestige and access to power. Spreading the false rumor that the grand vezir had decided to overthrow the sultan, the opposition secured his dismissal and execution in March 1653.[29] The ill-fated Tarhoncu Ahmed Paşa was followed by a series of weak grand vezirs who were subservient to the mother of the sultan and the chief eunuch, Süleyman Ağa. For the next three years the political situation deteriorated as the *celâli* revolts continued to disrupt rural and urban life in Anatolia. As peasant farmers fled their villages, agricultural production declined and government revenue decreased. With roads controlled by the rebels and bandits, food supplies could not reach the capital. The specter of famine and starvation spread panic among the populace in Istanbul. In June 1656, the Venetian navy once again blockaded the Dardanelles after inflicting a humiliating defeat on the Ottoman fleet.[30] Under these dire circumstances, in September, the young sultan Mehmed appointed the elderly reform-minded Mehmed Köprülü (Köprülü Mehmed Paşa) as grand vezir, thereby ushering in the reign of a family of statesmen who would dominate Ottoman politics for the remainder of the seventeenth century.[31]

The son of an Albanian father, Mehmed Köprülü had been recruited through the *devşirme*.[32] He had served many masters and patrons both within the palace and in various provinces and acquired a reputation for competence and honesty. Aware of the grave risks that came with such a high position, he asked the sultan for certain promises and commitments before he assumed the position of grand vezir. He knew that the commanders of the *janissary* corps and the palace officials regularly interfered with the management of the state. If the sultan wished to restore power, prosperity, and peace for his subjects and neutralize the threat posed by the Venetians and their blockade, it was essential for the new grand vezir to have a free hand.[33] He requested and received a promise from his royal master that all appointments and dismissals be made by the grand vezir, and that the sultan refuse to listen to any story accusing his chief minister of malice and treachery.[34] Having secured the support of the sultan, Mehmed Köprülü began a policy of purging present and future opponents and replacing them with his own clients and protégés. The chief eunuch, the imperial treasurer, the commander of the navy, and the chief *mufti*, who had accumulated a great deal of wealth and influence in the court, were banished.[35] With his position secured in Istanbul, Köprülü embarked on the expulsion of the Venetians from the Dardanelles, which was achieved in July 1657.[36] Although the grand vezir had planned to further his victory over the Venetians by an invasion of Crete, events in Transylvania forced him to focus his attention northward. Prince George Rákoczi (Rakoczy) had established an alliance with Sweden, Moldavia, and Wallachia to conquer and unify Poland and Hungary under his own rule. In alliance with the Crimean khan, the Ottomans invaded from the south while the Tatars attacked from the east, defeating Rákoczi and replacing him with Ákos Barcsay (Barkczai). The defeated Prince Rákoczi sought refuge in Habsburg territory, where he died in 1660. By 1662, the Ottomans had defeated Rákoczi's successor, Janos Kemény, reestablishing their suzerainty under the new prince, Mihail Apafi (Apaffy).[37]

In the autumn of 1658, Köprülü focused his military campaigns on the rebellion staged by Abaza Hasan Paşa in Anatolia. The conditions that had given rise to the *celâli* revolts were reignited by the arrival of *sipâhis* and *janissaries*, who were fleeing the regime of the new grand vezir in Istanbul. Despite efforts to suppress Abaza Hasan, the revolt gained momentum as an increasing number of officials and troops who were sent to Anatolia from Istanbul joined the rebels. As the grand vezir assumed command of the army, he paid his troops their wages in advance and distributed bribes among the members of the rebel army, forcing Abaza Hasan and his supporters to retreat eastward toward the Anatolian heartland. Forced to sue for peace, Abaza Hasan and his immediate followers were invited to a banquet on February 17, 1659 where they were slaughtered by their host and his armed agents. The rebellion crushed, the grand vezir sent his agents and troops to Anatolia where they were ordered to kill every individual, including members of the *ulema*, the army, and the professional class, who might be entertaining antigovernment sympathies. According to one source, some 12,000 heads were sent back to Istanbul.[38] Back in Istanbul, the ailing grand vezir, who had lost his mobility, resigned in favor of his son, Köprülüzâde Fazil Ahmed Paşa, who rushed from his post as the governor of Damascus to replace his father, who passed away on October 29, 1661.

For the next fifteen years, Fazil Ahmed Paşa would dominate Ottoman politics. Trained as a member of the *ulema*, the new grand vezir shared the ruthlessness of his father. His education and sophistication, however, allowed him to achieve his objectives through diplomacy and negotiations rather than brutality and violence. He also patronized arts and scholarship. As with his father, Fazil Ahmed pursued a foreign policy that aimed at checking the Habsburg intervention in Transylvania. After his demand for non-intervention was rejected by Vienna, the grand vezir led "an army of 100,000 through Buda" and conquered the fortress of Neuhäusel (Ujvar) on September 24, 1663.[39] In response, a Holy League was organized under the leadership of Pope Alexander VII, allowing the Habsburgs to take the offensive.[40] When the Christian army and Ottoman forces clashed near the village of St. Gotthard on August 1, 1664, the Ottomans were defeated and lost many more men and equipment than the troops of the Holy League, which included Habsburg, Spanish, and French units. However, when the peace treaty was negotiated at Vasvár on August 10, the Habsburgs agreed to evacuate their troops and Ottoman rule over Transylvania was once again secured.[41]

Following the signing of the treaty with the Habsburgs, Fazil Ahmed led the Ottoman fleet in an invasion of Crete. The Ottoman blockade of Iraklion (Herakleion) as well as the conflict between the Venetians and the French allowed the grand vezir to secure the evacuation of the island by the Venetian defenders. The Ottoman–Venetian peace treaty of September 5, 1669 allowed the Ottomans to establish their rule over Crete. Fazil Ahmed then led his troops northward against Poland. After a series of wars with Russia over the control of Dnieper Cossacks, the Poles had succeeded in establishing a strong military presence on the northern shores of the Black Sea, posing a direct threat to Ottoman hegemony. The Cossacks, however, "revolted against Poland and made common cause with the Crimean Tatars" and appealed to the sultan for support and assistance.[42] Determined to resist Polish military might, Mehmed IV assumed leadership of the campaign against Poland, which would span five important years of his reign. In 1672, the sultan succeeded in establishing Ottoman rule over the strategic forts of Podole (Podolya). With Sweden threatening from the north and the Russian specter looming in the east, the Poles agreed to a tactical peace treaty in 1672. The death of the Polish king, Casimir, in 1673 and the rise of the charismatic Jan Sobieski, who invaded the Ukraine, however, broke the peace treaty. Ottoman forces crossed into Polish territory, defeating the Poles at the battle of Żurawno on September 27, 1676. Shortly after the end of Polish campaigns, the grand vezir Fazil Ahmed died and was immediately replaced by his foster-brother, Merzifonlu Kara Mustafa Paşa. The new threat from Sweden forced Poland to agree to a peace treaty with the sultan, which was signed at Żurawno (Zorawno) on October 27. Poland ceded Podole and western Ukraine to the Ottoman Empire.[43] The conquest of western Ukraine forced the Ottomans to confront the emerging Russian power. Indeed, the new grand vezir began his tenure with a new military campaign against Russia, which lasted from 1677 to 1681. Alarmed by the recent Ottoman territorial gains, Czar Alexis gained the support of Cossacks and struck back. Distracted by the anti-Habsburg uprising in Hungary and the prospect of using it as an opportunity to invade and conquer the city of Vienna, and having failed to establish a military foothold along the key region between Dnieper and Bug, the new grand vezir opted for a quick peace with Russia, renouncing the Ottoman claim to the Ukraine.[44] Signed in February 1681, the treaty established the Dnieper as the border between the two states. Kara Mustafa Paşa could now focus exclusively on Hungary, where the leader of the anti-Habsburg revolt, Imre Thököly, sought Ottoman protection and promised to accept the sultan's suzerainty in return for his support.[45] The anti-Habsburg uprising was also supported by the sultan's principal ally to the west, the French, who hoped to ease the pressure on themselves as they fought the emperor. Ironically, the Habsburgs' attempt to avoid a military confrontation with the sultan and renew the Treaty of Vásvar was construed in the Ottoman camp as a sign of weakness.

Convinced that the Habsburg military was on the verge of collapse and encouraged by the French who viewed an Ottoman invasion as essential to their victory in the west, Kara Mustafa Paşa moved with a large army against Vienna in June 1683. By July, the Habsburg capital was under Ottoman siege. The Habsburg emperor, however, had organized a coalition that included Jan Sobieski, the Pope, the Spaniards, and the Portuguese. The defenders' determined resistance, the poor generalship of the Ottoman grand vezir, and a surprise attack by a German relief force and an even larger Polish army led by Sobieski, made an Ottoman defeat inevitable.[46] In a fierce battle on September 12, the Ottoman forces were routed.[47] More than 10,000 Ottoman soldiers were killed.[48] The Ottoman army disintegrated and lost any semblance of organization and discipline, leaving behind its heavy cannon and badly-needed supplies.[49] The shocked grand vezir tried to rally his army in Belgrade, but it was already too late. His enemies in Istanbul had convinced the sultan that his chief minister was solely responsible for the humiliating debacle at the gates of Vienna. On December 25, 1683, the grand vezir was executed by the order of his royal master.[50]

The execution of Merzifonlu Kara Mustafa Paşa only exacerbated the crisis. Without a commander capable of rallying the troops and facing a shortage of equipment and supplies, the Ottoman forces fell into disarray. Worse, a new Holy League was formed in 1684, which included the Habsburgs, Venice, Poland, the Pope, Malta, Tuscany, and later Russia. The Habsburgs began to push southward, moving their forces into Hungary and capturing Buda in September 1686. With the disintegration of Ottoman defenses in Hungary, the troops, who were suffering from low morale and lack of pay, revolted. The revolt spread as angry *sipâhis* who had lost their *timars* to the invading Habsburg army crossed the Danube searching for new sources of income and seeking government officials responsible for the Ottoman defeat. The panic-stricken officials who were facing not only the Habsburgs, but also their own angry troops, fled to Belgrade.

The devastating defeats exposed the weaknesses of the Ottoman Empire and opened the door to aggressive European campaigns on all fronts. The Habsburgs concentrated their attacks on Hungary, Serbia, and Bosnia, while Poland invaded Podole and Moldavia, and the Venetians targeted Albania, Morea, and the Dalmatian coast. To the surprise and dismay of their European foes, the Ottomans fought courageously against Sobieski and his Polish army, beating back his efforts to take Kamenec in September 1687 and establish a foothold in Moldavia. From 1684 to 1687, despite assistance and support from Russia and the Cossacks, the Poles failed to breach the Ottoman defenses, which were reinforced and strengthened by the Crimean Tatars. To the south and southwest, however, the Venetians managed to score several impressive victories. While the initial attempt to establish a foothold in Bosnia was beaten back by Ottoman troops in 1685, Venice eventually occupied several strategic forts on the Dalmatian coast. Venetian forces also used the Morea as a base to invade mainland Greece. By September 25, 1687, they had stormed and occupied Athens. As the news of the defeats and loss of territory spread, the members of the ruling elite, as well as the populace in Istanbul, became increasingly aware of the gravity of the situation. The continuation of attacks by the Habsburgs from the north and the Venetian push into Morea and mainland Greece triggered a massive influx of refugees fleeing their homes for the capital.

A sharp drop in agricultural production and the subsequent loss of revenue for the central government worsened the situation. The policy of recruiting peasant farmers for the army had already depopulated many rural communities in Anatolia and southeast Europe, which began to face the prospect of famine and starvation. Despite the alarming situation, which threatened the very survival of the state, Mehmed continued with his daily hobbies of hunting and enjoying the pleasures of the royal *harem*. In the dying days of 1687 (November 8), in a gathering attended by Köprülüzâde Fazil Mustafa Paşa, prominent notables, and the *ulema* of the capital, the *şeyhülislâm*, issued a *fetva* deposing the sultan and replacing him with a son of Sultan Ibrahim, who ascended the Ottoman throne as Süleyman II.[51]

After forty years of living in the isolation of the royal *harem*, the new sultan could not rule without the support and guidance of those who had installed him on the throne. The *janissaries* stationed in the capital used the transition of power as justification for plundering shops and small businesses and exacting revenge against government officials they blamed for the empire's defeat on European battlefields. The disturbances in Istanbul emboldened the Habsburgs, who had already established a highly centralized rule over Hungary, to march toward Belgrade and capture the city on September 8, 1688. The fall of Belgrade and the collapse of Ottoman defenses in Croatia and Slovenia ignited a series of anti-Ottoman revolts in Serbia, Bulgaria, and Wallachia, where the prince threw in his lot with the Habsburgs. Süleyman II panicked and sued for peace, which the Habsburg emperor Leopold was prepared to sign. While the Habsburgs were willing to consider peace negotiations with the agents of the sultan, the Russians, the Poles, and the Venetians (all of whom did not have to worry about a threat from France) insisted on the continuation of the campaign against the disintegrating Ottoman army.[52] Thus, the peace negotiations collapsed and the Habsburgs resumed their offensive, occupying Bosnia, Niş, Vidin, and Skopje in the summer and fall of 1689. Another Habsburg offensive targeted Transylvania and Wallachia where Ottoman defenses were collapsing rapidly.[53] At this juncture, with the situation seemingly hopeless, another member of the Köprülü family, Fazil Mustafa Paşa, agreed to assume power and embark on a major campaign to reverse the losses that the empire had suffered.[54] As the new grand vezir began his reorganization of the Ottoman army, he followed the tradition set by previous Köprülü ministers and introduced badly needed reforms within the government and the army. *Janissary* units incapable of performing on the battlefield were fired, and competent administrators and commanders were appointed.[55] In the summer of 1690, the grand vezir and his newly reorganized army advanced northward, recapturing Niş on September 9 and Belgrade on October 8, and establishing the Danube as a defensive line. The following summer, after Süleyman II died and was replaced by Ahmed II, the grand vezir embarked on his second campaign against the Habsburgs, who routed his army at Slankamen on August 19, 1691. Fazil Mustafa Paşa was shot and killed on the battlefield. For the next four years, as the two sides wrangled over the terms of a possible peace treaty, Venice, Poland, and Russia tried to expand their territorial gains against the Ottoman state, which was further weakened by the death of Ahmed II and the accession of Mustafa II. Mustafa waged three campaigns against the Habsburgs, which finally ended in the devastating defeat at Zenta on September 11, 1697 at the hands of Eugene of Savoy. By then, the Habsburgs were not the only power gaining territory at the Ottoman Empire's expense. To the east, the Russian state under the charismatic leadership of Peter the Great (1689–1725) had embarked on an ambitious campaign to establish a foothold on the northern shore of the Black Sea, capturing Azov on August 6, 1696. The Ottomans recognized that it was impossible to fight several European powers simultaneously. In November 1698, an Ottoman delegation began to negotiate a peace treaty with representatives of the Holy League Powers, namely, the Habsburg monarchy, Poland, Russia, and Venice, at the Serbian town of Karlowitz.[56] The Treaty of Karlowitz (Sremski Karlovci), signed on January 26, 1699, was negotiated based on the principle of *uti possidetis* (as you possess), "a phrase used to signify that the parties to a treaty are to retain possession of what they have acquired by force during the war."[57] The Habsburgs remained in control of Hungary and Transylvania while the Ottomans maintained their rule over the Banat of Temeşvar. Poland received Podole, and Russia established its rule over Azov and the territory north of the Dniester. Venice emerged as the master of Dalmatia, the Morea, and several strategic islands in the Aegean.[58] The sultan was also forced to guarantee the freedom of religion for his Catholic subjects. The humiliating treaty marked the beginning of a new era.[59] The Ottoman Empire ceased to be the dominant power courted by all European powers. Indeed, with the signing of the Treaty of Karlowitz, the Ottoman state emerged as a retreating power adopting a defensive posture against the rising power of the Habsburg and Russian empires. Other European states were quick to recognize the altered balance of power. With the loss of territory also came a significant reduction of revenue generated from collection of taxes as well as unemployment for those who, until recently, served the Ottoman government in areas now lost to European states.

Thus, the Ottoman state entered the eighteenth century in turmoil and decline. The past glory of its able and charismatic sultans had become, by 1700, an empty shell. Long wars against the Habsburgs, Venice, Poland, and Russia had drained the resources of the state, which could not even pay the salary of its officials and troops. Consequently, corruption and nepotism became rampant. Against this disheartening and demoralizing background, the Ottoman elite once again appealed to a member of the Köprülü family to save the empire. Amcazâde Hüseyin Paşa became the grand vezir in September 1697 and embarked on another series of reforms that aimed at reducing the financial burdens of the state without punishing the members of the subject class with heavier taxes. Taxes on basic consumer goods such as oil, soap, tobacco, and coffee were reduced. Similarly, tax incentives were provided to peasants to return to the cultivation of land. The new grand vezir also restored discipline within the army, reduced the size of the *janissary* corps and the *sipâhis*, and reorganized and modernized the Ottoman naval forces under a new command structure. He clamped down on corruption within the palace and among the ruling elite and tried to address the abuses by *timar* holders.[60] But, as would happen again and again in the next two hundred years, the grand vezir ran into formidable opposition from the traditional elite. The opposition led by the *şeyhülislâm*, Feyzullah Effendi, forced the reform-minded grand vezir to step down in September 1702. With the rise of Feyzullah Effendi and his family to power, the process of decline accelerated. Taxes remained uncollected and government officials and troops were not paid their wages. The treasury was drained and corruption spread to all levels of the civil administration. As the sultan spent much of his time in Edirne, he did not even realize the severity of the political and economic crisis in the capital where the *janissaries*, who were being sent on a military campaign to the southern Caucasus, refused to obey orders unless they were paid. With the army taking the lead, artisans, shopkeepers, merchants, and students from various religious schools joined a rebellion in July 1703. Mustafa responded by dismissing Feyzullah Effendi, but the rebels, emboldened by the concessions from the sultan, began their march from Istanbul to Edirne. The sultan himself could only lead his troops against the rebels, but the fatal clash was avoided when the troops marching with the sultan defected and joined the rebels. With Mustafa forced to abdicate in favor of his brother Ahmed III on August 22, the rebels exacted their revenge by executing Feyzullah Effendi and his supporters.

Ahmed tried to buy time and reorganize the Ottoman army by keeping the empire out of war. Every effort was made to increase the revenue generated by the central government and reduce state expenditures. Many who had participated in recent intrigues and disturbances were captured and killed, their landed estates and personal properties confiscated in the name of the state. The *janissary* units were also purged. Despite these efforts, the Ottomans were once again pulled into European power politics and eventually open warfare, first with Russia and then with the Habsburgs. The drive to convince the Ottoman Empire to confront the Habsburgs and Russia came from France, which needed an ally in the battle against the Habsburg emperor. The Swedish monarch, Charles XII, also sought allies in his confrontation with Peter the Great of Russia. Additionally, the khan of Crimea, Devlet Giray, was anxious to mobilize the Ottoman forces behind his efforts to resist Russian incursion into the northern Black Sea region. Initially, the Ottomans resisted the temptation to confront the Russian and Habsburg threat. The memory of recent defeats and the humiliating Treaty of Karlowitz were still fresh in the minds of many Ottoman officials who wished to avoid another military debacle.

The Ottoman refusal to form an alliance with Sweden, however, emboldened the Russians, who defeated Charles XII at Poltava in the summer of 1709. Following his defeat, the Swedish king sought refuge at the Ottoman court and was joined by the Cossack leader Mazepa, who also fled into the sultan's territory.

The Ottoman court emerged once again as a center of intrigue and corruption. The Swedish king, the Crimean khan, and the French ambassador established close ties with elements within the sultan's inner circle and his *harem*, distributing gifts and bribes to secure a declaration of war by the sultan against Russia. The Russian and British ambassadors countered by offering financial contributions to those within the court who were willing to espouse and support the cause of peace. With the war party beating the drums of war, the sultan sacked his grand vezir and appointed the governor of Aleppo, Baltaci Mehmed, as his new chief minister in 1710. The grand vezir was an advocate for war, but the problem was that the war party itself was internally divided between those who called for a campaign against Russia as the highest priority and a second faction advocating an attack on Venice to recover the Morea.[61] The partisans of war against Russia, supported by the Swedish king and the Crimean khan, triumphed. The Russian czar had already used the presence of the Swedish monarch at the Ottoman court as a convenient justification to mobilize his army. He had also sought and received commitments of support from the princes of Wallachia and Moldavia. As the news reached Istanbul of Peter's military plans, hostilities became unavoidable and the Ottoman government declared war on Russia in December 1710.

Fortunately for the Ottomans, the Habsburgs did not provide any support to Peter. Having recognized the threat from an aggressive Russia, the Tatars and Cossacks came together with the goal of coordinating their raids against Peter's army. With his rear threatened and the princes of Wallachia and Moldavia reneging on their promise to provide support for his troops, Peter, who had crossed the Pruth into Moldavia in July 1711, was forced to retreat. As the Russian army was about to cross the Pruth on its return journey, however, the Ottoman forces struck and surrounded the czar and his troops. The founder of modern Russia and his army were at the mercy of the Ottoman grand vezir who could have annihilated them in one blow. Recognizing the severity of his situation, Peter promised to surrender his cannons, return the Ottoman-held territories he had occupied, and remove the forts he had built along the frontier with the Ottoman Empire. In return, the Ottomans allowed Russian merchants to trade freely in their territory and agreed to mediate a peace treaty between Russia and Sweden.[62] One of the most important implications of the Russo-Ottoman war was the change in the political structure of the Principalities. The secret negotiations between the princes of Wallachia and Moldavia and the Russian government convinced the sultan that he should remove the native princes and have governors appointed directly by the Porte.[63] The new governors were selected from the Greek Phanariote families of Istanbul who had played an important role within the Ottoman state as the dragomans of the sultan.[64] With the rise of these new governors to power, the population in the two Principalities began to develop a deep resentment toward the ascendancy of the Greek language and culture in their administrative system.[65]

Despite the Ottoman peace with Russia, the internal court intrigues continued. The Swedish king and the Crimean khan, supported by the French, Polish, and Venetian ambassadors, advocated the continuation of war against Russia, while the Dutch and the English, backed by the Russian ambassador, distributed bribes to secure a treaty between the sultan and the czar. The advocates of peace between Russia and the Ottoman Empire triumphed when a new treaty was signed between the two powers on June 24, 1713. The czar promised to abandon the territories he had occupied on the northern shores of the Black Sea, withdraw his forces from Poland, and allow Charles XII of Sweden to return to his country.[66] The Russian retreat only emboldened the anti-Venice war party, who began to advocate a series of fresh military campaigns to recapture the Morea. While the Ottoman forces attacked Venetian positions and regained their control over the Morea in 1715, their advances against Croatia forced the Habsburgs to ally with the Venetians and declare war on the sultan.

Once again the confrontation between the Ottoman forces and the Habsburg army led by Eugene of Savoy proved to be disastrous for the sultan and his overly confident grand vezir, Damad Silahdâr Ali Paşa, whose forces were routed at Petrovaradin (Peterwardein or Pétervárad) on August 5, 1716. The Ottoman defenses collapsed and they lost Temeşvár in September followed by Belgrade, which fell into the hands of the Habsburgs on August 18, 1717. The demoralizing defeats undermined the position of the war party in the court and allowed the sultan to appoint his closest advisor, Nevşehirli Damad Ibrahim Paşa, as his new grand vezir in May 1718. The peace negotiations resulted in the signing of the Treaty of Passarowitz on July 21, 1718, with both sides agreeing to maintain possession of the territory they had conquered. The Habsburgs received the Banat of Temeşvar and northern Serbia, which included Belgrade and Oltenia (Wallachia west of the river Olt).[67] They also received assurances that their merchants could operate freely in the sultan's domains. Catholic priests also regained their old privileges, which allowed the Habsburg emperor to interfere in the internal affairs of the Ottoman Empire by acting as the champion and protector of the Catholic community.[68] The Treaty of Passarowitz dealt a deadly blow to the self confidence of the Ottoman ruling elite. The Habsburg's victory attested to the military, technological, and organizational supremacy of modern European armies. It was essential now for the Ottoman state to avoid continuous warfare, to establish a peaceful relationship with its European neighbors, and to use this opportunity to rebuild its shattered economy and demoralized army.

The new grand vezir, Damad Ibrahim Paşa, was the ideal Ottoman official to lead the empire at the time when warfare had to give way to negotiations and diplomacy. He purged the sultan's inner circle and installed his own men in key positions within the royal *harem* and the central administration. To divert the sultan's attention to sexual desires and personal fantasies, he ordered the construction of a palace named *Sa'dabad* (Place of Joy), which was to serve as the center for various royal entertainments. Designed after Fontainebleau, *Sa'dabad* emerged as the model for other palaces later built by the wealthy members of the ruling elite along the banks of the Bosphorus. Ibrahim Paşa built a palace for himself on the Anatolian side of the Strait. It contained gardens and fountains that imitated the French. The tulip emerged as the flower of the time, which later came to be known as *Lale Devri* (the Tulip Period).[69] During late night garden parties, turtles with candles on their backs moved through the tulip beds while entertainers, including poets and musicians, performed their latest lyrics and songs for a dazzled audience that included foreign dignitaries and diplomats.[70] If the lower classes could not afford to build palaces with gardens and fountains, they could still enjoy the increasing number of taverns and coffeehouses that served as centers of public entertainment.[71] Thus, the sultan and his grand vezir used "sumptuous consumption" to "enhance their political status," and to establish themselves as "models for emulation" and the cultural leaders of a new era in Ottoman life.[72]

The new grand vezir was not simply a man of extravagant taste but also an intelligent politician and diplomat with a new approach to diplomacy and foreign policy. In private negotiations with European diplomats, he reassured them of his peace strategy and convinced them of his good intentions by offering tantalizing concessions. He won the friendship and confidence of the Russian czar by promising his ambassador in Istanbul that he would no longer interfere in the conflict between Russia and Sweden. To further reassure the Russians, he asked the Tatars to stop their raids into Russian and Polish territories. The grand vezir understood that the empire needed to adopt a new approach toward Europe, using diplomacy as the principal means of resolving conflicts and warfare only as the last resort. He also appreciated the need for collecting information on European political and military affairs. Not surprisingly, therefore, he dispatched Ottoman ambassadors to European capitals, where he used them not only as diplomats on foreign policy issues but also as informants who visited European factories, hospitals, and zoos, reporting back to him on the latest European fort building techniques and other innovations.[73] Ottoman officials who had always believed in the superiority of their system took up residence in European capitals, where they were exposed to new customs, practices, ideas, beliefs, and technology. They soon recognized the need to borrow selectively those innovations that could help the Ottoman state to catch up with its European contenders. One of these innovations was the first printing press in 1727, which was initially opposed by the *ulema* and the scribes, who feared that it would put an end to their relevance in society. The grand vezir assured them that the printing press would be only used for non-religious publications, particularly in the arts and sciences.[74]

A crisis in Safavid Iran and Ottoman intervention in the country's internal affairs brought the Tulip Period to a sudden end. Ottoman–Iranian relations had remained peaceful following the campaigns of Sultan Murad IV and the signing of the Treaty of Qasr-i Shirin in 1639. However, in October 1722, an Afghan army led by Mahmud, a leader of Ghalzai tribesmen in southern Afghanistan, who had rebelled against the Safavid monarchy in Iran, marched to the Iranian capital Isfahan and deposed the Safavid monarch, Shah Sultan Hussein.[75] The sudden collapse of the Safavid state created opportunities as well as anxieties for the Ottomans. Battered by the wars with the Habsburgs and the treaties of Karlowitz and Passarowitz, they now had an opportunity to regain their lost credibility by scoring a quick and easy victory in Iran. Ahmed and Ibrahim Paşa could use the vacuum created by the disintegration of the Safavid state to occupy its western provinces and increase the revenue collected by the central government. But the sultan was not the only sovereign determined to conquer valuable territory. Having successfully triumphed over Sweden, the Russian czar Peter was also determined to profit from the sudden disappearance of the Safavid dynasty in Iran, a country that could serve Russia as a land bridge to the warm waters of the Persian Gulf and the riches of India.

Using Astrakhan and the river Volga, Peter transported his armies through Daghistan to capture Darbend on the western shores of the Caspian Sea, claiming all along that he had invaded Iran to rescue the Iranian shah from his Afghan captors. The Ottomans invaded to prevent the Russians from occupying Azerbaijan, Armenia, and Georgia. Jointly recognizing the need to avoid a military conflict over Iran, in 1722, the Ottoman and the Russian governments began to negotiate an agreement that allowed the sultan to move his troops into Georgia. The Ottomans sent two armies to the east, the first entering the capital of Georgia, Tiflis (Tbilisi), in July 1723 and the second occupying the western Iranian town of Kermanshah in October.[76] In a treaty signed on June 24, 1724, the sultan and the czar effectively partitioned northern and western Iran into a Russian and an Ottoman sphere of influence.[77] The partition allowed Russia to claim the southern Caspian provinces of Gilan and Mazandaran as well as the eastern and central Caucasus all the way to the confluence of the Aras and Kur rivers. All the territory west of this partition line, including the Iranian provinces of Azerbaijan, Kurdistan, and Luristan, along with the important cities of Tabriz, Kermanshah, and Hamedan, were to be annexed by the Ottomans.[78] The treaty allowed Ottoman forces to occupy Hamedan in August 1724 followed by Erivan in October. On August 3, 1725, the Ottomans entered Tabriz while a second and smaller force captured the town of Ganja in the southern Caucasus in September. Meanwhile, Afghans remained in occupation of Isfahan, Shiraz, and most of southeastern Iran. Iranians who wished to resist the foreign occupation began to rally around the Safavid prince Tahmasp, who had declared himself the shah and was living in hiding in northern Iran. To put the Ottomans on the defensive, the Afghan leader Ashraf sent an emissary to Istanbul to criticize the sultan for forming an alliance with a Christian power and helping the Shia Safavids against the Sunni Afghans.[79] The response from the Ottomans to this accusation was swift. The sultan declared war on the Afghans and ordered his troops to move on the capital, Isfahan. Having seized the city of Maragheh in Azerbaijan and Qazvin west of present-day Tehran, the Ottoman army was moving south toward Isfahan when it suffered defeat at the hands of the Afghans who, despite their victory, sued for peace.[80] In return for the Afghans recognizing the Ottoman sultan as the caliph of the Islamic world, the Ottoman sultan recognized the Afghan leader Ashraf as the shah of Iran.[81] The newly established Afghan rule in Iran was, however, short-lived. The Safavid prince, Tahmasp, was now joined by Nader Qoli, a man who emerged as the savior of Iran and the last great Iranian conqueror.[82] Using the northeastern Iranian province of Khorasan as his base of operation, Nader routed the Afghans twice in 1729.[83] With the Afghans in flight, Nader moved against the Ottomans in July 1730, forcing them to withdraw from Hamedan and Nihavand. The defeat jolted the Ottoman capital.

In September 1730, as the Ottoman army was preparing another campaign against Iran, Patrona Halil, an officer of Albanian origin, staged a revolt, which was joined by the *ulema* and a large number of soldiers and civilians after they denounced the sultan and Ibrahim Paşa for mismanaging the war and losing territory to the Shia infidels. To save his throne, the sultan ordered the execution of his grand vezir on October 1, but the rebellion did not subside. The sultan then agreed to abdicate in favor of the oldest living prince of the Ottoman dynasty, who ascended the throne as Mahmud I.[84] The uncertainty of the transition period and the weakness of the new sultan allowed Patrona Halil and his supporters to impose a reign of terror in Istanbul, burning and destroying the palaces that had been built during the Tulip Period and killing their wealthy owners. The crisis spread to towns across the empire, and rebels began to extort money from business and home owners in the capital and demanded a voice in the everyday affairs of the central government. By mid-November, the new sultan and his advisors had to put an end to the rebellion. Patrona Halil and his supporters were invited to the palace where they expected to discuss the next campaign against Iran. Instead, they were attacked and killed by the agents of the sultan. Peace or some facsimile thereof was once again restored.

Mahmud was determined to continue with reforms that had started during the Tulip Period. He was particularly determined to reorganize the Ottoman army by recruiting European advisors and trainers. In their search for a capable European advisor, the Ottomans recruited the French officer, Claude-Alexandre Comte de Bonneval (d.1747), who had served Louis XIV and later Eugene of Savoy.[85] As he could not serve the sultan and at the same time retain his Christian faith, Bonneval converted to Islam and assumed the name of Ahmed. Because of the formidable opposition from the *janissary* corps, Bonneval's reforms were primarily confined to the reorganization of the artillery corps.[86] Other French officers as well as Scottish and Irish mercenaries joined Bonneval in training Ottoman army units, but as long as the government failed to pay regular salaries and pensions, the officer corps would not view military service as a career.[87] European advisers were also dependent on the support of the central government, which could change with the appointment of a new grand vezir. Despite these obstacles, reforms in the military structure forced the government to introduce modern educational institutions, such as a military engineering school where modern sciences were taught. The Ottomans, however, continued to believe that the old army could be reformed. They refused to accept the unpleasant reality that to catch up with Europe, they would have to discard the traditional army and replace the *janissaries* with units commanded by young officers trained in Western military techniques.

Despite his determination to focus on reform, much of Mahmud's reign was spent fighting. The revolt of Patrona Halil and the emergence of a new sultan did not end the hostilities between the Ottoman Empire and Iran. The skirmishes between the two Muslim states continued in Iraq, eastern Anatolia, and the southern Caucasus. Having liberated Iran from occupation forces, the Safavid prince Tahmasp declared himself the shah. The real power, however, rested with the shah's chief minister and commander, Nader, the hero of the hour, who enjoyed the loyalty of the Iranian army. While the Safavid monarch wished to take the credit, it was Nader's genius and charisma as a tactician, leader, and commander that was responsible for the independence of the country. After pushing Ottoman forces out of western Iran, Nader had been forced to abandon his campaign and return to northeastern Iran to quell a rebellion. In his absence, the shah attacked the southern Caucasus in 1731 but was pushed back and subsequently defeated near Hamedan. The territories that Nader had regained from the Ottomans were lost, although the shah managed to retain control over Azerbaijan, Luristan, and Iranian Kurdistan. More to the point, the defeat allowed Nader to portray the shah as weak and incompetent. He denounced the treaty that the shah had signed and sent an ultimatum to the Ottoman government demanding the restoration of the provinces Iran had lost. Having excited and prepared his army and the population for a new war with the Ottoman Empire, Nader marched to Isfahan in 1732, removed the shah from the throne, and replaced him with an infant son. He then proclaimed himself the regent and led his army in another war against the Ottomans. Nader's first target was Baghdad, which he surrounded in 1733. The Ottomans, realizing the power and popularity of Nader, assembled a large force in northern Iraq. The two armies clashed near Kirkuk in Iraqi Kurdistan. In his first assault on the Ottoman forces, Nader was soundly defeated by the Ottoman commander, Topal Osman Paşa, near Mosul, but to the shock and amazement of his commanders and officials, he managed to reorganize his troops and attack the Ottoman forces three months later and at a time when Topal Osman Paşa had fallen victim to palace intrigues in Istanbul and had not received the men, arms, and provisions he had requested.[88] Thus, when the two armies met again in northern Iraq, the re-supplied and re-energized Iranian force routed the Ottomans. Topal Osman Paşa was captured and killed by Nader's soldiers.[89] In Istanbul, the sultan and his advisors could not accept the loss they had suffered. A new army was organized and dispatched against Nader, who immediately laid siege to Tiflis, Erivan, and Ganja in the southern Caucasus with the hope of forcing the Ottomans into an open engagement. The Ottomans took the bait and dispatched their army against Nader, who crushed it in the battle. The Ottoman commander was captured and killed, and the southern Caucasus was once again occupied by Iran. In October 1736, the two powers finally agreed to a peace treaty, which restored Iranian control over the southern Caucasus and recognized the borders as defined by the Treaty of Qasr-i Shirin in 1639.

The Iranian victory over the Ottoman forces served to convince the Russians to withdraw their remaining troops from Iran, allowing Nader to remove the Safavid monarch and ascend to the throne as Nader Shah in 1736. Although both sides were exhausted by continuous campaigns, the Ottomans were determined to punish Nader and regain the territory they had lost. After several years of peace, they organized a massive army in the summer of 1745, which marched from Kars in eastern Anatolia against Iranian positions near Erivan. After several days of fierce fighting, Nader once again defeated the larger Ottoman force. The Ottoman artillery was captured by Nader's men and thousands of Ottoman soldiers were killed. The two sides agreed to sign a peace treaty in September 1746, restoring the borders established in the Treaty of Qasr-i Shirin, which had been signed between Murad IV and the Safavids almost a century earlier.

While the conflict with Iran raged on, the Ottoman Empire became once again engaged in a series of military campaigns against Russia and the Habsburgs. With the defeat of Sweden and establishment of a pro-Russia ruler in Poland, the Russians could focus on a campaign against the Ottoman Empire. The dream of Russia was to establish its rule over the northern shores of the Black Sea and subdue the Crimean Tatars. The Habsburg objective was to push the Ottomans as far south as they could and incorporate Bosnia-Herzegovina into their empire. With the two European powers agreeing to divide the spoils of war, the Russians attacked the Crimea and captured Azov in May 1736. Their rapid advance, however, cut them off from their supply lines and caused famine and death among their troops. The Ottoman defenses also held them back from pushing into Moldavia in 1737. Meanwhile, the Ottomans organized a counteroffensive against the Habsburgs, who had invaded Bosnia and Serbia, recapturing Banja Luka, Vidin, and Niş in the summer of 1737. The Habsburgs did not have any other alternative but to retreat to Transylvania. Building on these victories, the Ottomans refused French mediation and attacked, retaking Belgrade. Recognizing that the war with the Ottoman Empire would allow Russia to push its forces into Moldavia, the Habsburgs signed the Treaty of Belgrade on September 18, 1739. The peace between the Ottomans and the Habsburgs forced the Russians, who had moved their forces through Polish territory into Moldavia and Wallachia, to stop their advance. They recognized that peace with the Habsburgs would allow the Ottomans to concentrate their forces against the Russian army. Even without an Ottoman counteroffensive, the Russians were suffering from a shortage of supplies. Thus, the czar renounced his territorial ambitions and agreed to evacuate Azov. In return, the sultan agreed to prevent future attacks by the Tatars against

Russian territory. The sultan also consented to permit Russian subjects to conduct trade in his domains and visit Christian holy places.

With the end of the wars with Russia and the Habsburgs, the Ottoman Empire entered a long period of peace. In the last years of Mahmud's reign, as well as the reigns of the next two sultans, Osman III (1754–1757) and Mustafa III (1757–1774), the Ottomans refused to play a role in the War of Austrian Succession (1740–1748) and the Seven Years' War (1756–1763).[90] Even the murder of the Iranian monarch Nader Shah in 1747 could not entice them to invade their old Shia nemesis to the east. Instead of using the long period of peace to reorganize the central administration and the army, however, the Ottomans fell into a deep sleep. They were awakened in 1768, when Russia, under Catherine the Great (1762–1796), embarked on an aggressive campaign to establish Russian rule on the northern shores of the Black Sea.

Notes

1. V.J. Parry, "The Period of Murad IV, 1617–1648" in *A History of the Ottoman Empire to 1730*, 137.

2. Sykes, *A History of Persia*, 2:210.

3. Imber, *The Ottoman Empire*, 80. Shaw, *History of the Ottoman Empire*, 1:196.

4. Ibid.

5. Ibid., 81.

6. Shaw, *History of the Ottoman Empire*, 1:198. Imber, *The Ottoman Empire*, 81.

7. Sykes, *A History of Persia*, 2:211.

8. Mohammad Ma'sum ibn Khajegi Isfahani, *Khulasat us-Siyar* (Tehran: 1990), 268–75.

9. J.C. Hurewitz, *Diplomacy in the Near and Middle East: A Documentary Record 1535–1956* (Princeton: D. Van Nostrand Company, Inc., 1956), 1:21–3.

10. Shaw, *History of the Ottoman Empire*, 1:199–200.

11. Parry, "The Period of Murad IV," 155.

12. Shaw, *History of the Ottoman Empire*, 1:201.

13. Ibid. See also Imber, *The Ottoman Empire*, 83.

14. Parry, "The Period of Murad IV," 155. Shaw, *History of the Ottoman Empire*, 1:201.

15. Shaw, *History of the Ottoman Empire*, 1:202.

16. Alderson, *The Structure of the Ottoman Dynasty*, 65.

17. Ibid.

18. Shaw, *History of the Ottoman Empire*, 1:203.

19. Ibid., 200.

20. Ibid., 203. Finkel, *Osman's Dream*, 236.

21. Ibid., 204.

22. Ibid.

23. Ibid. Kurat, "Mehmed IV," 162.

24. Ibid.

25. Kurat, "Mehmed IV," 163.

26. Ibid., 162–3. Shaw, *History of the Ottoman Empire*, 1:205.

27. Shaw, *History of the Ottoman Empire*, 1:205–6.

28. Ibid., 1:205. Kurat, "Mehmed IV," 163.

29. Ibid.

30. Ibid., 207. Kurat, "Mehmed IV," 163.

31. Finkel, *Osman's Dream*, 253. Shaw, *History of the Ottoman Empire*, 1:207–8. There is no consensus on Mehmed Köprülü's age, as the year of his birth is unknown.

32. McCarthy, *The Ottoman Turks*, 182.

33. Shaw, *History of the Ottoman Empire*, 1:209.

34. Ibid.

35. Kurat, "Mehmed IV," 164.

36. Ibid., 165.

37. Ibid., 165–8.

38. Shaw, *History of the Ottoman Empire*, 1:211.

39. Kurat, "Mehmed IV," 169.

40. Ibid., 169–170.

41. Shaw, *History of the Ottoman Empire*, 1:212.

42. Sugar, *Southeastern Europe under Ottoman Rule*, 198.

43. Ibid.

44. Kurat, "Mehmed IV," 171.

45. Ibid., 172.

46. Sugar, *Southeastern Europe under Ottoman Rule*, 199.

47. Finkel, *Osman's Dream*, 286.

48. Kurat, "Mehmed IV," 176.

49. Shaw, *History of the Ottoman Empire*, 1:214–15.

50. Finkel, *Osman's Dream*, 287.

51. Shaw, *History of the Ottoman Empire*, 1:219.

52. Ibid., 1:220.

53. Ibid.

54. Ibid.

55. Ibid.

56. Rifa'at Ali Abou-El-Haj, "Ottoman Diplomacy at Karlowitz" in *Ottoman Diplomacy: Conventional or Unconventional*, ed. A. Nuri Yurdusev (New York: Palgrave Macmillan, 2004), 89.

57. Henry Campbell Black, *Black's Law Dictionary*, Sixth Edition (St. Paul: West Publishing Company, 1990), 1546. Abou-El-Haj, "Ottoman Diplomacy at Karlowitz," 91.

58. Sugar, *Southeastern Europe Under Ottoman Rule*, 200.

59. Jelavich, *History of the Balkans*, 65.

60. J. S. Bromely and A. N. Kurat, "The Retreat of the Turks 1683–1730" in *A History of the Ottoman Empire to 1730*, 200.

61. Shaw, *History of the Ottoman Empire*, 1:229.

62. Ibid., 231. See Hurewitz, *Diplomacy in the Near and Middle East*, 1:39–40.

63. Jelavich, *History of the Balkans*, 101–2.

64. Ibid., 102. See also Charles and Barbara Jelavich, *The Establishment of the Balkan National States, 1804–1920* (Seattle: University of Washington Press, 1977), 10, 84. Donald Quataert, *The Ottoman Empire, 1700–1922* (Cambridge: Cambridge University Press, 2005), 47–8.

65. Shaw, *History of the Ottoman Empire*, 1:231.

66. Ibid.

67. Jelavich, *History of the Balkans*, 68.

68. Shaw, *History of the Ottoman Empire*, 1:232–3.

69. Quataert, *Ottoman Empire*, 43–4.

70. Shaw, *History of the Ottoman Empire*, 1:234.

71. Ibid.

72. Quataert, *Ottoman Empire*, 44.

73. Shaw, *History of the Ottoman Empire*, 1:235.

74. Ibid., 236–7.

75. Roemer, "The Safavid Period," 324.

76. Ibid., 327.

77. Ibid.

78. Sykes, *A History of Persia*, 2:237–8.

79. Ibid., 239.

80. Ibid., 240.

81. Ibid.

82. See Mirza Mehdi Khan Astarabadi, *Dorre-ye Nadereh: Tarikh-e Asr-e Nader Shah* (Tehran: 1988), 175–183.

83. Ibid., 202–243.

84. Bromely and Kurat, "The Retreat of the Turks," 218–19.

85. Jelavich, *History of the Balkans*, 116.

86. Ibid.

87. Shaw, *History of the Ottoman Empire*, 1:241–2.

88. Mehdi Khan Astarabadi, *Dorre-ye Nadereh*, 313–23. Sykes, *A History of Persia*, 2:251–2.

89. Ibid., 323–43. Sykes, *A History of Persia*, 2:252.

90. Jelavich, *History of the Balkans*, 68.

CHAPTER 6

European Imperialism and the Drive to Reform

During the seventeenth century and the first half of the eighteenth century, the Habsburg monarchy was the principal nemesis of the Ottoman Empire in southeast Europe. Starting with Peter the Great, this pattern changed as Russia began to expand southward toward the Black Sea. By the 1760s, Russia had replaced the Habsburgs as the principal threat to Ottoman rule in the Crimea and the Balkans.[1] The conflict between the Ottoman Empire and Russia began after Catherine the Great embarked on a campaign to establish Russian rule over the Black Sea, the Crimea, and Poland.[2] She used the death of the Polish king August III to install her former lover, Stanislaw Poniatowski, as the new ruler.[3] The Polish nobles, who opposed Russian and Prussian intervention, organized an uprising and appealed for support from the sultan.[4] Painfully aware of the Russian designs on their territory, the Crimean Tatars echoed the Polish plea for assistance. After Russian forces, who were pursuing Polish rebels, crossed the Ottoman frontier and burned a village, the Ottomans demanded that Russia withdraw its forces from Poland. When the demand was rejected, the Ottoman Empire, with strong encouragement from France and the Crimean Tatars, declared war on Russia on October 8, 1768.[5] The Ottoman declaration of war provided Catherine with the justification to order her troops to mobilize against the Muslim enemy. The Russian armies attacked Ottoman positions on several fronts. They first targeted Moldavia, destroying Ottoman defenses on the Danube and then pushing into Wallachia in September 1769. The native elite, who resented the Greek governors ruling on behalf of the sultan, joined the Russians and called on the populace to rise in support of the invading army. When the Ottomans finally managed to organize a counteroffensive, their army was literally destroyed by the Russians on August 1, 1770 at Kagul (Danube Delta). The Principalities had been lost and the Russian army was poised to invade Bulgaria and even Istanbul. A second front for the Russian invasion was the Caucasus. The occupation of Georgia allowed Russia to enter Ottoman territory from the northeast, forcing the sultan to divide his army and engage in a much wider conflict.

The most successful front for the Russians, however, proved to be the Crimea. Encouraging division and infighting among the Tatar leadership and in the absence of the Tatar army, which was fighting with Ottomans in the Principalities, Russia pushed deep into the Crimea and installed its puppet as the new khan of an autonomous Tatar state under Russian protection in the summer of 1771.[6] Many Tatars and their leaders who resented and opposed Russian occupation fled to the Ottoman territory and settled in Rusçuk, dreaming of a day when they could return and reclaim their homeland.[7] The last and perhaps the most surprising front was the Mediterranean, which provided the setting for a series of naval encounters between the two powers. Using the English port of Portsmouth and receiving direct support from English naval officers, the Russian fleet, which had embarked on its journey from the Baltic, sailed through the Atlantic into the Mediterranean and attacked several Greek islands while Russian agents fanned the flames of an anti-Ottoman rebellion in the Morea. The decisive battle took place at the harbor of Çeşme on July 6–7, 1770 when the Russian fleet, under the command of Admiral Orlov, destroyed the Ottoman naval force and killed a large number of its sailors and officers.

The occupation of the Principalities and Crimea alarmed Prussia and the Habsburgs. To calm them, Russia agreed to the first partition of Poland in 1772. To the relief of the European powers and the Ottoman Empire, the Pugachev Rebellion (1773–1775) distracted the Russians and forced Catherine to suppress the peasants and the Cossacks who had revolted. Both sides were ready for peace, but the sultan was insistent on retaining his suzerainty over the Crimea. Catherine ordered her capable commander, Suvorov, to attack Ottoman positions in the southern Balkans. The Russian forces defeated the Ottoman army in 1774, forcing the sultan and his grand vezir to sue for peace and a new treaty, which was signed on July 21 at Küçük Kaynarca south of the Danube in present day Bulgaria[8] (see Document 2).

The defeat at the hands of the Russians proved to be a turning point in the history of the Ottoman Empire. According to the treaty, both sides recognized the independence of the Crimean Tatars and promised that "neither the Court of Russia nor the Ottoman Porte shall interfere with the election" of the Crimean Khan or "in the domestic, political, civil, and internal affairs" of the country.[9] The Ottomans gained an important concession in the treaty: "As to the ceremonies of religion, as the Tatars profess the same faith as the Mahometans [Muslims], they shall regulate themselves, with respect to His Highness, in his capacity of Grand Caliph of Mahometanism [Islam], according to the precepts prescribed to them by their law."[10] Thus, the title of Caliph was revived to establish the Ottoman claim to the religious leadership of the Islamic world. The Russians withdrew their forces from Wallachia and Moldavia and the Caucasus. In return, the sultan agreed to the establishment of Russian protection over all Orthodox Christians in the Ottoman Empire, "especially in the Danubian Principalities."[11] The Ottomans also agreed to pay a large war indemnity, which drained the central government's treasury.

One of the most important consequences of the defeat was the loss of the central government's authority and credibility in the provinces, which were already in a state of chaos and rebellion. As the authority of the state waned, the power of the local notables (the *ayans*) increased. Serving as the sultan's representatives and tax collectors, the *ayans* used their newly acquired position as the intermediary between the state and the population to rise in stature and power, establishing local dynasties and acting as the protectors of the local population against the arbitrary policies and actions of the central government. Even in Arab provinces, local elites such as the Mamluks in Egypt created their own power structure, which nominally accepted the suzerainty of the sultan, but for all practical purposes acted as an independent state. By the beginning of the nineteenth century, in the remote and arid Arabian Peninsula, the Ottoman authority was challenged by the puritanical Wahabi religious movement, which enjoyed the political and military support of the Saud family. Using Najd as their operational base, the Wahabi movement spread its virulent anti-Shia message by attacking the holy Shia cities of southern Iraq such as Najaf and Karbala and killing thousands of Shia residents and pilgrims in 1802.

The failure of Ottoman garrisons to protect the life and the property of the sultan's ordinary subjects undermined the legitimacy of the central government and enhanced the power and authority of local notables who could render services and offer protections the sultan and his government could not. The sultan and his advisors adopted a policy of playing one notable against the other, hoping that the infighting would prevent the rise of formidable power centers in the provinces. Sultan Abdülhamid I, who ascended the throne at the death of his brother, Mustafa III in January 1774, was appalled by the performance of the Ottoman forces in the war against Russia and recognized the urgent need for immediate reforms both in the army and the navy. These reforms were confined to the introduction of new weapons and advisors. The sultan tried to break away from traditional biases and employed European military trainers and advisors without requiring them to convert to Islam.[12] However, the resistance from traditional-minded elements within the government, the *sipâhis* and the *janissary* corps, prevented the introduction of a new military based on modern training and organization.

The empire's internal chaos and anarchy emboldened enemies in the Middle East and Europe. Iran, which had undergone its own anarchy and civil war after the assassination of Nader Shah, challenged Ottoman rule in eastern Anatolia and southern Iraq. The new leader of Iran, Karim Khan (1760–1779), who founded the Zand dynasty (1750–1794), was anxious to expand Iran's commercial ties with European states and particularly with the British in India.[13] In search of a port city that could serve as Iran's gateway to the Persian Gulf, Karim Khan dispatched his troops under the command of his brother, Sâdeq Khan, against Basra in southern Iraq. After a siege of thirteen months, the city surrendered in April 1776.[14] Karim Khan's army remained in control of the city until his death and the beginning of another civil war, which forced the Iranian garrison to evacuate in 1779. The greatest challenge to the territorial integrity of the Ottoman state, however, came from Russia and the Habsburgs. Successful suppression of the Pugachev rebellion allowed Catherine to complete her imperial designs in Crimea. According to the Treaty of Küçük Kaynarca, the Crimea had gained its independence. The Russians intended to install their puppet, Şahin Giray, as the new khan, but the Ottomans tried to overthrow him by sending the pro-Ottoman Tatar leader Selim Giray and his army back to Crimea. In response, the Russians attacked and destroyed the Ottoman-backed Tatar army in March 1778, forcing the sultan to accept Crimean independence under Şahin Giray in the Aynalikavak Convention of January 1779.[15] The Tatar khan was a weak leader who could only rule with the support of his Russian master. Thus, in July 1783, Russia dropped its political and diplomatic pretense and annexed Crimea. The Ottoman government, which could no longer mount an effective offensive against European powers, agreed to the Russian conquest of Crimea in January 1784.[16] With the establishment of direct Russian rule, tens of thousands of Crimean Tatars, who refused to be ruled by a Christian monarch, fled their homeland seeking refuge in the Ottoman Empire.

The grand vezir, Halil Hamid Paşa, tried to use the humiliating losses to Russia and the Habsburgs as the impetus for his reforms, but his attempts were once again rebuffed by a coalition of powerful forces that included the *ulema*, the *janissaries*, and the *sipâhis*, who viewed the introduction of reforms as a direct threat to their interests and privileges. The reforms were denounced as an attempt to abandon traditional Ottoman values, customs, and institutions in favor of newly imported innovations from Christian Europe, and the grand vezir was accused of plotting against the sultan. He hoped to convince his royal master that the only way to withstand the European onslaught was to strengthen the power and the authority of the central government by implementing reforms, including the creation of a new engineering school and a new "fortification school," as well as the modernization and expansion of the rapid-fire artillery corps that had been trained originally by French military advisors. Despite his best efforts, the grand vezir fell victim to court intrigues and was dismissed and subsequently executed in March 1785.[17]

Although a new war with Russia and the Habsburgs, which started in 1788, resulted in a series of military defeats, the empire was saved by the rivalries and conflicts among the European powers as well as the French Revolution that erupted in 1789. The Habsburgs captured Bosnia, parts of Moldavia, and eventually Belgrade in October 1789, while the Russians occupied Akkerman and entered Bucharest in November. The Ottomans could neither organize a counteroffensive nor maintain their defenses, particularly when Sultan Abdülhamid died in April 1789 and the new sultan, Selim III, removed the grand vezir Koca Yusuf from his post. Fortunately for the Ottoman Empire, both European powers were anxious to end the hostilities and seek a peaceful resolution. Catherine was disturbed by the Swedish attempt to incorporate Finland, and the Habsburgs were greatly alarmed by revolts in Hungary and the Netherlands, as well as the growing power and influence of Russia in the Balkans. Both shared a common concern over a new Triple Alliance between Prussia, the Netherlands, and Britain. The Habsburgs agreed to a new peace treaty with the Ottoman Empire, signed in Sistova on August 4, 1791. They returned Bosnia, Serbia, and the parts of the Principalities they had occupied in return for the Ottoman promise of fair treatment of the sultan's Christian subjects and the recognition of the Habsburg emperor as their protector. The peace with the Habsburgs encouraged the new sultan, Selim III, to organize a new campaign against Russia. This effort, however, led to a devastating defeat in April 1791. The Ottomans agreed to a new peace treaty signed at Jassy (Yassy) on January 9, 1792, which was based on the Treaty of Küçük Kaynarca. The sultan recognized the Russian annexation of the Crimea and sovereignty over Georgia, in return for Russian withdrawal from the Principalities and Dniester as the boundary between the two empires.

Despite this ominous beginning to his rule, Selim tried to introduce fundamental reforms in the government and the army. As a young prince, Selim had become fascinated with Europe and had organized a small group of friends and confidants who shared his fascination with European customs, ideas, and institutions.[18] The repeated defeats suffered by the Ottomans in the eighteenth century had convinced him of the urgent need to introduce reforms that would restore the power of the central government while preserving the territorial integrity of the empire against internal and external threats. Internally, the greatest challenge for the young sultan was to reduce the power of the local notables. Although they accepted the suzerainty of the Ottoman sultan, some *ayans* acted as quasi-independent rulers, maintaining private armies and conducting their own foreign policy. Externally, Russia posed the greatest threat to the territorial integrity of the Ottoman state.[19] Thus, shortly after the signing of the Treaty of Jassy with the Russians, the sultan implemented his ambitious reform agenda, the *Nizam-i Cedid* (New Order). Selim centered his reforms on the creation of a modern army or *Nizam-i Cedid Ordusu* (Army of the New Order), which was to restore central governmental control over provincial notables (*ayans*).[20] Initially, the sultan believed that the existing *janissary* and *sipâhi* corps could be modernized by introducing new methods of training and administration. He soon realized, however, that the reform would ignite fierce opposition from within the corps. Thus, he abandoned the plan and opted for the more radical approach of creating a new army altogether. The recruitment for the new army began in 1793–1794. By 1807 when Selim was forced out of power, the new army had nearly 30,000 well-armed and well-equipped men.[21]

In their attempt to create a new army, the sultan and his advisers soon recognized that they could not achieve their objective without providing the technological and organizational support that a modern military structure required. The establishment of a new army required modern weaponry, which had to be either purchased and imported from European countries or designed and manufactured in factories built by the Ottoman government. Furthermore, a new army could not come into existence without proper training from a highly educated and experienced officer corps, which in turn required the introduction of modern military schools and colleges with instructors and trainers who could only be recruited and imported from European countries. Thus, a military engineering school was created in 1795. Finally, the entire project required considerable funding and investment from a government that lacked the financial power to implement such ambitious restructuring. The revenue for the central government derived from the collection of taxes. However, the government lacked the ability to collect taxes in the provinces of the empire where the local *ayans* dominated the political and economic life. Without the support and collaboration of the *ayans*, the treasury could not generate tax revenues. Thus, in an attempt to centralize the power of the government, the sultan and his advisers empowered the very forces that stood for decentralization. Selim also resorted to policies that made his reforms increasingly unpopular among the population.[22] He debased the coinage and imposed new taxes on basic consumer goods such as coffee and tobacco, thereby creating additional financial burdens on a population already overtaxed.[23]

The introduction of the new army forced the Ottoman government to recruit instructors and trainers, mostly from France. The arrival of French officers created a new cultural environment where Ottoman officials and army officers could mix and mingle with Europeans and learn the latest political, social, and cultural developments that were transforming European societies. The exposure to European ideas, values, and customs intensified with the establishment of permanent Ottoman legations to European capitals. Until the reign of Selim, the Ottoman government had negotiated with European powers through short-term embassies or the Greek dragomans. The introduction of permanent Ottoman embassies in European capitals gave rise to a new class of Ottoman diplomats, who spent a great deal of time interacting with European politicians, learning not only European languages and customs, but also European history, politics, and modern ideas.[24]

With the arrival of European trainers and the introduction of modern military schools, the anti-reform forces within the government and the society began to mobilize against the sultan. The new army was fiercely opposed by the *janissaries*, who viewed it as an open challenge to their traditional dominant role. The introduction of European education was also opposed by the religious classes led by the *şeyhülislâm*, who considered Selim's reforms to be fundamentally incompatible with Islam. Aside from the growing opposition among the *janissaries*, the *ulema*, and the conservative forces within his own government, Selim also faced a fluid and at times confusing international arena, which presented enormous challenges to the survival of the Ottoman state.

Selim had ascended the throne at a time when great events were unfolding in Europe. The French Revolution began on July 14, 1789 and diverted the attention of European powers from southeast Europe, allowing the Ottoman Empire to focus on internal reforms. From their fairly distant vantage point the Ottomans were obviously unaware of the political and ideological earthquake that was shaking the foundations of European (and indeed, world) power politics. For the Porte, the name of the game was survival in an international arena dominated by predatory European powers. As long as the revolution in France forced the European powers to fight among themselves, the Ottomans welcomed it. France had always enjoyed a close relationship with the Ottoman Empire and the sultan considered the French monarch, Louis XVI, with whom he had corresponded, a close ally.[25] It was natural, therefore, that the Ottoman court received the news of the arrest and trial of the French king, followed by his execution in January 1793, with shock and horror. However, the Porte responded to the new situation with a great deal of caution. In the short run, the sultan was relieved that the events in Paris had forced Russia and the Habsburgs to seek peace with the Ottoman state in order to shift their focus to the events in France. Once Napoleon attacked the Habsburgs, the Porte must have felt overjoyed by the news of French victory.

The Ottoman relationship with France, however, underwent a significant metamorphosis when a French army led by Napoleon landed in Egypt in early July 1798 and occupied Alexandria. The Mamluks, who ruled Egypt on behalf of the sultan, either fled or were crushed by the invading French force, which captured Cairo a few weeks later on July 22. Napoleon planned to challenge British hegemony by establishing a territorial foothold in North Africa, cutting "English trade routes," threatening "England's control of India," and constructing "a new French empire in the Middle East."[26] While the occupation of Egypt was accomplished with relative ease, the French fleet was destroyed by the British at Abukir (Aboukir) in August 1798. The French also failed in their attempt to establish their rule in Syria when the local notable Ahmed Cezzar Paşa defended Acre with significant support from the Ottoman forces and the British fleet between March and May 1799. Although the French defeated an Ottoman force at Abukir in July 1799, Napoleon abandoned his ambitious plans of conquest in the east and returned to France in August. After suffering a defeat at the hands of an Ottoman army backed by British naval forces, the remaining French troops evacuated Egypt in September 1801.[27] The French aggressive policy toward the Ottoman Empire, however, forced the sultan to seek a close alliance with England and Russia.[28]

Selim's reforms had threatened the *janissaries* more than any other group within the ruling elite. However, the *janissaries* were not alone in their opposition to *Nizam-i Cedid*. Indeed, they enjoyed the support of the religious classes, including the conservative *ulema* and their students, who had remained wedded to the traditional Ottoman beliefs and customs, and the inner governmental circles, who also feared that the sultan's reforms would undermine their power and status. In late May 1807, the rebellion that had been brewing finally erupted. Not surprisingly, the backlash began with the *janissary* corps stationed outside Istanbul killing a member of *Nizam-i Cedid*, who had urged them to wear new uniforms and receive modern military training. Instead of nipping the rebellion in the bud, Selim hesitated, encouraged by the *şeyhülislâm* to adopt a conciliatory approach toward the rebels.[29] The result was disastrous. The *janissary* units moved into Istanbul, gathering on their way other *janissaries* as well as the *ulema* and students. As they arrived in front of the palace, the sultan once again tried to negotiate with the rebels, promising them to abandon *Nizam-i Cedid* and throwing a number of his own supporters, including his grand vezir, into the crowd, who tore them into pieces. As in the past, appeasement merely emboldened the rebels.[30] The *ulema* supported the rebels and issued a *fetva* declaring that Selim's reforms were opposed to the laws of Islam and demanding that the sultan step down from the throne. Recognizing the serious nature of the revolt, Selim accepted his fate and returned to the palace cage. Selim's cousins, Mustafa and Mahmud, were the only princes of the Ottoman royal house who could ascend the throne. Since Mahmud was suspected by the rebels of being close to the deposed sultan and sympathetic to his reforms, Mustafa was brought out of the royal *harem* to ascend the Ottoman throne as Mustafa IV on May 29. Weak and incompetent, the new sultan was merely a convenient tool in the hands of the rebels, who used him to reverse Selim's military and governmental reforms.

Although many among the *ayans* opposed Selim's new army in the fear that a strong central government would attack and destroy their power, there were also powerful notables who had recognized the need to build a modern army capable of defending the empire against the Habsburg and Russian empires. Those *ayans*, who had fought with their armies against the Habsburgs and the Russians, recognized the urgent need for military reforms, which would slow down the process of territorial dismemberment by bringing the Ottoman military on par with modern European armies. They may have opposed the centralizing drive of the Ottoman government in Istanbul, but such centralization would still be preferable to being conquered and ruled by Christian European empires, which would swallow them whole. Among the provincial notables in southeast Europe opposed to the new regime in Istanbul, none was as powerful and influential as Bayrakdâr Mustafa Paşa, the powerful lord of Ruşçuk in present day Bulgaria. Mustafa Paşa, who supported the deposed sultan and opposed Mustafa IV, organized the Ruşçuk Committee, which brought some of the powerful *ayans* of southeast Europe under one umbrella. He then marched into Istanbul in July 1808 to reinstate Selim. As the news of the arrival and aims of the army from Ruşçuk reached the palace, Mustafa ordered the assassination of Selim and Mahmud, the only members of the Ottoman royal family who could replace him. Selim was killed, but Mahmud managed to escape through the roof of the palace and sought refuge with Bayrakdâr Mustafa Paşa and his forces.[31] The newly arrived army deposed Mustafa and installed Mahmud as the new sultan on July 28.

Mahmud II (1808–1839) was exceedingly weak and depended for his survival on Bayrakdâr Mustafa Paşa, who acted as the power behind the throne. To generate support for the new regime, Mustafa Paşa called for a meeting of the prominent *ayans* of the empire in Istanbul to discuss the political problems confronting the Ottoman Empire. A few powerful *ayans*, such as Tepedelenli Ali Paşa (Ali Paşa of Janina) and Muhammad Ali (Mehmed Ali) of Egypt, did not participate in the gathering. Many notables, particularly those from Anatolia, however, attended. After several days of discussions, the participants produced a "document of agreement" called *Sened-i İttifak*, which was signed on October 7, 1808.[32] The document allowed the provincial notables to reaffirm their loyalty to the sultan and his government, promising to support their royal master against any rebellion.[33] They also agreed to implement the Ottoman tax system throughout the empire without diverting any revenue that belonged to the sultan.[34] In return, the sultan made a commitment to "levy taxes justly and fairly."[35] Recognizing the need to defend the empire against foreign aggression, the participating *ayans* also made a commitment to support the central government in its efforts to recruit men for the new army.[36] Aside from making the above mentioned commitments to the sultan, the *ayans* also agreed to rule their provinces justly, to respect each other, and avoid interference in the internal affairs of fellow notables and governors.[37] Through the *Sened-i İttifak*, Bayrakdâr Mustafa Paşa and the *ayans* who were allied with him tried to impose a pact on the sultan and "legitimize their privileges and autonomy in the provinces."[38] Indeed, the agreement "recognized the land as the private property of the *ayans*" although the central government retained the authority to confiscate it.[39]

Bayrakdâr Mustafa Paşa reorganized the disbanded *Nizam-i Cedid* under the new name of *Seğban-i Cedid* (New Segbans, or the new Dog Keepers). He also tried to reform the *janissary* corps by prohibiting the sale of their positions, restoring the traditional system of seniority, and demanding that they receive modern training.[40] The notable from Ruşçuk was convinced that he had crushed the opposition, but he underestimated the power of the *janissaries*, the *ulema*, and the guilds. He also alienated the sultan, his government officials, and the population of the capital by adopting an arrogant attitude, refusing to consult Mahmud, and confiscating *timars* and land supervised by religious foundations.[41] Despite these difficulties, the opposition could not move against him as long as his forces remained in Istanbul. A revolt staged by rival *ayans* from Bulgaria forced the grand vezir to reduce the number of his men in the capital and to send a considerable segment of his army to Ruşçuk, which had been attacked by the rebels. Believing that he had full control over the capital, Bayrakdâr Mustafa Paşa had also allowed many of the *ayans* and their units who had marched with him to Istanbul to return to southeast Europe. The opposition seized this opportunity and struck again. *Janissary* divisions spread the rumor that Bayrakdâr Mustafa Paşa intended to disband their corps. Joined by an angry mob, they stormed the palace and trapped Bayrakdâr Mustafa Paşa in a powder magazine, where he blew himself up on November 15, 1808.[42]

The anti-reform forces believed that their coup had succeeded and that they had once again gained the upper hand. They were wrong. Having learned from the mistakes of his ill-fated cousin, Mahmud refused to concede to the demands of the rebels. He understood that offering concessions to the rebels would only embolden the opposition. Instead, he reacted quickly and swiftly, ordering his men to kill Mustafa IV. With the assassination of Mustafa, the sultan believed that the rebels had to accept him as the only remaining member of the Ottoman dynasty. Mahmud also called on the loyal commanders to rally to his support. As his troops arrived in the palace, Mahmud felt sufficiently confident to reject the demands of the rebels, who were then attacked by land and sea. The absence of an alternative to Mahmud and his ability to organize his forces against the *janissaries* convinced the rebels that they could not depose the sultan. Both sides agreed to talk. After extensive negotiations between the representatives of the sultan and the rebels, Mahmud agreed to disband the new *Segbans* (the new army units). In return the rebels agreed to Mahmud remaining on the throne. The anti-reform forces had gained a major concession from the sultan and they seemed to have scored a significant victory. But the sultan had also managed to survive. The events of November 1808 taught him that the *janissaries* could not be reformed and that they would do everything in their power to undermine the modernization of the Ottoman army. The only solution was to destroy the *janissary* corps altogether. Before destroying the *janissaries*, however, the Ottoman government had to confront the threat posed by nationalist rebellions in the Balkans, which were challenging the authority of the sultan.

The Ottoman system was built on the principle of dividing the population of the empire into separate and distinct religious communities. The *millet* system had worked well in an era when religious identity reigned supreme. Ironically, the preservation of national cultures within the framework of religious communities allowed distinct ethnic and linguistic feelings and identities to survive. By the end of the eighteenth century, under the influence of French revolution, a modern secular intelligentsia imbued with nationalistic ideas began to challenge the ideological hegemony of the traditional religious hierarchies, who had historically collaborated with the Ottoman regime. Nation was to replace God as the object of devotion, and the creation of a strong and independent state was proposed as the only alternative to collaboration with a foreign and alien sultan.

As a multi-ethnic, multi-linguistic, and multi-religious empire that recognized the supremacy of religious identity, the Ottoman state failed to develop an antibiotic for the bacteria called nationalism, which would ultimately destroy the territorial integrity of the empire. The political potency and popularity of nationalism among the subjects of the sultan were encouraged and intensified by the direct and open support it received from powerful European states. In nationalism they discovered an ideology with the capacity to challenge and destroy the Ottoman Empire from within. But nationalism proved to be a double-edged sword. Fomenting nationalistic revolts in the Balkans undermined the authority of the sultan and intensified the process of territorial disintegration. The emergence of independent nation states, however, posed a similar threat to others, such as the Russian and Austrian empires, which also contained within their borders an ethnically and linguistically diverse population.

The first nationalist movements to challenge the Ottoman power in the Balkans erupted in Serbia and Greece. The revolt in Serbia had already started in April 1804 during the reign of Selim III. The leader of the revolt, Kara George (Karajordje), denounced the abuses of *janissary* units stationed in Serbia.[43] The central government, which was planning to modernize the Ottoman army, did not oppose the rebellion and used it to remove *janissary* garrisons. The removal of the garrisons, however, allowed the revolt to gain momentum, emerging as a full-fledged movement for autonomy. Despite the support they received from the Russian government, which invaded Wallachia and Moldavia in 1806, the Serbs could not fight the superior power of the Ottoman army, which crushed their revolt in October 1813.[44] The suppression of the revolt did not address the underlying causes of discontent among the Serbian population. Two years later, in March 1815, a new revolt erupted, this time under the leadership of Miloš Obrenović, who intended to gain autonomy for a Serbian principality through negotiations with the Ottoman central government.[45] To neutralize the rebellion, the Ottoman government reached a settlement of the conflict with Obrenović. In return for recognizing the autonomy of a Serbian principality between Belgrade and Niş, the Ottomans maintained the right to preserve army garrisons in the important urban centers and receive an annual tribute.[46] Obrenović, called the "Serbian Paşa" by his "disgruntled countrymen," failed to gain independence for his people.[47] He did, however, demonstrate to other ethnic and linguistic communities in the Balkans the possibility of revolting and gaining limited autonomy from the central government in Istanbul.

The second revolt to challenge the Ottoman rule began in Greece and culminated in the establishment of an independent Greek state. Ironically the revolt began after the sultan clashed with the powerful *ayan*, Tepedelenli Ali Paşa (Ali Paşa of Janina), who at the height of his reign ruled a vast region that included much of present day Greece and parts of Albania.[48] In Istanbul, Mahmud, who was determined to impose the authority of the central government on the provincial *ayans*, had watched with some anxiety the emergence of Ali Paşa as a strong ruler. Indeed, the capable and ambitious notable had accumulated enormous prestige and conducted his own foreign policy. Many in the sultan's inner circle warned him against attacking the powerful magnate. The sultan, however, rejected their advice and ordered an invasion of Greece. He could not have known that by attacking Ali Paşa, the Ottoman government would provide a golden opportunity to the Greek nationalists, who had been organizing a movement to overthrow Ottoman rule and establish an independent Greek state. Indeed, the destruction of Ali Paşa removed the only power structure that enjoyed popular legitimacy among the native population capable of suppressing the Greek revolution.

The Greek nationalist movement was led and inspired by *Philiki Hetairia (Etairia)* or Friendly Society, which came into existence in Odessa in 1814.[49] From its inception the movement was supported by wealthy and influential Greek merchant families residing in Crimea.[50] Starting in 1820, Alexander Ypsilantis (Ipsilantis/Ipsilanti), a member of one of the most powerful Phanariote (named after the *Phanar* quarter) families of Istanbul who "claimed descent from the Byzantine princely dynasty of Comnenus," emerged as the leader of the secret society.[51] He had studied in Russia and joined the Russian army as an officer. Ypsilantis's original plan was to organize an anti-Ottoman revolt in Wallachia and Moldavia in order to divert the attention of Ottoman forces from Greece, where he was secretly training his supporters. He also hoped that the uprising in the Danubian Principalities would force Russia to intervene on behalf of the rebels.[52] The ultimate dream of Ypsilantis was to recreate the Byzantine Empire through a mass uprising of all peoples of the Balkans.[53] In March 1821, Ypsilantis and his supporters entered Moldavia, but the revolt they had hoped for did not materialize. The Romanian population was generally mistrustful or outright hostile toward the Greeks, who had ruled their country on behalf of the Ottoman sultan. Having failed to ignite a popular uprising against the Ottoman Empire, the Greeks were defeated in June 1821 and Ypsilantis was forced to seek refuge in Hungary.

Although the revolt in the Danubian Principalities failed, the efforts of Ypsilantis and *Hetairia* were successful in mainland Greece. In the Morea (Peloponnese), the Greek national movement benefited enormously from the confrontation between the Ottoman government and Ali Paşa. Though willing to accept the suzerainty of the sultan, Ali Paşa refused to give up on his dream of creating an autonomous state under his own rule. The Ottoman government was well aware that he had established close ties with *Hetairia*, cultivating the support of the Greek population by improving conditions in rural communities under his control.[54] The conflict between the central government forces and Ali Paşa's army created a golden opportunity for *Hetairia* to stage its revolution. The revolt began on February 12, 1821 in a series of attacks on Turkish rural communities, followed by a full-fledged uprising in Mani in April. For the Greeks, the act that marked the beginning of their revolution was Bishop Germanos raising the Cross at the monastery of Aghia Lavra at Kalavryta in the northern Peloponnese.[55] With the sultan's army focused on defeating Ali Paşa, the Ottoman response to the Greek revolt was slow. Their efforts to suppress it were further hampered by a new war with the Qajar dynasty in Iran, which began in November 1821 and did not end until July 1823 with the Treaty of Erzurum. The war with Iran forced the Ottomans to divert some of the army units needed in Greece to a new campaign in the east. In Istanbul, the news of the Greek revolt was received with shock and disbelief. The sultan, who continued to view Ali Paşa as his principal nemesis, demanded that the Greek Orthodox Patriarch of Istanbul denounce the rebels and restore peace and order among the members of his religious community. When the revolt spread, the sultan continued to blame the Patriarch, who was executed by hanging on Easter Sunday, April 22, 1821.[56]

In January 1822, Ali Paşa was caught and killed by Ottoman forces. The Greek revolt, however, refused to subside. The guerrilla attacks staged by Greek nationalists against Ottoman troops increased. As the military campaigns intensified, a growing number of villagers on both sides of the ethnic, religious, and linguistic divide were subjected to brutal attacks, losing their livelihood in the bloody clashes that took place between the sultan's troops and the Greek nationalist fighters. In April 1824, the sultan appealed to Muhammad Ali, the Ottoman governor of Egypt, for assistance and support. In return for dispatching his troops to Greece, Muhammad Ali's son Ibrahim Paşa was promised the governorship of the Morea and Crete.[57] After capturing Crete, the Egyptian forces under the command of Ibrahim Paşa landed in the bay of Methoni in February 1825 and stormed and occupied several strategically important forts in the Mani. Soon, much of the Peloponnese was under Ottoman control, with Missolonghi "at the entrance to the Gulf of Corinth" falling in April 1826 and Athens just over a year later in June 1827.[58]

Throughout this period, atrocities were committed by both sides, with Greek revolutionaries attacking Muslim Turkish villagers and Ottoman-Egyptian forces killing Greek civilians. The European newspapers and official circles, however, focused exclusively on "Turkish atrocities" against an unarmed and helpless Greek civilian population.[59] This sustained propaganda ignited intense pro-Greek and anti-Ottoman sentiments in Europe. Many European intellectuals, including some highly educated and enlightened romantics, such as the poet Lord Byron, became infatuated with the Greek cause and joined the Philhellenism movement. Lord Byron demonstrated his devotion to the Greek national movement by joining the battle against Ottoman forces and dying at Missolonghi in 1824.[60] The anti-Ottoman political campaign and the cry of genocide against a helpless population allowed Russia, France, and Britain to discard their differences and combine their forces in an attempt to impose a resolution on the warring parties. In the Greek revolt, the three European powers recognized an opportunity to intervene in the internal affairs of the Ottoman Empire and advance their own political, diplomatic, and commercial interests in the Balkans. When the three powers expressed their intention to mediate, the Greek nationalists expressed their support while the sultan rejected it.[61] In response, the three European states imposed a naval blockade on the Egyptian supply lines. The inevitable confrontation between the Ottoman-Egyptian forces and the combined naval forces of Russia, Britain, and France erupted in October 1827 at Navarino, where the European powers destroyed the entire Ottoman-Egyptian fleet. The refusal of the sultan and his advisors to accept the defeat and mediation allowed Russia to declare war on the sultan and invade Ottoman territory in April 1828. Russian forces crossed into eastern Anatolia from their bases in the south Caucasus and captured Erzurum in July 1829, while a second Russian army attacked and occupied Edirne in August. The destruction of the Ottoman and Egyptian naval forces and intense pressure from Russia and Great Britain forced Muhammad Ali to withdraw his troops from Greece in October. The sultan could only sue for peace. The Treaty of Edirne signed in September 1829 forced the sultan to recognize the independence of Greece and the autonomy of Moldavia, Wallachia, and Serbia, which was enlarged by receiving additional territory.[62] Although a new independent Greek state had been established, it did not incorporate all the territory and the districts that Greek nationalists had envisioned. Great Britain, France, and Austria did not wish the new Greek state, which was under strong Russian influence, to be a large and strong political entity. It would have been foolish for these European powers to further undermine the power and authority of the Ottoman sultan by rewarding the aggressive and expansionist Russia with a new base of operations in the Balkans.[63]

Even before the destruction of the Ottoman-Egyptian fleet at Navarino and the Treaty of Edirne, Mahmud had concluded that he could not establish the authority of the central government without building a new modern army. Perhaps his most important lesson was that as long as the *janissaries* survived, the anti-reform forces could always rely on their support to challenge governmental reforms. Learning from the mistakes of Selim III, Mahmud did not create a new and separate army that could be viewed as a direct challenge to the *janissaries*. Instead, he selectively modernized army units such as the artillery corps, which were crucial in any future confrontation. By June 1826, the sultan was ready to act. First, he demanded that the *janissaries* follow the model of other military units and reform. When they revolted and tried to challenge him by rallying the conservative forces, Mahmud, unlike his cousin, refused to budge. He knew full well that concessions to the rebels would be construed as a sign of weakness. When the grand vezir and the *ulema* rallied to the banner of their sultan and Mahmud's agents called on the people of Istanbul to rise against the corrupt and rebellious troops, the *janissaries* did not have any other alternative but to return to their barracks. Determined to use the revolt as a justification to destroy them, the sultan struck back, ordering his artillerymen to shower the *janissary* barracks with cannon balls and force the gates to open. This allowed the units loyal to the sultan to force their way into the barracks, mowing down every *janissary* they encountered. The victory was complete. The day after the massacre, the *janissary* corps was officially abolished. The attack on the *janissary* units stationed in Istanbul was replicated in other provinces of the empire. The message to the conservative forces was clear. You may challenge the will and policies of the sultan, but you will no longer have the military means to overthrow him. The destruction of the *janissaries* by Mahmud was celebrated throughout the empire as the *Vaka-ye Hayriye* or the beneficial event.[64]

The destruction of the *janissaries* may have removed a formidable obstacle to the creation of a modern army, which was the hallmark of the sultan's efforts to build a strong and centralized governmental authority, but it also created a vacuum that could not be filled overnight. The absence of a strong and well-trained army undermined Ottoman attempts to maintain their rule over Greece. But if the loss of Greece struck a devastating blow to Ottoman prestige and power, it was the revolt of Muhammad Ali, the governor of Egypt, that brought the empire to the verge of political extinction. Muhammad Ali, originally an Albanian from northern Greece, had emerged as the master of Egypt after building a strong and modern army with direct assistance and support from France. Mahmud, who was fully aware of Muhammad Ali's successes and his newly acquired military capability, asked for his support when the Greek revolution erupted. The defeat at Navarino, however, forced the governor of Egypt to withdraw his forces. He had lost his fleet and he could not receive any compensation for such a devastating loss from the sultan in Istanbul.[65] The battles of the Greek revolution had demonstrated that the Ottoman army was in a sorry state and could not prevent him from expanding his rule into neighboring lands and provinces. Initially, Muhammad Ali had thought of building his own kingdom in North Africa by attacking Algeria and Tunisia, but the French had acted faster by attacking and occupying Algiers in July 1830.

With North Africa falling into the hands of the French, Muhammad Ali and his son Ibrahim Paşa, who acted as his father's army commander, turned their attention eastward and attacked Palestine and Syria in October 1831.[66] In May 1832, the town of Acre fell, followed by Damascus in June. By July, Ibrahim Paşa had routed Ottoman forces twice, establishing his rule over the entire country.[67] As in the case of the Greek revolution, the sultan refused an offer for a negotiated settlement. With offers of peace rejected, the Egyptian army pushed into Anatolia and, in a battle near Konya in December, defeated the Ottoman army that had been sent from Istanbul. On February 2, 1833, the Egyptians reached Kütahya in western Anatolia.[68] Mahmud responded to the defeat by opening negotiations with European powers with the aim of securing their support against his rebellious and ambitious subject. When the British and the Austrians turned down the request, the sultan asked for military intervention from Russia. While the arrival of the Russian fleet in February 1833 prevented Muhammad Ali from marching his troops to Istanbul, it could not dislodge the Egyptian forces from their newly conquered territories in Anatolia. To end the crisis, the sultan agreed to sign the Treaty of Kütahya in April and appoint Muhammad Ali the governor of Syria. On July 8, he also signed the Treaty of Hünkâr Iskelesi with Russia, an eight-year defense pact, which confirmed the Treaty of Edirne.[69] According to this treaty, Czar Nicholas received a promise from the sultan that the Ottoman government would close the straits to all ships at the time of war between Russia and a foreign power. Thus, Russia succeeded in using the Ottoman Empire as a means of blockading any future attack by a hostile European power against its positions and establishing naval supremacy in the Black Sea.

The Treaty of Hünkâr Iskelesi has been lauded as a great victory for Russian diplomacy, for it emphasized a successful policy of controlling the Ottoman Empire "from within."[70] Despite the peace with Muhammad Ali, the sultan was anxious to strengthen his army and strike back at the disloyal and rebellious governor of Egypt. The British, who were greatly alarmed by the growing power and influence of Russia, viewed Muhammad Ali as an ally of France whose aggressive and expansionist policies toward the Ottoman Empire would force the sultan to depend on the Russians for his survival. Meanwhile, the sultan hoped to utilize British anxiety over Muhammad Ali to gain their support for a campaign against him. However, in 1834, when an Ottoman army began to move toward Syria, the British cautioned the sultan against the attack.

In 1838, the tension between the sultan and Muhammad Ali erupted again when the latter stated his intention to declare his independence from the Ottoman Empire. When this ambitious and provocative move was opposed by his closest ally, the French, Muhammad Ali backed down. The sultan was now determined to secure the support of Great Britain in a campaign to destroy Muhammad Ali. Using this opportunity to expand its economic and commercial interests in the region, the British prime minister, Palmerston, signed a commercial treaty with the Ottoman government in August 1838, which confirmed British capitulatory privileges and opened the Ottoman markets to British investment and trade.[71] The treaty has been interpreted as compensation to the British government for its support during the war against Mohammad Ali, and it has been identified as the principal cause for the collapse of the Ottoman economy in the nineteenth century.[72] Without British support, Mahmud mobilized a force, which was sent against Muhammad Ali's army in Syria. When the Ottoman army attacked Aleppo in June 1839, Egyptian forces under the command of Ibrahim Paşa destroyed it, killing most of the Ottoman soldiers and officers. Less than a week later, Mahmud died in Istanbul after a long battle with tuberculosis. It is believed that the news of the devastating defeat in Syria arrived after the ailing sultan had taken his last breath.

Despite his many failures on the battlefield, Mahmud introduced a number of important political, military, judicial, educational, and cultural reforms, which transformed the Ottoman Empire and laid the foundation for a group of government officials to push a far more ambitious program of reforms from 1839 to 1876. Indeed, one of the fundamental differences between the reforms of Mahmud and those that were introduced before his reign was the underlying commitment of the sultan to abandon the old institutions and replace them with new structures that were borrowed from various European countries.

Notes

1. William Hale, *Turkish Foreign Policy, 1774–2000* (London: Frank Cass, 2000), 21.

2. Jelavich, *History of the Balkans*, 68–9.

3. Shaw, *History of the Ottoman Empire*, 1:247. Aksan, *An Ottoman Statesman*, 115. Finkel, *Osman's Dream*, 374.

4. Jelavich, *History of the Balkans*, 69.

5. Ibid.

6. Shaw, *History of the Ottoman Empire*, 1:249.

7. Ibid.

8. Sugar, *Southeastern Europe under Ottoman Rule*, 140.

9. Hurewitz, *Diplomacy in the Near and Middle East*, 1:55.

10. Ibid., 55–6.

11. Aksan, *An Ottoman Statesman*, 167.

12. Shaw, *History of the Ottoman Empire*, 1:251.

13. See Mirza Mohammad Sadeq Mousavi Nami Isfahani, *Tarikh-i Guitygosha* (Tehran: 1988).

14. Ibid., 195–211.

15. Aksan, *An Ottoman Statesman*, 174–76.

16. Ibid., 184.

17. Shaw, *History of the Ottoman Empire*, 1:257.

18. Erik J. Zürcher, *Turkey: A Modern History* (New York: I.B. Tauris, 2004), 21.

19. Ibid.

20. Kemal Karpat, "Comments on Contributions and the Borderlands," in *Ottoman Borderlands: Issues, Personalities and Political Changes*, eds. Kemal H. Karpat with Robert W. Zens (Madison: The University of Wisconsin Press, 2003), 11.

21. Zürcher, *Turkey*, 22.

22. Ibid., 24.

23. Ibid.

24. Ibid., 23.

25. Ibid., 21.

26. Gordon Wright, *France in Modern Times: 1760 to the Present* (Chicago: Rand McNally & Company, 1960), 87.

27. Alan Palmer, *The Decline & Fall of the Ottoman Empire* (New York: Barnes & Noble, 1992), 59.

28. Zürcher, *Turkey*, 25.

29. Shaw, *History of the Ottoman Empire*, 1:273–4.

30. Ibid., 1:274.

31. Jelavich, *History of the Balkans*, 125–6.

32. Shaw, *History of the Ottoman Empire*, 2:2–3. Zürcher, *Turkey*, 28.

33. Zürcher, *Turkey*, 28.

34. Shaw, *History of the Ottoman Empire*, 2:2. Zürcher, *Turkey*, 28.

35. Ibid.

36. Finkel, *Osman's Dream*, 422.

37. Ibid.

38. Halil Inalcik, "An Overview of the Ottoman History" in *The Great Ottoman Turkish Civilization*, ed. Kemal Çiçek, 4 vols. (Ankara: 2000), 1:86.

39. Karpat, "Comments on Contributions and the Borderlands," 10.

40. Shaw, *History of the Ottoman Empire*, 2:4.

41. Ibid.

42. Ibid., 2:5. Zürcher, *Turkey*, 29.

43. Ibid., 1:271, 2:14. Zürcher, *Turkey*, 31.

44. Zürcher, *Turkey*, 31. See Jelavich, *History of the Balkans*, 196–202.

45. Jelavich, *The Establishment of the Balkan National States*, 54.

46. Zürcher, *Turkey*, 31.

47. Sugar, *Southeastern Europe under Ottoman Rule*, 208.

48. Finkel, *Osman's Dream*, 429.

49. Zürcher, *Turkey*, 31.

50. Shaw, *History of the Ottoman Empire*, 2:17.

51. Finkel, *Osman's Dream*, 430.

52. Jelavich, *History of the Balkans*, 216.

53. Zürcher, *Turkey*, 32.

54. Jelavich, *History of the Balkans*, 216.

55. Ibid., 217. Finkel, *Osman's Dream*, 429.

56. Finkel, *Osman's Dream*, 430.

57. Ibid., 432.

58. Ibid.

59. Jelavich, *History of the Balkans*, 217.

60. Ibid., 224.

61. Ibid., 226.

62. Zürcher, *Turkey*, 35.

63. Ibid.

64. Ibid., 40.

65. Ibid., 36.

66. Ibid.

67. Ibid.

68. Hale, *Turkish Foreign Policy*, 24.

69. Ibid., 25.

70. Jelavich, *The Establishment of the Balkan National States*, 23.

71. Zürcher, *Turkey*, 38. Shaw, *History of the Ottoman Empire*, 2:50.

72. Inalcik, "An Overview of the Ottoman History," 1:87.

CHAPTER 7

FROM TANZIMAT TO AUTOCRATIC MODERNIZATION

On November 3, 1839, the new Ottoman sultan Abdülmecid ordered his ministers and dignitaries as well as representatives of foreign powers to gather in the rose garden of the Topkapi Palace where his foreign minister, Mustafa Reşid Paşa, read a decree entitled *Hatt-i Şerif-i Gülhane*, the Noble Edict of the Rose Garden (see Document 3).[1] Though written under pressure from European powers, the issuance of this imperial edict signaled the beginning of a period of governmental reforms that came to be known as *Tanzimat* (Reorganization).[2] The document guaranteed the subjects of the sultan security of life, honor, and property.[3] It also promised a regular system for assessing and levying taxes as well as a just system of conscription and military service.[4] The decree committed the central government to a number of essential reforms, such as establishing a new penal code, eradicating bribery, and creating a regular and just tax system that would eliminate inequities and special privileges, such as tax farming. Thus, the imperial decree demonstrated a new commitment by the sultan and his advisors to the rule of law, the equality and fair treatment of all Ottoman subjects regardless of their religion and ethnicity, and the establishment of a new justice system that protected their life and property against arbitrary attacks and confiscation.[5] The period of *Tanzimat* represented a systematic attempt by the central government to strengthen the authority of the Porte by "promoting the notion of a state based on law" and efficient administrative practices.[6]

In the traditional system, the Ottoman state had a limited number of obligations toward its subjects, such as the maintenance of security and order, and protection against outside aggression.[7] In the age of

Tanzimat, however, as the Ottoman central government adopted the European model, the role and responsibilities of the state expanded significantly. For the first time, the government had declared itself responsible for building a modern economic infrastructure and providing basic social and economic services ranging from the building of new schools to constructing roads and railways, which would connect various urban and rural communities of the empire, stimulate cross regional commerce, and create a more integrated economic system.[8]

The introduction of reforms, which were to be implemented from above, required the creation of a highly centralized bureaucracy. In emulating the European system, the government was divided into several ministries with specific tasks and responsibilities. A council of ministers was created to act as the highest advisory body to the sultan in his effort to save the empire from further disintegration by imposing the authority of the Porte over the remotest provinces. Building new roads and railways was viewed as one of the most important priorities of the central government. Armies sent to quell internal rebellions and confront foreign invaders could reach their destination much faster using a modern road or riding on a train. Telegraph services were introduced as a means of communicating orders from Istanbul and receiving the latest news from various provinces. The improvement of the transportation and communication systems also stimulated the economy and intensified commercial ties between various regions of the empire.

In addition to the modernization of the empire's infrastructure, the *Tanzimat* period also witnessed a significant transformation in the Ottoman educational system. During the reign of Mahmud II, the Ottoman government had introduced the *Ruşdiye* (adolescence) schools, which provided a secular education for male students who had completed the *mekteps* (the traditional schools devoted to the study of the Quran).[9] The principal objective for the creation of modern schools was to train a new educated elite capable of administering an empire. The religious schools did not teach modern sciences and humanities, but despite these deficiencies, the reformers did not wish to attack Islamic schools and propose their closure. Such a move would have been vehemently opposed by the *ulema* and it would have exposed the men of *Tanzimat* to the accusation of heresy from the religious classes. Indeed, the fear of opposition from the conservatives continued to slow down educational reforms and forced the reformers to attach modern schools to various governmental ministries and bureaus. Thus, the first medical and engineering schools in the Ottoman Empire were introduced as integral components of a military school.[10] The introduction of modern educational institutions also suffered from a lack of adequate funding and the absence of well-trained teachers and instructors. Despite these difficulties, a new bureaucracy, which was four to five times larger than the imperial administration and relied heavily on graduates from the modern schools, was created.[11] Finally, the men of *Tanzimat* tried to create a modern financial structure and an efficient tax collection system that would provide the central treasury with sufficient funds to implement its reform program. The "main thrust" of their financial reforms was "to simplify the collection of revenues" by centralizing the treasury and delegating "the responsibility of tax collection to the salaried agents of the government, rather than governors, holders of prebendal grants, or other intermediaries of the classical system."[12]

Despite their best efforts to focus on reforms, the men of the *Tanzimat* faced serious challenges from both internal rebellions and foreign aggression, which ultimately undermined their efforts and resulted in the disintegration of the empire. In October 1840, the Ottomans and the British began to exert military pressure on Muhammad Ali, forcing his troops to evacuate Palestine and Syria in February 1841. The sultan, however, issued a decree granting Muhammad Ali and his family the right to rule Egypt. Meanwhile, a new crisis in Lebanon began to occupy the attention of the Ottoman leadership in Istanbul. Lebanon was divided among numerous religious communities, such as the Maronite Christians, the Orthodox Christians, the Druze, the Sunni Muslims, and the Shia Muslims, who had developed their own separate leadership and unique identity in opposition to their neighbors. To maintain peace and security over this internally fragmented entity, the Ottoman government had empowered the Shihabi family to rule Lebanon on behalf of the sultan. Though corrupt and inefficient, Emir Bashir II had maintained a fragile peace among the various communities by playing one against another.[13] This tenuous arrangement was, however, undermined when Muhammad Ali's army invaded Lebanon under the leadership of his son, Ibrahim Paşa, and began showing favor to the Maronite Christians over the local Muslims, who had remained staunchly loyal to the sultan.[14] Outside interests compounded the situation. The French found friends among the Maronite Christians, while the British supported the Druze, a heretical branch of the Shia sect.[15] In October 1840, Emir Bashir was deposed. Open warfare between the Maronite and the Druze communities erupted a year later, in October 1841. The Ottoman government, under pressure from European powers, intervened and imposed a division of the country into a Maronite and a Druze *sancak* under an Ottoman administration in January 1843. Local representatives of each community were empowered to collect taxes from their own peasant population, and councils with mixed representation were organized to respond to appeals. A general agreement was finally reached in October 1846. Peace was restored but the tension between the religious communities continued to cause serious difficulties for the Ottoman authorities.

The second important foreign policy crisis of the *Tanzimat* era was the Crimean war, which forced the Ottoman Empire to declare war on Russia on October 4, 1853.[16] By claiming to protect Serbia, the Danubian Principalities, and the sultan's Orthodox Christian subjects, Russia intended to replace both the Ottoman Empire and Austria as the dominant power in the Balkans. The ultimate goal of Russian foreign policy was to create a series of satellite states that were dependent on Russian protection and support for their political survival. Parallel to this was the debate between the Catholic and Orthodox churches over their rights to various holy sites in Jerusalem, with Russia championing the Orthodox position and France that of Rome. In 1852, the Ottoman government announced its decision on the question of Christian Holy Places in Palestine and sided with the French position. The Russian government was outraged, and Czar Nicholas I ordered a partial mobilization of his army to back a new series of demands, including the Russian right to protect the sultan's Christian Orthodox subjects, which constituted a direct threat to the sovereignty of the Ottoman state. Confident that it would be supported by several European powers (such as Great Britain, France, and Austria), the Ottoman government refused to accept the Russian demands. When the czarist forces invaded the Danubian Principalities, the Ottoman Empire declared war on Russia.

As the British and the French naval forces crossed the Straits on their way to the Black Sea, the Ottoman fleet fought the Russian navy at Sinop on November 30. Most Ottoman ships that fought in the naval confrontation were destroyed, and thousands of sailors were killed. In March 1854, France and Great Britain declared war on Russia after negotiations collapsed. Fearing an attack from Austria, the Russian forces withdrew from Wallachia and Moldavia, which were then occupied by a joint Austro-Ottoman force.[17] The military campaigns that followed, particularly the attack on Sevastopol, which was occupied in October 1855, forced Russia to sue for peace.

As the representatives of European powers began to arrive at the peace conference in Paris in February 1856, the sultan, under pressure from France and Great Britain, issued a second major reform decree, the *Hatt-i Hümâyun*, or the Imperial Edict committing his government to the principle of equality of all Ottoman subjects. On an international level, the Treaty of Paris, signed on March 30, 1856, forced Russia to withdraw from Wallachia and Moldavia, which along with Serbia were to regain their autonomy under Ottoman rule. By surrendering southern Bessarabia to Moldavia, Russia's access to the Danube was blocked. That famous river as well as the Turkish Straits were declared open to ships of all countries, and the Black Sea was demilitarized. Russia was also obliged to withdraw its forces from eastern Anatolia, including the city of Kars, which it had occupied during the war. Perhaps most importantly, however, was that the Crimean War and the Treaty of Paris had resulted in the de facto inclusion of the Ottoman Empire in the "Concert of Europe," which had tried to maintain the balance of power in the continent since the defeat of Napoleon and the convening of the Congress of Vienna in 1814.[18] The territorial integrity of the empire was thus theoretically preserved, and Russia's expansionism into southeast Europe was contained. With Russian aggression neutralized, the leaders of *Tanzimat* could once again focus on the implementation of their reform agenda. The presence of large British and French contingents in Istanbul had exposed the city and its population to European manners and customs, allowing for the emergence of a more tolerant cultural environment that helped the leaders of *Tanzimat*. On the negative ledger, however, was the sad fact that the Crimean War had been very costly and forced the Ottoman government to apply for high interest loans that would eventually undermine the economic independence of the state. The accumulation of significant debt to European banks and the continuous struggle to generate sufficient revenue to repay them would undermine the efforts to reform the government for the remainder of the nineteenth century.

Although the Ottoman Empire received guarantees of support for its territorial integrity in the Treaty of Paris, inter-communal tensions and nationalist uprisings by the sultan's Christian subjects continued to undermine the authority of the central government. In May 1860, tensions between the Maronite and the Druze communities in Lebanon erupted into a civil war, with thousands of civilians massacred on both sides and the carnage soon spilling into Damascus with even greater losses. Despite Ottoman attempts to suppress the violence, the French viewed the crisis as an opportunity to intervene and expand their influence in the Levant by sending their troops to Beirut. This alarmed London, which organized an international conference that resulted in the withdrawal of Ottoman troops, the stipulation that all taxes collected be used locally and that the people of Lebanon enjoy equality before the law. Most significantly, however, was that the Organic Statute for Lebanon reorganized the country as a special *sancak* governed by its own Christian governor, albeit one appointed by the sultan and confirmed and supervised by European powers.[19]

Shortly after the resolution of the crisis in Lebanon, in June 1861, Sultan Abdülmecid died. During the reign of the new sultan, who ascended the Ottoman throne as Sultan Abdülaziz on June 25, the Ottoman Empire continued to face new nationalist revolts, such as the one that erupted in May 1866 on the island of Crete. While the sizable Muslim community on the island had remained loyal to the sultan, the Greek-speaking Orthodox Christian community which constituted the majority of the population maintained close political, commercial, and cultural ties to mainland Greece. As in the Balkans, the revolt did not begin as a nationalist uprising of a people demanding their independence. Rather, the principal complaint of the Greek population of the island was centered on corruption and mismanagement by Ottoman authorities. Once the news of protests became public, however, Greek nationalists called for the union of the island with mainland Greece and began to recruit volunteers to join the battle against Ottoman troops. As the conflict intensified, the Russian government called on European powers to intervene and secure the separation of Crete from the Ottoman Empire and its union with Greece. Cognizant of the objectives of the Russian policy, the European states refused to intervene. The failure of the Greek nationalists to mobilize European support allowed the Porte to restore order and, by 1868, reestablish the authority of the central government on the island, at least for a time.

It was neither the communal strife among the diverse Arabic-speaking communities in Lebanon nor the uprising of Greek nationalists in Crete that destroyed the territorial integrity of the Ottoman Empire. Rather, it was the revolt of the Slavic subjects of the sultan, backed by Russia, which ultimately ended Ottoman rule in southeastern Europe. Acting as the centers of Pan-Slavic agitation, Serbia and Montenegro provided support and inspiration to the protests against Ottoman administrative mismanagement and corruption in neighboring Bosnia-Herzegovina, directing them toward a more nationalistic and Pan-Slavist agenda. When Christian peasant uprisings erupted against the predominantly Muslim landowning class in 1853, 1860–1862, and 1875, Serbia and Montenegro supported the rebels and fanned the flames of anti-Ottoman and anti-Muslim sentiments, hoping to overthrow Ottoman rule and cleanse the area of Muslim presence and influence, thus creating a greater Serbian state.[20] The threat posed to Ottoman rule in Bosnia-Herzegovina was not, however, confined to agitation from Russia and Serbia. Inside Bosnia, the old landowning families (former *timar* holders as well as former *sipâhis* and *janissaries*), who had settled in the province after being forced out of Hungary by the Habsburgs, exercised a great deal of power and influence. While they viewed themselves as the first line of defense against

Austrian southward expansionism, they also resented the centralizing reforms of the men of *Tanzimat*, preferring a looser system that would allow them to maximize the taxes they collected from peasant farmers without the expectation of increasing their contribution to the central treasury in Istanbul. Conflict was almost inevitable. Starting in 1850 with the arrival of Ömer Paşa as the new governor, the Ottoman forces embarked on a sustained drive to impose central government authority over Bosnia-Herzegovina. Three years later, Ömer Paşa attacked Montenegro in a successful campaign, which was brought to an end only after Austria intervened and delivered an ultimatum to the Porte.[21] The conflict in Bosnia-Herzegovina erupted again in 1874 and 1875, allowing Serbia and Montenegro to intervene and declare war on the Ottoman state in 1876.

The era of *Tanzimat* was dominated by government officials who had received their education and training at the translation bureau, followed by service at Ottoman embassies in European capitals. Under the leadership of Mustafa Reşid Paşa and his protégés Fuad Paşa and Ali Paşa, the center of power shifted from the palace to the Porte, and particularly the ministry of foreign affairs. With the death of Ali Paşa in September 1871, the *Tanzimat* era came to an end. For the next three years, six grand vezirs came and went as Sultan Abdülaziz became increasingly involved in running the everyday affairs of the empire, thus introducing an element of chaos. Then, in the early hours of Tuesday, May 30, 1876, a small group of officials and army commanders led by the energetic and reform-minded statesman Midhat Paşa, who had served as governor of Niş (1861–1868) and Baghdad (1869–1872), carried out a peaceful military coup.[22] A nephew of Abdülaziz, Prince Murad, was brought out of his residence to the ministry of war and declared the new sultan. The legality of the putsch was provided by the *şeyhülislâm*, Hayrullah Effendi, whose *fetva* of deposition justified the coup on the grounds of Abdülaziz's "mental derangement, ignorance of political affairs, diversion of public revenues to private expenditure, and conduct generally injurious to state and community."[23]

Before the new sultan could establish himself, however, the news of Abdülaziz's sudden death was announced to a shocked populace on June 4. The body of the deposed sultan had been discovered in his private bedroom, his wrists slashed with a pair of scissors, leading many to conclude that he had been murdered. To diffuse the rumors of assassination, the government called on doctors from several foreign embassies in Istanbul to examine the body and offer their medical opinion on the cause of death, which was officially declared a suicide. The events profoundly affected the new sultan Murad, who suffered a nervous breakdown. Accordingly, Midhat Paşa and his colleagues decided to depose Murad in favor of his brother, who ascended the Ottoman throne on August 31 as Abdülhamid II. Meanwhile, Midhat was appointed grand vezir on December 19, and four days later the first Ottoman constitution was introduced by the new grand vezir.[24]

These momentous events took place in the context of major developments in European power politics. In addition to another crisis in the Balkans, which had erupted when Serbia and Montenegro attacked the Ottoman Empire in July 1876, there was the slow-burning issue of Ottoman–Russian affairs which ultimately included all the powers of the day. For starters, the Franco-Prussian war, which began in the summer 1870, had left a profound impact on the Russian policy makers who viewed the Prussian victory and the emergence of a strong and unified German state as a direct challenge to the Russian hegemony in eastern Europe. Russian pride had not recovered from the defeat in the Crimean War, which had forced the czar to relinquish his control over southern Bessarabia and accept the demilitarization of the Black Sea and the loss of its dominant role in the Slavic populated lands of the Balkans such as Serbia, Montenegro, and Bulgaria, all of which had begun to intensify their agitation for a more aggressive and interventionist Pan-Slavic foreign policy under Russia. In July 1875, several uprisings erupted in Bosnia-Herzegovina, which the Ottoman government failed to suppress, providing the justification for the Three Emperor's Alliance (Russia, Germany, and Austria) to intervene and demand the implementation of fundamental reforms. The Ottomans accepted the first reform proposal in December 1875, which was rejected by the rebels. A second proposal submitted in May 1876 as the Berlin Memorandum was rejected by the Porte. With chaos and uncertainty reigning in Istanbul and the revolt and instability spreading to the rural communities in Bosnia-Herzegovina, Russia began to push for military intervention by Serbia and Montenegro. This Pan-Slavic project designed by Russia and implemented by Serbia failed miserably, however, when Ottoman troops struck back, defeating the Serbs and forcing them to sue for peace on July 24. Russia then instigated a nationalist uprising in Bulgaria, which was crushed by Ottoman forces with heavy casualties and massacres of the civilian population, allowing Russia to demand that the Ottoman Empire introduce reforms and grant autonomy to the Bulgarian people. Recognizing the threat of Russian intervention in the eastern Balkans, the British government intervened and called for the convening of an international conference to meet in Istanbul with the intention of diffusing the possibility of another war between Russia and the Ottoman Empire. However, on the first day of the conference, December 23,

1876, the Ottoman delegation shocked the European participants by announcing that a constitution had been promulgated and that any attempt by European powers to pressure the Ottoman state to introduce reforms in its European provinces were unnecessary because, under the constitution, all Ottoman subjects would be treated as equals with their rights protected and guaranteed by the new government.[25]

The Ottoman constitution did not, however, prevent another military confrontation with Russia. Continuous palace intrigues convinced Abdülhamid to dismiss his prime minister, who was sent into exile in February 1877, an event that was soon followed by a Russian declaration of war on April 24. The Ottoman forces delayed the Russian southward incursion for several months at Plevna in Bulgaria, but by December, the czarist army was encamped a mere twelve kilometers outside Istanbul.[26] On March 3, 1878, the Treaty of San Stefano was signed between Russia and the Ottoman Empire. Among other things, it called for the establishment of an autonomous Bulgarian state, stretching from the Black Sea to the Aegean, which Russia would occupy for two years. Serbia, Romania, and Montenegro were also to be recognized as independent states, while Russia received the districts of Batumi, Kars, and Ardahan in eastern Anatolia. Additionally, the Ottoman government was obliged to introduce fundamental reforms in Thessaly and Armenia. But the rapid growth of Russian influence in the Balkans and the Caucasus could not be tolerated by other European powers, forcing them to intervene. The Treaty of San Stefano was nullified, and the European powers agreed to meet in Berlin at a new congress designed to partition the European provinces of the Ottoman Empire in such a way as to prevent the emergence of Russia as the dominant power in the region.

The Congress of Berlin, which began in June 1878, was a turning point in the history of the Ottoman Empire and southeast Europe. When the Congress ended a month later, the Ottoman Empire was no longer a political and military power in the Balkans.[27] The Ottomans lost 8 percent of their territory and 4.5 million of their population.[28] The majority of those who left the empire were Christians, while tens of thousands of Muslim refugees from the Balkans and the Caucasus fled into the interior of the empire. The large Bulgarian state that had been created at the Treaty of San Stefano was divided into three separate entities.[29] The region north of the Balkan Mountains and the area around Sofia were combined into a new autonomous Bulgarian principality that would recognize the suzerainty of the sultan but for all practical purposes act as a Russian satellite. The region lying between the Rhodope and Balkan Mountains, which corresponded with Eastern Rumelia, was established as a semi-autonomous region under its own

Christian governor, who was to be appointed by the sultan and super-vised by European powers.[30] The third area of Thrace and Macedonia remained under Ottoman rule.[31] The Congress did not provide Greece with any new territory. Instead the powers asked that Greece and the Ottoman Empire enter into negotiations on establishing the future of their boundaries, which also involved the status of Thessaly and Epi-rus. Austria was granted the right to occupy and administer Bosnia-Herzegovina as well as the *sancak* of Novi Pazar, a strip of land that separated Serbia from Montenegro.[32] Although the new territorial enti-ties nominally remained part of the Ottoman Empire, all participants in the Congress, including the Ottoman delegation, were fully aware that they had been permanently lost.[33]

And more: while the Congress recognized Serbia, Romania, and Montenegro as independent states, the Romanian state was forced to hand southern Bessarabia to Russia and in return receive Dobrudja and the Danube Delta.[34] Russia also received the districts of Batumi, Kars, and Ardahan, thereby establishing military control over the east-ern shores of the Black Sea and an important strategic land bridge to eastern Anatolia.[35] The British received the island of Cyprus, which contained a Greek majority and a Muslim Turkish minority popula-tion. By handing Albanian populated areas and towns to Montenegro and Greece, the European powers ignited a new nationalist movement among a proud people who had faithfully served the Ottoman state on many occasions in the past.[36] Thus Albania, with its emerging national movement, would replicate the model set by the Serbs, the Romanians, and the Bulgarians and demand independence.

Although Serbia, Montenegro, Romania, and Bulgaria gained their independence or autonomy in 1878, the Congress of Berlin left the newly independent states dissatisfied and hungry for more terri-tory. The Romanians were angry because they were forced to cede the rich and productive Bessarabia in return for gaining the poor and less productive Dobrudja. The Bulgarians were outraged because they lost the greater Bulgarian state that had been created by the Treaty of San Stefano. Serbia gained limited territory, but it did not satisfy the vora-cious appetite of Serbian nationalists who dreamt of a greater Serbia with access to the sea. Montenegro received a port on the Adriatic, but, as in the case of Serbia, it did not get the towns and the districts it had demanded. Of all the participants in the Congress, Russia was perhaps the most frustrated. In return for its massive human and financial investment in the war against the Ottoman Empire, it had only received southern Bessarabia in the Balkans while the Austrians, who had opportunistically sat on the sidelines, had been awarded Bosnia-Herzegovina. These frustrated dreams turned the Balkan Peninsula into a ticking bomb. By carving the Ottoman Empire in the Balkans into small and hungry independent states, the European powers laid the foundations for intense rivalries. Thirty-six years after the conclusion of the Berlin Congress, the Balkan tinderbox, which had already gone off twice in 1912 and 1913, exploded on June 28, 1914, when Serb nationalists assassinated the Austrian crown prince Archduke Franz Ferdinand in Sarajevo, sparking the First World War.

With the removal of the grand vezir Midhat Paşa, the center of power began to shift back from the Porte to the Palace. Despite the defeat at the hands of the Russians and the territorial losses imposed by the Congress of Berlin, the new sultan, Abdülhamid II, began his reign as a highly energetic and intelligent monarch committed to the reforms introduced during the *Tanzimat* period. Indeed, it was during the reign of Abdülhamid that a new and Western-educated officer corps emerged. Ironically, the same officers would play an important role in deposing the sultan in April 1909. In addition to military training, the reform-minded sultan expanded elementary and secondary education (including the opening of a new school for girls in 1884), introduced a modern medical school, and established the University of Istanbul. To create a modern communication system for the empire, he developed telegraph services and the Ottoman railway system, connecting Istanbul to the heartland of the Arab world as far south as the holy city of Medina in Hijaz.[37] The Hijaz railroad, which was completed in July 1908, was justified as a means of promoting Islamic practices such as the *hajj*, or the annual pilgrimage to the holy city of Mecca. But the new railway line also served the goal of centralizing power in the hands of the sultan and his government, enabling the state to send its troops to the Arab provinces in case of rebellion.

As with the reforms introduced by the *Tanzimat*, the principal objective of Abdülhamid's modernization schemes was to establish a strong centralized government capable of maintaining the territorial integrity of the empire. In practical terms, this meant suppressing uprisings among the sultan's subjects and defending the state against the expansionist and interventionist policies of European powers. Despite the sultan's best efforts, however, the empire continued to lose territory.

Building on their occupation of Algeria in 1830, the French imposed their rule on Tunisia in May 1881. Never fully incorporated into the Ottoman system, Tunisia was ruled by a *bey* who had become increasingly dependent on financial assistance from European states. His failure to pay his debts allowed European powers to intervene and organize an International Debt Commission in 1869, which seized control of Tunisia's finances. Fearing Italian designs for an African empire, France then moved in forces and established a protectorate over the province. When the Ottoman government reminded the signatories at the Congress of Berlin that they had promised to respect the territorial integrity of the empire, none of the European powers responded.

In imposing colonial rule over Tunisia, the French enjoyed the support of the British, who were anxious to establish control over Egypt, which had also suffered from mismanagement and indebtedness to European powers. During the reigns of Khedive Said and Khedive Ismail, the Egyptian government granted numerous concessions to European banks and governments and received high interest loans to pay for the expensive lifestyles of its rulers. These loans eventually forced Egypt into bankruptcy, providing the European powers with an excuse to intervene in the name of reorganizing the country's finances. European states seized control over the collection of taxes by administering custom houses and the railway system. When the resentment over European imperial intervention triggered an uprising by a group of army officers led by Ahmad Urabi Paşa in September 1881, Abdülhamid tried to intervene and negotiate a settlement by inviting Urabi Paşa to the Ottoman capital. The sultan's attempts failed when the arrival of British ships resulted in bloody clashes between the Egyptians and Europeans in Alexandria. The killing of European nationals in Alexandria provided the convenient justification for the British navy to shell the city and land troops on July 11, 1882. A few days later, they were in Cairo. In September, the British defeated the nationalist forces at Tel el-Kebir.[38] The Ottoman government did not possess the political and military capability to challenge the British. By 1885, the British and the Ottomans had reached an agreement on the fiction of sultan's suzerainty over Egypt, and an Ottoman and a British commissioner were assigned responsibility to advise the Khedive. Regardless of these formal arrangements, however, it was the British who were now the true masters of Egypt, a country they would dominate for the next seventy years.

While Tunisia and Egypt were seized by France and Great Britain, the Ottoman Empire was also losing territory in the Balkans. After the Congress of Berlin, the only territory left under Ottoman rule was a relatively narrow corridor south of the Balkan Mountains that stretched from the Black Sea in the east to the Adriatic in the west, incorporating Thrace, Thessaly, Macedonia, and Albania.[39] Greece, Serbia, Montenegro, and Bulgaria coveted the remaining territory of the dying Ottoman Empire. In accordance with the promises made at the Congress of Berlin, the Ottomans handed much of Thessaly and a district in Epirus to Greece in July 1881. Despite these new gains,

Greece continued to push for additional territorial concessions, including the island of Crete.

The rise of Bulgarian nationalism in East Rumelia, which had also been created at the Congress of Berlin, began to cause serious anxiety in Istanbul. From the time of its demarcation, the province of East Rumelia was denounced by local nationalists as a conspiracy to prevent the emergence of a strong and unified Bulgarian state. Having used Russia to gain their independence, the Bulgarians were determined to remove Russian influence and create a larger and stronger state by staging a unionist revolt in East Rumelia. In September 1885, nationalists in East Rumelia called for the unification of their province with Bulgaria and invited Prince Alexander to assume leadership. The prince, who had promised the Russian government that he would not advocate unification, was caught in a terrible dilemma.[40] On one hand, he did not wish to alienate his Russian allies. On the other, if he did not assume leadership of the unification movement, he could be deposed by the nationalists.[41] Ultimately, he threw in his lot with the Bulgarian nationalists. Like Russia, the Ottoman Empire was outraged. After all, East Rumelia had been created by the European powers at the Congress of Berlin. The province had accepted the suzerainty of the sultan, paying much of its taxes to the central treasury in Istanbul. Sultan Abdülhamid, who could have intervened, rejected the idea of military action and pinned his hopes on the European powers preserving the territorial integrity of his empire. The Russian czar also expressed his opposition.[42] But the British, who were initially opposed to the unification of Bulgaria and East Rumelia, switched their position. As long as the Bulgarians had acted as the puppets of Russia, the British opposed unification, believing that a Russian-dominated Bulgaria could be used by the czar as a land bridge to invade and conquer Istanbul. But with Prince Alexander acting as an independent monarch and refusing to collaborate with Russian imperial designs, the British were pleased to support the emergence of a strong Bulgaria that would act as a bulwark against Russian expansionism in the Balkans.[43] While the debate raged among European powers, Serbia sent its troops to prevent the unification of the two Bulgarias. In response, the Bulgarians joined forces and fought the invading Serbian army, defeating it in November 1885 and forcing the powers to recognize the unification of East Rumelia.[44] After Prince Alexander abdicated in 1886, a German prince, Ferdinand of Saxe-Coburg, was chosen in 1887 as the new ruler of Bulgaria.[45] Initially, the new monarch ruled with strong support from prominent nationalists but soon realized that as long as he was identified with their cause, he could not gain Russian support or achieve his ultimate dream of a greater Bulgaria that would include Macedonia.[46]

As the Ottoman Empire disintegrated in the Balkans, the Albanians, who had historically remained loyal to the sultan, began to organize their own national movement as a means of protecting their communities from encroachments by their Greek and Slavic neighbors. In the earlier part of the nineteenth century, Albania had been divided between two *paşaliks*, who enjoyed a great deal of autonomy from Istanbul. Ali Paşa of Janina and the Buşati family of Shkodër had dominated Albanian politics for decades. In 1820, Mahmud II, who was determined to impose the authority of the central government, dismissed Ali Paşa and attacked his territory. Ironically, the suppression of Ali Paşa, who was killed by Ottoman agents in 1822, allowed Greek nationalists to stage their revolution against the Ottoman Empire. Following Ali Paşa's demise, the government then turned against the head of the Buşati family, Mustafa Paşa, and the *beys* and *ağas* who supported him. After suffering defeat at the hands of Ottoman forces, Mustafa Paşa accepted his fate and settled in Istanbul where he lived the rest of his life as a loyal servant of the sultan.[47]

The establishment of direct Ottoman rule allowed the government to introduce a series of reforms. The principal objective of these reforms was to remove the intermediary class of notables and replace it with a new administrative organization run by officials sent from Istanbul. The Porte also intended to bring the local landowners who had converted the old *timars* into privately owned estates under its control and create a more efficient tax collection system, which would increase revenue. The central government also wished to establish a new recruitment system, which would provide troops for a new military force. In implementing this ambitious agenda, the sultan abolished the *timars* in 1832 and created two *eyâlets* of Janina and Rumelia, which were reorganized into the three *vilâyets* of Janina, Shkodër, and Bitola in 1865.[48] These reforms were vehemently opposed by the notables, who preferred being ruled by their own local *beys*. But it was the inability of the central government to protect Albanian communities from Greece, Serbia, and Montenegro that forced the Albanians to organize their own independent national movement.

The Ottoman defeat at the hands of the Russians in 1878 and the Treaty of San Stefano, which rewarded Serbia, Montenegro, and Bulgaria with Albanian populated areas, marked the beginning of a transformation in the relationship between Albania and the central government in Istanbul. Until 1878, the Ottoman government, which viewed the Albanians as members of the Muslim community, had not treated them as a separate national group. Muslim Albanians who attended school studied Arabic, the language of the holy Quran, and Turkish, the language of the government and the army. Christian

Albanians, on the other hand, were viewed as members of the Christian Orthodox *millet* who studied Greek as the principal language of their religious community.[49] In response to the signing of the Treaty of San Stefano, a group of prominent Albanian leaders organized a secret committee in Istanbul and called for a larger gathering at Prizren in June 1878.

Determined to transcend their religious and regional differences, the meeting at Prizren brought together Muslim and Christian Albanians who agreed to create the League of Prizren, which enjoyed the authority to collect taxes and organize an army.[50] The League also sent an appeal to the European powers participating in the Congress of Berlin, which was ignored.[51] With Serbia and Montenegro emerging as independent states, the Ottoman government was forced to begin negotiations on the delineations of its new borders with the two countries. Since several towns and districts, such as Bar, Podgorica, and Plav that were handed to Montenegro had a significant Albanian population, the League of Prizren turned to resistance. The Ottoman government was caught in a dilemma. It had to abide by the terms of the Berlin Congress, but it was also determined to benefit from Albanian resistance and use it as a means of reducing its territorial losses.[52]

With arms from the Ottoman government, the Albanians resisted the occupation, forcing the European powers to recognize and respect the power of the newly emerging nationalist movement. Realizing the intensity of Albanian national sentiments and the potential for eruption of ethnic conflicts, the European powers reversed their position and agreed to allow Plav and Gusinje to remain within the Ottoman Empire. Instead, they offered a port, namely Ulcingi (Dulcigno), to Montenegro.[53] Nor was the Albanian resistance confined to the towns and districts that were handed to Montenegro. There was also a very strong opposition to handing any Albanian territory to Greece. The Albanian resistance against Greek occupation of Epirus bore positive results. The European powers agreed in the spring of 1881 that, aside from Thessaly, the Greeks would only receive the district of Arta in Epirus. Despite the successes of the Albanian resistance and the support it enjoyed from the Ottoman government, the sultan remained bound by provisions of the agreement to hand Ulcinji to Montenegro, even if it meant crushing the Albanian League. An Ottoman army was, therefore, dispatched to occupy Prizren, which fell in April 1881.[54] Another Ottoman force routed the Albanian resistance at Ulcinji before the town was handed to Montenegro. Despite its suppression, the League of Prizren had accomplished a great deal. European powers had recognized that Albanian lands could not be partitioned among their Balkan allies without serious repercussions and resistance from the local population.[55]

After Bulgaria received East Rumelia in 1885, Greece, which had seized Thessaly and parts of Epirus, tried to counter the rise of a stronger and more unified Bulgaria by occupying the rest of Epirus. As with the Serbs and the Bulgarians, the Greeks were also determined to incorporate Macedonia into their territory. The control of Macedonia could decide which of the three states would emerge as the most powerful nation in the Balkans. To appease nationalistic sentiments and to compensate for the failure to capture Macedonia, the Greek government began to agitate for an anti-Ottoman uprising in Crete. The island, which had remained under Egyptian occupation from the early 1820s, had been returned to the sultan in 1840. In 1878, the Ottoman government agreed to the formation of an assembly that would be led by the Christian leaders of the island. However, clashes between the Christian and Muslim communities convinced the sultan to disband the assembly and send Muslim governors to run the island. In 1894, the *Ethnike Hetairia* (The National Society), which had a significant following within the Greek army, became actively involved in organizing a mass uprising aimed at unifying the island with Greece. The Cretan revolt finally broke out in 1896, providing the justification for the Greek government to send a fifteen-hundred–man army to the island. In the clashes that followed many civilians on both sides were killed. Building on nationalistic feelings that had erupted throughout the country, the Greek government ordered its army to attack Ottoman territory in April 1897. To the surprise of many, however, the Ottoman forces pushed back the Greek army, capturing sizable territory in Thessaly and forcing Athens to sue for peace and to pay a war indemnity of a hundred million francs. A peace treaty signed on December 4 ended hostilities.[56] Remarkably, it was Greece that emerged as the victor in Crete. Under pressure from European powers, the sultan agreed to the creation of an autonomous government for the island, along with a high commissioner, Prince George, the second son of the Greek monarch.[57] In 1913, Crete was finally unified with Greece.

But of all the Ottoman provinces to demand the attention of the sultan, none was as challenging as Macedonia. With a mixed population that included Bulgarians, Greeks, Vlachs, Jews, Serbs, and Muslims, the province emerged as the breeding ground for contending nationalist movements financed and armed by different neighboring states. Bulgaria, Greece, and Serbia in particular were determined to incorporate Macedonia by any means.[58] Historians and linguists were mobilized to weave "scientific" and "scholarly" justifications for these romantic and nationalistic claims. Bulgarian scholars emphasized the close linguistic ties between the Slavic population of Macedonia and the Bulgarian people. The Greeks utilized the religious commonalities by arguing that any Christian who followed the "ecumenical patriarch was Greek."[59] Finally, the Serbs used common festivals and ceremonies to assert that Macedonians were in reality a branch of the Serbian people.[60]

While the scholars were busy manufacturing new identities, the politicians in various Balkan countries were engaged in organizing political movements and terrorist organizations, which would fight in the name of unifying Macedonia with either Bulgaria or Serbia or Greece.[61] There were pro-Bulgaria, pro-Serbia, and pro-Greece organizations, which used churches, schools, and at times, terrorism, to advance their cause. From 1900 onward, as these political and paramilitary groups intensified their activities, Macedonia was ravaged by internal strife, violence, and bloodshed, forcing many Macedonians (including thousands of Muslims) to flee their homes and seek refuge in Istanbul and other more secure cities. As in previous cases, European powers, particularly Russia and Austria, used the instability created by some of their own allies as a pretext to intervene, and in October 1903, the two powers proposed their own reform program that called for an Ottoman inspector to be joined by Russian and Austrian advisers who would respond to the complaints filed by various Christian communities in Macedonia. The sultan was also asked to provide financial assistance to those who had lost their homes and farms during the civil strife. The Ottoman government was also responsible for the creation of mixed Muslim and Christian courts in the districts where the two communities lived side by side. The reform proposal was accepted grudgingly by the sultan, who wished to do anything to avoid military intervention by European powers. The Greeks and Vlachs, however, denounced the program as favoring the Slavs and discriminating against them. While pro-Bulgaria groups continued with their attacks, the Greek-backed organizations emerged as the most active in Macedonia. As Europe began to slide toward the First World War, Macedonia remained a tinderbox where the resurgence of nationalistic rivalries could ignite a civil war.

Despite the military disasters and territorial losses that the empire suffered, the reign of Abdülhamid proved to be a period of significant social, economic, and cultural transformation. The autocratic sultan continued with the reforms that had been introduced by the men of *Tanzimat*. There was, however, a fundamental difference. The statesmen of the *Tanzimat* had begun their governmental careers as translators and diplomats attached to Ottoman embassies in Europe, and thus wished to emulate European customs and institutions. Abdülhamid, in contrast, may have been a modernizer, but one who believed strongly in preserving the Islamic identity of the Ottoman state. With the loss of its European provinces, the number of Christian subjects of the sultan decreased and Muslims began to emerge as the majority population.[62] The Muslim population was not only loyal to the sultan, but also felt a deep anger toward the sultan's Christian subjects for allying themselves with the imperial powers of Europe in order to gain their independence. Abdülhamid understood the new mood among his Muslim subjects and appealed to Pan-Islamism, or the unity of all Muslims under his leadership as the caliph of the Islamic world, to counter European imperial designs.

Within the Ottoman Empire, Pan-Islamic ideas can be traced back to 1774, when the Ottomans first used Islam as a political and ideological weapon not only to counter the threat posed by Europe, but also to secure their religious and cultural influence in the Muslim populated Crimea.[63] The loss of Crimea, which they had ceded to Czarist Russia after suffering defeat in the Russo-Ottoman war of 1768–1774, did not deter the Ottomans from trying to preserve their historical and religious ties with the Muslim and Turkic-speaking Tatar population. In the absence of Turkish nationalistic feelings, which were alien to their political and cultural thinking, the Ottomans appealed to Islam and revived the idea of the caliphate, maintaining that the Ottoman sultan was not only the ruler of his own domain, but also the religious and spiritual leader of the entire Islamic world.[64] Thus, in the Treaty of Küçük Kaynarca, signed in 1774 after the conclusion of the war with Russia, the sultan claimed the title of caliph of all Muslims and the religious representative of the Crimean Tatars.[65] In order to strengthen their claim to the caliphate, the Ottomans also manufactured the myth that the last Abbasid caliph, who lived in Cairo at the time when Selim I conquered Egypt, had passed the title and the insignia of the caliphate to the family of Osman.[66]

During the nineteenth century, the Ottoman Empire lost most of its European and North African provinces as a result of nationalist uprisings or direct military and diplomatic interventions by European powers. But the Ottoman Empire was not the only Islamic state to lose vast territories. The first half of the nineteenth century also witnessed the victory of the Russian empire over the Qajar dynasty in Iran and the occupation of the Caucasus by the czarist state, while the second half of the century saw the colonization of Muslim-populated Central Asia by Russian forces.[67]

As a result of military defeats suffered at the hands of European powers, the loss of vast territories, and the decline of political and economic power and prestige, a new sense of Ottoman patriotism began to emerge in the last decade of the *Tanzimat* period. The first to advocate Islamic unity were the Young Ottomans, a group of Muslim intellectuals, who believed that the modernization of the Ottoman state was the principal means through which the empire's independence and territorial integrity could be preserved.[68] Concerned with the disintegration of the Ottoman Empire, humiliated by the inability of the state to defend itself against foreign aggression, and inspired by the unification of Germany and Italy, the Young Ottomans believed it was necessary to modernize the political, military, and economic institutions of the empire. At the same time, they agreed on the need to retain their society's basic Islamic characteristics.[69] For the Young Ottomans, it was necessary that the Ottoman state not only introduce modern political institutions such as a parliament, but also assume a leading role in unifying and guiding the rest of the Islamic world as it struggled to maintain its independence.

The Pan-Islamic ideas of the Young Ottomans were most probably responsible for the introduction of the third article of the Ottoman constitution of 1876, which referred to the sultan as the caliph of the Islamic world.[70] Starting with the reign of Abdülhamid II, Pan-Islamism began to play a significant role in shaping the ideology and the foreign policy of the Ottoman state.[71] After all, the Russian czar used the defense and protection of the sultan's Orthodox Christian subjects to promote Pan-Slavism and justify his intervention in the internal affairs of the Ottoman state. Likewise, the sultan could use the protection of Muslims in Russia and British India to justify Pan-Islamism and legitimize interventions in regions under Czarist or British control. It was also during the reign of Abdülhamid II that Sayyid Jamal ud-Din Afghani (al-Afghani or Assadabadi), the Iranian-born Shia Muslim activist and revolutionary, arrived in Istanbul to propagate Islamic unity under the leadership of the sultan as the caliph of all Muslims.[72] Having recognized the threat posed by Russia, Great Britain, and France to the security and the territorial integrity of the Ottoman Empire, Abdülhamid also adopted a closer relationship with Germany, seeking the support of the Kaiser to modernize and centralize the Ottoman state. When the Ottomans began to build a railway system, which would connect the capital to Anatolia and the Arab Middle East, the sultan awarded the contract to the German government. Although he established closer ties with Germany, the intelligent and shrewd sultan maintained friendly relations with all European powers, "without forming an alliance with any of them."[73]

Notes

1. Roderic H. Davison, *Reform in the Ottoman Empire, 1856–1876* (New York: Gordian Press, 1973), 36. Zürcher, *Turkey*, 50–1.

2. Finkel, *Osman's Dream*, 447. Quataert, *The Ottoman Empire*, 66.

3. Davison, *Reform in the Ottoman Empire*, 36–8.

4. McCarthy, *The Ottoman Turks*, 297.

5. Ibid., 296–7. Shaw, *History of the Ottoman Empire*, 2:59–61. Zürcher, *Turkey*, 50–1.

6. Somel, *Historical Dictionary of the Ottoman Empire*, 289.

7. McCarthy, *The Ottoman Turks*, 297. Shaw, *History of the Ottoman Empire*, 2:55.

8. Ibid.

9. Zürcher, *Turkey*, 62.

10. McCarthy, *The Ottoman Turks*, 299.

11. See Carter V. Findley, *Bureaucratic Reform in the Ottoman Empire: the Sublime Porte 1789–1922* (Princeton: Princeton University Press, 1980). Karpat, "Comments on Contributions and the Borderlands," 11.

12. Reşat Kasaba, *The Ottoman Empire and the World Economy: The Nineteenth Century* (Albany: State University of New York Press, 1988), 50.

13. Zürcher, *Turkey*, 52.

14. Shaw, *History of the Ottoman Empire*, 2:133–4.

15. Ibid.

16. Finkel, *Osman's Dream*, 456–8.

17. Jelavich, *The Establishment of the Balkan National States*, 107.

18. Zürcher, *Turkey*, 54. Shaw, *History of the Ottoman Empire*, 2:140–1.

19. Shaw, *History of the Ottoman Empire*, 2:143. Zürcher, *Turkey*, 55.

20. Zürcher, *Turkey*, 56.

21. Jelavich, *History of the Balkans*, 252.

22. Davison, *Reform in the Ottoman Empire*, 335–38. Roderic H. Davison, *Nineteenth Century Ottoman Diplomacy and Reforms* (Istanbul: Isis Press, 1999), 99–100.

23. Ibid., 336.

24. McCarthy, *The Ottoman Turks*, 304.

25. Zürcher, *Turkey*, 74.

26. Ibid.

27. See Hurewitz, *Diplomacy in the Near and Middle East*, 1:189–91.

28. Kemal H. Karpat, *Ottoman Population 1830–1914: Demographic and Social Characteristics* (Madison: University of Wisconsin Press, 1985), 28. Finkel, *Osman's Dream*, 491. Shaw, *History of the Ottoman Empire*, 2:191. Shaw writes that "the Ottoman Empire was forced to give up two-fifths of its entire territory and one-fifth of its population, about 5.5 million people, of whom almost half were Muslims."

29. Shaw, *History of the Ottoman Empire*, 2:190–1.

30. Ibid., 2:191.

31. Jelavich, *History of the Balkans*, 360.

32. Ibid.

33. Ibid., 361.

34. Ibid., 360. Zürcher, *Turkey*, 75.

35. Hurewitz, *Diplomacy in the Near and Middle East*, 1:190.

36. Jelavich, *History of the Balkans*, 361–6.

37. Zürcher, *Turkey*, 77. Shaw, *History of the Ottoman Empire*, 2:226–30.

38. P. M. Holt, "The Later Ottoman Empire in Egypt and the Fertile Crescent" in *The Cambridge History of Islam*, 1:388.

39. Shaw, *History of the Ottoman Empire*, 2:195.

40. Jelavich, *History of the Balkans*, 370.

41. Ibid.

42. Ibid.

43. Ibid., 371.

44. Ibid.

45. Ibid., 372.

46. Ibid., 372–3.

47. Ibid., 362.

48. Ibid., 362–3.

49. Shaw, *History of the Ottoman Empire*, 2:199–200.

50. Ibid., 199. Jelavich, *History of the Balkans*, 363–4.

51. Jelavich, *History of the Balkans*, 364.

52. Ibid., 364–5.

53. Ibid., 365.

54. Ibid., 366.

55. Ibid.

56. Jelavich, *The Establishment of the Balkan National States*, 175.

57. Shaw, *History of the Ottoman Empire*, 2:207.

58. Ibid., 2:208.

59. Jelavich, *The Establishment of the Balkan National States*, 208.

60. Ibid.

61. Ibid.

62. Donald Quataert, "Age of Reforms, 1812–1914" in *An Economic and Social History of the Ottoman Empire*, Halil Inalcik with Donald Quataert, 2 vols. (Cambridge: Cambridge University Press, 1994), 1:782–4.

63. Mehrdad Kia, "Pan-Islamism in Late Nineteenth Century Iran", *Middle Eastern Studies* 32:1 (1996), 30.

64. Ibid.

65. Ibid. See Hurewitz, *Diplomacy in the Near and Middle East*, 1:54–61.

66. Shaw, *History of the Ottoman Empire*, 1:85.

67. Kia, "Pan-Islamism in Late Nineteenth Century Iran," 31.

68. See Şerif Mardin, *The Genesis of Young Ottoman Thought* (Princeton: Princeton University Press, 1962).

69. See Albert Hourani, *Arabic Thought in the Liberal Age: 1798–1939* (London: Oxford University Press, 1962), 103–7. Bernard Lewis, "The Ottoman Empire in the Mid-Nineteenth Century: A Review," *Middle Eastern Studies*, vol. 1, No. 3 (April, 1965). Bernard Lewis, *The Emergence of Modern Turkey* (London: Oxford University Press, 1968), 138–9. Shaw, *History of the Ottoman Empire*, 2:130–1.

70. Robert G. Landen, *The Emergence of the Modern Middle East* (New York: Van Nostrand Reinhold, 1970), 99. Lewis, *The Emergence of Modern Turkey*, 336.

71. Lewis, *The Emergence of Modern Turkey*, 342–3. Shaw, *History of the Ottoman Empire*, 2:157–8, 259–60.

72. See Elie Kedourie, *Afghani and Abduh: An Essay on Religious Unbelief and Political Activism in Modern Islam* (London: The Humanities Press, 1966). Nikkie R. Keddie, *An Islamic Response to Imperialism: Political and Religious Writings of Sayyid Jamal ad-Din al-Afghani* (Los Angeles: University of California Press, 1968). Nikkie R. Keddie, *Sayyid Jamal ad-Din al-Afghani* (Los Angeles: University of California Press, 1972).

73. Hale, *Turkish Foreign Policy*, 31.

CHAPTER 8

THE YOUNG TURK REVOLUTION AND THE FALL OF THE OTTOMAN EMPIRE

Despite his attempt to modernize the Ottoman state, Abdülhamid could not neutralize the opposition of the secular-minded intelligentsia and young army officers who opposed his autocratic rule and Islamic ideology. In a government where power was the monopoly of the monarch and a small clique of tradition-minded government officials, the members of the modern educated class, who served in the army and the bureaucracy, felt excluded and marginalized. On May 21, 1889, a small group of students at the army medical school organized the *İttihâd-i Osmâni Cemiyeti* (Ottoman Unity Society), which became the nucleus of the *İttihâd ve Terakki Cemiyeti* or Committee of Union and Progress (CUP), a secret society that would lead the movement to restore the constitution for the next two decades.[1] The unity referred to the unity of all ethnic, linguistic, and religious groupings under a constitutional system of government, which would save the empire from further disintegration by allowing all citizens of the Ottoman state to be included in a political system that granted them equal rights and legal protections. By 1896, CUP, which recruited primarily the young, urban, and educated civil servants, army officers, teachers, and students, had accumulated sufficient organizational strength to plan a *coup* against Abdülhamid.[2] The plot was, however, discovered and smashed by the sultan's secret police. While many were arrested and sent to the remote corners of the empire, some managed to flee to European countries, particularly France and Switzerland, where they joined the anti-government intellectuals who were already publishing newspapers that were critical of the sultan and his regime. Thus, the opposition that was neutralized inside the empire found a voice in the émigré community in Europe. The leaders of the movement that came to be called the Young Turks believed in the restoration of the 1876 constitution and insisted that the preservation of the empire depended on guaranteeing equal rights for all subjects of the Ottoman state. As with the Young Ottomans of the 1860s and 1870s, the Young Turks believed that the establishment of a constitutional government would neutralize the national aspirations of the non-Turkish minorities, allowing them to identify themselves as members of the larger Ottoman family.[3] They had concluded that the alienation of the Christian subjects of the sultan was caused by the absence of political rights and corrupt administrative practices. If the Ottoman government provided constitutional rights to its citizens and eliminated corruption, then the empire could be saved.[4] Beyond these commonly shared principles, however, a great deal of divergence and conflict existed within the movement. Indeed, the Young Turk movement in Europe was internally fragmented. One wing was led by Ahmed Riza, a former civil servant who emerged as the most prominent Young Turk leader after he fled to France in 1889.[5] A devout follower of the French thinker Auguste Comte (1798–1857) and his positivist philosophy, Ahmed Riza, who published the newspaper Meşveret (Consultation), was an ardent materialist, scientist, and atheist who refused to appeal to popular religious sentiments as a means of organizing the masses against the sultan.[6] One rival was Murad Bey, the publisher of the anti-government newspaper Mizan (Balance) and the head of the Geneva branch of Young Turks, who challenged Ahmed Riza's leadership and emphasized the need to preserve the movement's Islamic identity. Furthermore, as an Ottoman nationalist, Ahmed Riza believed in a strong centralized state and rejected the idea of foreign intervention as the means of removing Abdülhamid from the throne, while another faction within CUP, led by Prince Sabaheddin (Sabaheddin Bey), advocated a decentralized form of government and agreed with the Armenian faction within CUP that foreign intervention could be used as a legitimate means to overthrow the sultan's autocratic rule.[7]

In 1905 and 1906, the opposition reorganized itself, particularly in Salonica where a secret organization managed to recruit a significant number of army officers stationed in the Balkans and particularly in the tinderbox of Macedonia.[8] In sharp contrast to the liberal-minded Young Turk leaders in Europe, many of the young army officers who joined the opposition came from the Balkans, where they had experienced first-hand the disintegration of the empire. Many were the children of the Ottoman borderlands where they had lived or served as members of the Muslim minority side by side with non-Turkish, non-Muslim communities and had witnessed how the Christian subjects of the sultan had revolted successfully against the Ottoman Empire with the financial and military support of European powers. Any illusion that the Christian communities of the empire wished to live side by side with the Muslim subjects of the sultan and remain loyal to the authority of the Ottoman state had evaporated in front of their eyes.

Revolution came unexpectedly from Macedonia in July 1908, when army officers loyal to CUP revolted, demanding the restoration of the 1876 constitution.[9] After a faint effort to suppress the rebellion, Abdülhamid concluded that resistance was futile. On July 23 he restored constitutional rule and ordered parliamentary elections.[10] As the news of revolution spread, massive celebrations erupted, particularly in Istanbul, where Turks, Jews, Armenians, and Arabs joined hands and embraced in the streets of the capital.[11] Among the deputies in the new parliament, which opened on December 17, there were 142 Turks, 60 Arabs, 25 Albanians, 23 Greeks, 12 Armenians, 5 Jews, 4 Bulgarians, 3 Serbs, and one Romanian.[12] Although the Young Turk movement had aimed at ending the autocratic rule of Abdülhamid, the sultan was not removed from the throne. The leaders of CUP were well aware that the autocratic monarch enjoyed enormous popularity among the Muslim masses, particularly in rural Anatolia, and his removal would alienate the religious classes in Istanbul and other cities.

The Young Turks had convinced themselves that the restoration of the parliamentary regime would secure the support of European powers for the preservation of the territorial integrity of the Ottoman Empire.[13] They were wrong. Shortly after the victory of the revolution, the Austro-Hungarian Empire formally annexed Bosnia-Herzegovina, which had maintained its nominal affiliation with the empire by accepting the suzerainty of the sultan.[14] Greece annexed the island of Crete, while Bulgaria unified with Eastern Rumelia, which had remained an autonomous province under the nominal rule of the Ottoman sultan.[15]

Aside from Abdülhamid and his supporters, the new constitutional regime had other formidable opponents. Prince Sabaheddin and his liberal pro-British faction opposed the more authoritarian and militaristic elements in the CUP, who advocated centralization of power. The urban religious classes such as *şeyhs* and *dervişes*, as well as students from religious schools, viewed the leadership of CUP as secular atheists who were trying to limit the power of the sultan/caliph by introducing alien European rules and laws, thereby undermining the *Şeriat* or the legal code of Islam. On April 12, 1909, several army divisions, which had been brought recently from Macedonia to Istanbul, rose in rebellion and were joined by students from religious schools.[16] The demonstrators marched to the parliament, where they demanded the dismissal of the grand vezir and the president of the chamber of deputies, Ahmed Riza. They also called on the government to replace a number of CUP officers and banish several deputies from Istanbul. Finally, they called for the restoration of Şeriat and asked for amnesty for the troops who had mutinied.[17] The government in Istanbul panicked, unsure how to respond. Every effort had to be made to avoid bloodshed and infighting between pro- and anti-CUP army units. By April 15, the troops loyal to the CUP, particularly those stationed in Macedonia and led by Mahmud Şevket Paşa, and primarily Albanian units headed by Niyazi Bey, struck back and began to march toward the capital using the Ottoman railway system to transport their troops. Despite a last-ditch effort by the government to delay their entry into the capital, the pro-CUP divisions entered Istanbul without confronting any armed resistance. On April 27, the two chambers of parliament deposed Abdülhamid and replaced him with his younger brother, who ascended the throne as Mehmed V.[18] A new era in Ottoman politics had been inaugurated. The center of power had shifted once again, this time from the palace to the army, the bureaucracy, and the parliament.

There were other political transformations, too. Although CUP dominated both the government and the parliament, it was the Ottoman army that emerged as the most powerful institution within the state. Neither the cabinet nor CUP and the parliament could challenge the power of the army and its commander, Mahmud Şevkat Paşa, who had saved them from political extinction.[19] The army allowed CUP to dominate the legislative branch and introduce new laws that significantly cut the budget for the palace and restricted the power of the sultan by granting him only the right to appoint the grand vezir and the şeyhülislâm. In return, CUP let the army do what it wanted as it undertook the purging of the senior commanders and officers who had served Abdülhamid.[20] The growing power of junior officers who were rising in rank and their interference in the political life of the empire allowed the opposition to reorganize. Initially, the army and CUP did not prevent the creation of new political parties, including the Ottoman Socialist Party. However, as the new parties coalesced into a unified opposition, the army and CUP felt compelled to act. The Albanian uprising, which began on April 1, 1910, and the assassination of the influential journalist Ahmed Samim, who had criticized CUP, on June 10, energized the opposition parties. In October 1911 Italy invaded Libya by landing troops in Tripoli and Benghazi.[21] The grand vezir and his cabinet were forced to resign as the opposition forces unified in a coalition, which included both conservative and liberal parties. CUP responded by dissolving the parliament and calling for new elections. Massive fraud and intimidation allowed CUP to win the majority of seats in the new parliament.[22] Despite the convening of the new CUP-dominated parliament, the political situation continued to deteriorate. The central government was so weak that it failed to respond effectively to growing unrest in Albania, the uprising of Imam Yahya in Yemen, and the Italian invasion and occupation of Libya.[23] To their credit, a group of Ottoman officers affiliated with CUP and under the leadership of Major Enver (later Enver Paşa) rushed to Libya and organized a defense with assistance from the Sanusiya religious order against the Italian occupiers. An Italian attack on the Dardanelles and the occupation of the Dodecanese islands in May 1912, however, forced the Ottoman government to sue for peace.[24]

The Italian victory emboldened the neighboring Balkan states, which had been waiting for an opportunity to invade and occupy the remaining Ottoman provinces in Europe. After series of negotiations, Serbia and Bulgaria formed an alliance in March 1912.[25] Shortly after, in May, Bulgaria signed a similar agreement with Greece.[26] Finally, in October, Serbia and Montenegro formed an alliance.[27] Using the imperial rhetoric of European powers, the four Balkan states demanded the implementation of fundamental reforms in Macedonia, knowing full well that they were weaving a convenient justification for their joint invasion of Ottoman territory.[28] On October 8, the Balkan states dropped their pretense and declared war. The Bulgarians soon defeated the Ottomans at the battles of Kirklareli/Kirkkilise (October 22–24) and Lüleburgaz (October 22–November 2), followed by a Serbian victory at the battle of Kumanovo (October 23–24).[29] Meanwhile, the Greeks captured Salonica on November 8. Without a coordinated plan, and in the absence of a unified command, the Ottomans were forced either to retreat or to take defensive positions. The major urban centers of the empire in Europe (Edirne, Janina, and Shkodër) were surrounded by the invading Balkan armies. By December, the Ottoman government sued for peace. As the discussions dragged on in London, Bulgaria demanded the city of Edirne. This was too much for a group of young officers in Istanbul, who staged a military coup on January 23, 1913, killing the minister of war and forcing the grand vezir to resign. The former commander of the army, Mahmud Şevket Paşa, assumed the post of grand vezir and the minister of war.[30] When the news of the coup in Istanbul reached London, the Balkan states resumed their military campaigns. Despite a promise to adopt an offensive posture, the new government in Istanbul failed to repulse the Bulgarian forces, who captured Edirne on March 28, and the Serbs, who seized Shkodër on April 22. On May 30, the Ottoman government was forced to sign the Treaty of London, which resulted in the loss of much of its territory in Europe, including the city of Edirne. Disaster seemed to be complete with the murder of the new grand vezir, Mahmud Şevket Paşa, on June 11.

Fortunately for the Ottomans, intense rivalries and jealousies among the Balkan states erupted shortly after the signing of the Treaty of London. Romania, which had not participated in the war, demanded territory from Bulgaria. The Greeks and Serbs also expressed dissatisfaction with the division of territory in Macedonia. As the negotiations for the creation of an anti-Bulgarian alliance began, Bulgaria attacked Serbia, which ignited a new Balkan war between the victors of the first. The Ottomans used the opportunity to recapture Edirne under the leadership of Enver, forcing Bulgaria to sign the Treaty of Constantinople on September 29, 1913.[31]

The military coup of January 1913 brought the government under the control of CUP, which soon began suppressing the activities of opposition parties with arrests and death sentences. As CUP began to consolidate its power over the organs of the state, a triumvirate comprising Cemal Paşa, Enver Paşa, and Talat Paşa began to rule the empire with the support of an inner circle, which represented the various factions within CUP. With the clouds of war gathering over Europe, the beleaguered Ottoman government appraised its various options, none of which looked very promising, given the predatory nature of European powers. Then, on August 2, 1914 the Ottoman Empire signed a secret treaty of alliance with Germany. According to this treaty, the Ottoman Empire and Germany agreed "to observe strict neutrality" in the "conflict between Austria-Hungary and Serbia."[32] However, "in the event that Russia should intervene with active military measures and thus should" pose a threat to Germany, this threat "would also come into force for Turkey."[33] In the case of a threat or a war, Germany committed itself to defending the Ottoman Empire by "force of arms."[34] The decision to enter the war on the side of Germany and the Austro-Hungarian Empire brought the Ottoman state into open military confrontation with France, Czarist Russia, and the British Empire, which used the hostilities to terminate the nominal suzerainty of the Ottoman Empire over Egypt, depose the Khedive Abbas Hilmi II, and establish a protectorate over the country on December 18, 1914.[35] The British also annexed the island of Cyprus and occupied Basra in southern Iraq.

Nor was this the worst. In the Constantinople Agreement of 1915, the three Entente powers agreed to the complete partition of the Ottoman Empire after the end of the war.[36] The Allied expectation that the "sick man of Europe" would be destroyed with one single military blow proved to be wishful thinking. The British attempt to oust the Ottoman Empire called for a massive landing of allied troops at the foothills of Gallipoli on the European shores of the Dardanelles. After establishing a bridgehead, the troops planned to climb the hills and destroy the Ottoman force, which defended the heights. To the dismay of the British, the Ottomans, supported by German officers, fought back heroically, inflicting an impressive defeat on the enemy who retreated with heavy casualties in January 1916. The sick man of Europe was ailing, but it was not prepared to die.

Another advancing British front in southern Iraq also met unexpected resistance. With their military efforts coming to an unexpected halt, the British resorted to the more devious strategy of fomenting internal rebellions amongst the sultan's Arab subjects. Two Arab leaders stood out. The first, Abdulaziz ibn Saud, was the master of Najd in Central Arabia. As the principal protector of the Wahabi religious movement, Ibn Saud could rally the tribes of central and eastern Arabia against the Ottoman state. However, the British cast their lot with another ambitious Arab leader, Sharif Husayn of Mecca. Claiming direct lineage from the Prophet Muhammad, Sharif Husayn and his two sons, Faisal and Abdullah, dreamt of carving a united Arab state from the Arab provinces of the Ottoman Empire in the Middle East. In negotiations between Husayn and the British High Commissioner in Egypt, Sir Henry McMahon, the British government made a critical promise to the Sharif and his family that if they organized a revolt against the Ottoman Empire, at the end of the war the British would support the creation of an independent Arab kingdom under their leadership (see Document 4). Unknown to Sharif Husayn and his sons was the fact that the British were also negotiating about the fate of the Arab provinces of the Ottoman Empire with their principal ally in Europe, the French. In negotiations between Sir Mark Sykes, who represented the British government, and his French counterpart, Charles François Georges Picot, the two European powers carved the Arab provinces of the Ottoman Empire into British and French zones of influence. According to the document which came to be known as the Sykes–Picot Agreement (May 16, 1916), the British promised Greater Syria to France, which included the present day country of Lebanon, and the Ottoman province of Mosul in present day northern Iraq. In return, the British gained control over the provinces of Baghdad and Basra with an adjacent territory that stretched to the Mediterranean towns of Acre and Jaffa, including the imprecisely defined Holy Land, or Palestine[37] (see Document 5).

In November 1917, the British government made a third critical promise which would have a long-lasting impact on the political life of the Middle East. In a letter addressed to one of the leaders of the Zionist movement in Europe, Lord Rothschild, the British Foreign Secretary Arthur James Balfour expressed the support of his government for the Zionist movement's aim to establish a Jewish National Home in Palestine. The Balfour Declaration stated that the British government viewed "with favour the establishment in Palestine of a national home for the Jewish people" and that it would use its "best endeavours to facilitate the achievement of this object, it being clearly understood that nothing shall be done which may prejudice the civil and religious rights of existing non-Jewish communities in Palestine, or the rights and political status enjoyed by Jews in any other country"[38] (see Document 6). The map of the Arab Middle East was redrawn as the British government tried to fulfill the promises it had made to the Arabs, the French, and the Zionists during the First World War while at the same time maintaining its hegemony over the region after terminating Ottoman rule.

The Ottomans faced a far greater and more immediate challenge in the east, where the Russians were pushing toward Erzurum in 1915. With the Ottoman defenses collapsing in eastern Anatolia, the Russians were poised to occupy the entire region. The Bolshevik revolution of October 1917 and subsequent withdrawal of Russia from the war, however, saved the Ottoman state, allowing its forces to march into the southern Caucasus region and all the way to the city of Baku on the Caspian. During the war against Russia in eastern Anatolia, a large number of Armenians were killed and many were deported from their ancient homeland. The so-called "Armenian question" had started in the nineteenth century when the Armenian communities both in the Ottoman Empire and the Caucasus experienced a cultural revival.[39] The study of Armenian language and history became increasingly popular, the Bible was published in the vernacular, and Armenian intellectuals developed a new literary language, which made their works accessible to the masses.[40] Wealthy Armenian families began to send their children to study in Europe, where a new class of young and educated Armenians became fluent in European languages and politics. By the time they returned, they had been imbued with modern European ideas such as nationalism, liberalism, and socialism. Influenced by the rise and success of the nineteenth century nationalist movements in the Balkans, a small group of Armenian intellectuals and activists began to question the leadership of the Armenian Church and called for the introduction of secular education.[41] Some went one step further and joined the Young Ottomans in their demand for the creation of a constitutional form of government that would grant all subjects of the sultan equal rights and protection under law. When the Congress of

Berlin granted independence and autonomy to several Balkan states, a small group of Armenian officers, who served in the Russian army, began to advocate the creation of an independent Armenian state with support from the Russian czar.[42] Two Armenian organizations, the Bell (*Hunchak*) founded by Armenian students in Switzerland in the summer of 1886 and the Hay Heghapokhakan Dashnaktsutiun (Armenian Revolutionary Federation, ARF) created in the summer of 1890 in Tiflis, played a central role in advocating Armenian independence.[43]

Starting in the 1890s, the tension between the Armenian population and the Muslim population in eastern Anatolia intensified as Armenian nationalists and Ottoman forces clashed. Abdülhamid II ordered a crackdown on the wealthy Armenian families in Istanbul and organized the *Hamidiye* regiment, which included Kurdish tribal units. As the conflict intensified from 1890 to 1893, the *Hamidiye* regiments were unleashed against the Armenian communities with devastating results. Thousands of Armenians living in Sasun were murdered in the summer of 1894. The attacks and mass killings continued in "Trebizond, Urfa, and Erzurum in the fall of 1895, and Diarbekir, Arabkir, Kharpert, and Kayseri in November 1895."[44] In response, the *Hunchaks* organized demonstrations in Istanbul appealing to European embassies to intervene. Similar protests were organized in towns across eastern Anatolia. The situation worsened in 1895 and 1896 as the clashes between the *Hamidiye* regiments and Armenian nationalists intensified. On August 24–26, 1896, armed Armenians seized the Ottoman Bank in Istanbul, threatening to blow it up. Other terrorist attacks against government offices and officials followed. The sultan himself was attacked when bombs were set off as he walked to Aya Sofya for his Friday prayer. Some twenty Ottoman policemen were killed in the attack. Throughout the conflict with the Ottoman government, the Armenians had pinned their hopes on intervention by European powers, particularly the British and the Russians. But Czar Nicholas II opposed British intervention in a region that he viewed as a sphere of Russian influence. He also feared the establishment of an Armenian state led by revolutionaries who could infect his own Armenian subjects with such revolutionary ideas as nationalism and socialism.

As the First World War began and fighting erupted in eastern Anatolia, many Armenians officers and soldiers serving in the Ottoman army defected, joining the Russians with the hope that the defeat and collapse of the Ottoman state would fulfill the dream of establishing an independent Armenian state.[45] The defections were followed by an uprising of the Armenians in the city of Van in April 1915. Alarmed by the rise and popularity of the Armenian national movement, the central committee of CUP adopted a policy of forcibly relocating the

Armenian population to the Syrian desert.[46] Starting in May 1915, virtually the entire Armenian population of central and eastern Anatolia was removed from their homes. This policy was then replicated in western Anatolia. Hundreds of thousands of Armenians perished from starvation, disease, and exposure, and many more were brutalized by Ottoman army units and the irregular Kurdish regiments who robbed, raped, and killed the defenseless refugees.

Today, after the passage of almost ninety years, the plight of the Armenian people continues to ignite intense emotional debate between Armenians and Turks, centering on the number of casualties, the causes for the deportations, and the intent of the perpetrators.[47] Armenians claim that nearly 1,500,000 lost their lives in a "genocide" designed at the highest levels of the Ottoman government. Turks, in contrast, posit the "disloyalty" and "traitorous activities" of many Armenians who defected from the Ottoman army and joined the Russians who had invaded the Ottoman homeland. They also claim that the majority of Armenian deaths were caused by the irregular armed Kurdish units, which felt threatened by the prospect of living as a minority community under a newly established Armenian Christian state.[48] According to this argument, the Ottoman government can be held responsible for failing to prevent the inter-communal violence between the Kurds and the Armenians, but it cannot be blamed for atrocities that were committed by the local Muslim population during the fog and agony of civil war. Regardless, there is little doubt that a small inner circle within CUP's central committee known as *Teşkilât-i Mahsusa* or Special Organization, which operated under the Ottoman ministry of defense since January 1914, designed and implemented the plan for relocating the Armenian population in order to effect a "permanent solution" to the question of Armenian nationalism in Ottoman lands.[49]

For the Ottomans, World War I came to an end when British troops supported by Arab fighters under the leadership of Prince Faisal entered Damascus in August 1918. The British had already occupied Baghdad on March 11 and Jerusalem on December 9, 1917. The three Young Turk leaders, Enver Paşa, Talat Paşa, and Cemal Paşa, fled the country for Berlin. The Ottoman Empire sued for peace in October 1918. With Russia out of the picture, the British were the only power with troops in the Middle East who could dictate the terms of an Ottoman armistice. After a week of negotiations on the British ship *Agamemnon*, the terms of the Armistice of Mudros were presented to the Ottoman government on October 31.[50] They included allied occupation of Istanbul as well as the forts on the Bosphorus and Dardanelles.

On May 15, 1919, with support from the British, the French, and the Americans, the Greek government, which had joined the allies at the end of the World War I, landed troops in Izmir.[51] In the midst of this chaos and humiliation, Mustafa Kemal Paşa (1881–1938) was appointed "Inspector General of Ottoman forces in northern and northeastern Anatolia" and was dispatched by the sultan to disarm and disband the remaining Ottoman army units and pacify the local population.[52] An Ottoman army officer, who had fought with distinction at Gallipoli (1915), the Caucasus (1916), and Palestine (1917), Mustafa Kemal had emerged as a hero of the First World War and was considered to be the ideal officer capable of diffusing a rebellion against the sultan and the allies. Having enrolled in the Ottoman military academy, Mustafa Kemal had joined the Young Turks before the 1908 revolution, but had refused to assume political office even after the triumvirate of Enver, Talat, and Cemal had seized control of the government. It was rumored that he had opposed and criticized Enver Paşa.

On May 19, when Mustafa Kemal arrived in Samsun on the northern coast of Anatolia, he had already decided to disobey his orders and organize a national resistance movement.[53] Support came from other Ottoman commanders and officers who shared his determination to remove foreign forces, particularly the Greeks, from western Anatolia and prevent Armenian nationalists from establishing an independent state in eastern Anatolia. By June, Kemal's activities and telegraphic correspondence with other commanders and officers had aroused the suspicions of the British, who pressured the government in Istanbul to recall him.[54] Though dismissed from his post in June, Mustafa Kemal continued his efforts, with the primary focus being the creation of a national congress to serve as a quasi alternative government to that in occupied Istanbul, even while he and his associates continued to express their allegiance to the sultan-caliph. The establishment of a national congress could also resolve internal rivalries and disagreements within the nationalist movement and provide Kemal with the legal authority to act on behalf of the Muslim people of Anatolia. Throughout the summer of 1919, the Congress met, first in Erzurum (July–August) and then in Sivas (September), discussing and devising a program for the liberation of Ottoman Turkish lands.

Recognizing the growing popularity of the nationalist movement, the imperial government in Istanbul tried to counter it by calling for elections to an Ottoman parliament, which convened in Istanbul on January 12, 1920. Neither the sultan and his officials nor the British and their strategists recognized the depth of anti-foreign sentiments in the new parliament, which issued a "National Pact" (*milli misak*) on February 17, replicating the demands of the nationalist movement.[55] Allowing that the destiny of the portions of the Ottoman Empire "populated by an Arab majority" should be determined in accordance with the will of the native population, the pact emphatically declared that the Anatolian heartland, an area "inhabited by an Ottoman Muslim majority, united in religion, in race, and in aim" constituted "a whole" and could not be divided and partitioned.[56] The pact also insisted on the security and protection of the city of Istanbul, "the capital of the Sultanate, and the headquarters of the Ottoman government."[57]

By March, the British, who had awakened to the threat posed by the Ottoman parliament in Istanbul, forced the removal of the grand vezir and imprisoned a large number of the deputies, sending some one hundred fifty to exile on the island of Malta. [58] The new grand vezir, Damad Ferid Paşa, declared Mustafa Kemal and his lieutenants to be in rebellion against the sultan and deserving of execution for treason. In collaborating with the foreign occupiers and in condemning the leaders of national resistance to death, the sultan and his advisors had demonstrated that they lacked the will and determination to fight against the occupation and domination of the Ottoman homeland by European powers. Worse, they had decided to collaborate with the occupying armies against nationalist officers who were fighting to liberate the Ottoman homeland. Instead of intimidating the nationalists, the actions of the British government generated popularity for the resistance movement, which convened a Grand National Assembly in Ankara on April 23, 1920. The newly convened assembly elected Mustafa Kemal Paşa as its president, but reiterated the loyalty of the people to the sultan-caliph. The nationalist movement knew full well that after being ruled by sultans for several hundred years, the majority of the population, particularly in rural Anatolia, retained a deep emotional and religious loyalty to the Ottoman dynasty. To appease popular sentiments and at the same time diminish the power and influence of the sultan over his subjects, the Assembly declared that because the sultan lived under foreign occupation, all power and authority had to rest in the Congress as the representative of the people. Britain and France, meanwhile, moved forward with their plan of partitioning the Ottoman Empire, imposing the humiliating Treaty of Sèvres on August 10, on the imperial government in Istanbul. The treaty, which was immediately condemned by Mustafa Kemal and the national resistance movement, forced the sultan to surrender all the non-Turkish provinces of the empire and partitioned Anatolia among European powers, Greeks, Armenians, and Kurds. With the National Assembly behind him, Mustafa Kemal focused on the two most immediate threats; the Armenians to the east and the Greeks to the west, creating a centralized and unified military command structure under the leadership of one of his most trusted and capable commanders, Ismet Paşa (later Ismet Inönü), who was appointed the chief of the general staff.[59]

Mustafa Kemal first turned his attention to the east. The national resistance forces under the command of Kâzim Paşa (Karabekir) attacked the forces of the Armenian Republic, which had established itself as an independent state with its capital in the city of Erivan. As they pushed back the Armenian forces, the Turkish nationalists regained Ardahan and then Kars in October 1920, which the Ottomans had lost to czarist Russia in 1878. The Treaty of Gümrü, signed between the Republic of Armenia and the nationalist movement in December 1920, confirmed Turkish territorial gains, setting the borders at the pre-1878 boundary between Russia and the Ottoman Empire. Shortly after signing the peace treaty, the republics of southern Caucasus, namely Georgia, Azerbaijan, and Armenia, were attacked and occupied by the Soviet Red army. All three lost their independence and soon emerged as reconstituted Soviet Socialist republics under the direct rule of the Bolshevik communist party in Moscow. Despite the occupation of the south Caucasus by the Red Army, the Soviet government did not challenge the new boundaries set by the peace treaty between the Turks and the Armenians. Under siege and sanction itself, the new communist regime in Moscow was anxious to support the Turkish nationalist movement as a means of pushing British, French, and Italian forces as far back from Soviet territory as possible. It could also justify its support of Mustafa Kemal and his movement in the name of solidarity with anti-imperialist national liberation movements. On March 16, 1921, the nationalist government signed a treaty of friendship with the Soviets, which recognized the frontiers between the two states and provided Kemal's army with badly-needed funds and war material.

The second battle for control of Anatolia was centered in the southern region of Cilicia which had been occupied by the French forces shortly after the end of World War I. The French, like the British, initially supported the establishment of an Armenian state in eastern Anatolia. The principal objective of the French policy in the Middle East was not, however, to gain territory in Anatolia but to establish firm control over Syria. The units that the French moved from Syria into Cilicia were, therefore, small and could only control the urban centers, while Turkish and Armenian armed bands fought over the control of the countryside. The Armenian Legion, which intended to seize southern and eastern Anatolia for a future independent state, was strengthened further when thousands of Armenian refugees, who had been displaced during the war, joined its ranks. The skirmishes between Turkish forces and Armenian Legionnaires culminated in a battle at the town of Maraş where the Turks scored a victory, forcing French and Armenian forces to evacuate the district. The

French, who were anxious to consolidate their control over Syria and Lebanon and not lose credibility in front of their newly acquired Arab subjects, entered into negotiations with the Turkish nationalist forces, which culminated in the signing of a treaty on October 20, 1921. Recognizing the power and popularity of the nationalist movement, the French agreed to withdraw their forces from Cilicia while at the same time disavowing the Treaty of Sèvres and accepting the legitimacy of the emerging Turkish government.[60] But, the struggle for the liberation of the Ottoman Turkish homeland could not be completed without the removal of Greek forces from western Anatolia.

With direct support from the British and French naval forces, the Greek government had landed troops in Izmir on May 15, 1919. The initial agreement with the Allies allowed the Greek forces to occupy the city and the immediate surrounding region for five years before a plebiscite determined whether the territory could remain under Greek rule.[61] Having recognized the absence of a significant Ottoman military presence and an organized resistance, the Greek forces advanced quickly beyond Izmir and occupied the entire west Anatolian province of Aydin. As they moved farther inland, the Greeks met with little resistance with the exception of a few skirmishes that could not be sustained by remaining Ottoman divisions because they lacked leadership, manpower, and war material. As the Greek forces occupied Turkish towns and villages, Ottoman officials and representatives were either arrested or executed while the local population was forced out of their homes and businesses, which were often set on fire. More than one million ethnic Turks became refugees as Greek forces swept through western Anatolia.[62] With the British refusing to stop their expansion, the Greek forces occupied Bursa and Izmit while a second Greek army invaded eastern Thrace in the summer of 1920, concentrating its efforts on capturing Edirne. With their confidence at an all time high, the main Greek force focused on Ankara, the new capital of the nationalist movement under the leadership of Mustafa Kemal. The nationalist forces under the command of Ismet Paşa managed to repulse a Greek army advancing toward Ankara at the river Inönü in January 1921, replicating the feat again in April.[63] Although they could not exploit their victories, the two successful military campaigns boosted the confidence of the nationalist forces and enhanced the prestige and popularity of Mustafa Kemal. As the Greek forces mounted another offensive in the summer of 1921, the Grand National Assembly requested that Mustafa Kemal assume the leadership of the army. At the battle of Sakarya in August, the Turkish nationalists scored an impressive victory against the Greeks, who fled on September 13.[64] A year passed before the Greeks could mount a new campaign. The historic battle, which sealed the fate of Anatolia, began on August 26, 1922 and ended with the total defeat of Greek army on August 30. Overextended and suffering from inadequate supply lines, the Greek forces were routed while their commanders surrendered on September 2 and 3. The result was a total collapse of the Greek imperial idea. Officers and soldiers fled to Izmir, where they and many Greek residents of the city boarded British and French ships that transported them to mainland Greece. At the last moment, the city was set on fire. On September 9, 1922, the nationalist army entered Izmir. A few days later, the Greek forces evacuated northwestern Anatolia, including the city of Bursa, the first Ottoman capital.[65] The victory was complete. Turkey had gained its independence, and Mustafa Kemal had succeeded in establishing full Turkish sovereignty over Anatolia.

The Turkish victory resulted in a shift of attitude by the European powers, who recognized the new reality on the ground and began a more conciliatory policy toward the nationalist movement. The only remaining European power, Great Britain controlled Istanbul and the Straits. Having witnessed the decisive defeat of Greek forces and realizing that their allies, particularly the French, did not intend to fight the Turkish nationalists, the British convinced the Greek government to withdraw from eastern Thrace and sign an armistice (the Armistice of Mudanya) with the Turks on October 11, 1922. On October 27, the allies invited the nationalist government in Ankara and the imperial government in Istanbul to attend a peace conference in Lausanne, Switzerland.[66] The Turkish nationalists, however, announced that the sultan in Istanbul no longer represented the new Turkish nation, and on November 1 the Grand National Assembly in Ankara abolished the Ottoman sultanate.[67] Shortly after, on November 20, a Turkish delegation led by the hero of the war of independence, Ismet Paşa, arrived in Lausanne to negotiate a peace treaty. The Turkish nationalist government intended to negotiate on the basis of the National Pact that had been drafted and ratified by the Grand National Assembly, which clearly stated that the Turkish nationalist movement was willing to accept the loss of Arab provinces. But it was not willing to compromise on the preservation of the territorial integrity of Anatolia, the security and restoration of Istanbul under Turkish sovereignty, the participation of the government of Turkey in establishing a new arrangement for the Straits, and the abolition of the capitulations.[68] When the treaty was finally concluded many months later, on July 24, 1923, the final document represented significant compromises by the new Turkish government and the allies. Exhausted by the war and anxious to end all hostilities, both sides had realized that they had to give up some of their demands in order to achieve a lasting and meaningful peace. The Turkish side had clearly recognized that they could not revive the Ottoman Empire and that their former Arab provinces, occupied by the British and the French during and after World War I, were permanently lost. They also renounced their claim on the island of Cyprus, which was under British occupation, as well as several other islands including Rhodes, Lispos, and Cos, which remained under Italian rule. The Turks also guaranteed the civil and political rights of their non-Muslim minorities, agreeing to the principle that "all inhabitants of Turkey, without distinction of religion, shall be equal before law."[69] The Turks renounced their claims on Mosul in present day northern Iraq and the region of Hatay, which was occupied by the French until 1938 when it was returned to the Republic of Turkey. Despite such compromises, however, the Turkish side emerged from Lausanne as the principal victor.

After the signing of the Treaty of Lausanne, the British troops evacuated Istanbul in October 1923, and Mustafa Kemal and his army entered the city. The time had come to deal with the Ottoman royal family, who had collaborated with foreign occupation forces throughout the war of national liberation and had condemned Mustafa Kemal to death in absentia. The Grand National Assembly proclaimed the establishment of the Republic of Turkey with Mustafa Kemal as its first president on October 29, 1923, while a member of the Ottoman ruling family, Abdülmecid, remained the caliph. Determined to cut the country's ties with its Ottoman past, the new government moved the capital from Istanbul to Ankara, and on March 3, 1924 the Grand National Assembly abolished the caliphate and the last member of the Ottoman royal family was sent into exile. The 600-year Ottoman Empire had ceased to exist, replaced by the modern Republic of Turkey.

Notes

1. Erik-Jan Zürcher, "The Young Turks: Children of the Borderlands?" in *Ottoman Borderlands*, 276. Shaw, *History of the Ottoman Empire*, 2:256.

2. Shaw, *History of the Ottoman Empire*, 2:257.

3. Feroz Ahmad, *The Young Turks* (Oxford: Clarendon Press, 1969), 16.

4. Ibid.

5. Ibid., 177.

6. For a discussion of Auguste Comte, see Irving M. Zeitlin, *Ideology and the Development of Sociological Theory* (Englewood Cliffs, New Jersey: Prentice Hall, 1968), 70–9.

7. Finkel, *Osman's Dream*, 505–6.

8. Zürcher, "The Young Turks: Children of the Borderlands?", 277. See also Şükrü Hanioğlu, *Preparation for a Revolution. The Young Turks, 1902–1908* (New York: Oxford University Press, 2001); Aykut Kansu, *The Revolution of 1908 in Turkey* (Leiden: E.J. Brill 1997); and David Kushner, *The Rise of Turkish Nationalism 1876–1908* (London: Frank Cass, 1977).

9. Shaw, *History of the Ottoman Empire*, 2:266–67.

10. Ahmad, *The Young Turks*, 12. Andrew Mango, *Atatürk: The Biography of the Founder of Modern Turkey* (New York: Overlook Press, 1999), 77–8.

11. Shaw, *History of the Ottoman Empire*, 2:273.

12. Mango, *Atatürk*, 85

13. Ibid.

14. Jelavich, *The Establishment of the Balkan National States*, 215–16.

15. Zürcher, *Turkey*, 104.

16. Mango, *Atatürk*, 86–7.

17. Shaw, *History of the Ottoman Empire*, 2:280.

18. Zürcher, *Turkey*, 98.

19. Ibid., 99–100.

20. Ibid., 100.

21. Jelavich, *The Establishment of the Balkan National States*, 216.

22. Zürcher, *Turkey*, 103.

23. Ibid., 105–6.

24. Ibid.

25. Jelavich, *The Establishment of the Balkan National States*, 216–17.

26. Zürcher, *Turkey*, 106.

27. Ibid.

28. Ibid.

29. Ibid., 107.

30. Ibid., 108.

31. Ibid.

32. See Hurewitz, *Diplomacy in the Near and Middle East*, 2:1–2.

33. Ibid.

34. Ibid.

35. Ibid., 2:5–7.

36. Ibid., 2:7–11.

37. Zürcher, *Turkey*, 143.

38. Hurewitz, *Diplomacy in the Near and Middle East*, 2:26.

39. Simon Payaslian, *The History of Armenia* (New York: Palgrave MacMillan, 2007), 117–19. Shaw, *History of the Ottoman Empire*, 2:202.

40. Ibid. Shaw, *History of the Ottoman Empire*, 2:202.

41. Ibid. Shaw, *History of the Ottoman Empire*, 2:202.

42. Shaw, *History of the Ottoman Empire*, 2:202.

43. Payaslian, *The History of Armenia*, 119–20.

44. Ibid., 120.

45. Zürcher, *Turkey*, 114.

46. Ibid., 114–15.

47. Ibid., 115.

48. Ibid.

49. See Taner Akçam, *From Empire to Republic: Turkish Nationalism and the Armenian Genocide* (London: Zed Books, 2004), 143–5, 158–75. Guenter Lewy, *The Armenian Massacres in Ottoman Turkey* (Salt Lake City: The University of Utah Press, 2005), 82–9.

50. Hurewitz, *Diplomacy in the Near and Middle East*, 2:36–7.

51. Mango, *Atatürk*, 217.

52. McCarthy, *The Ottoman Turks*, 377.

53. Mango, *Atatürk*, 218–21.

54. Ibid., 225–6.

55. McCarthy, *The Ottoman Turks*, 378. Mango, *Atatürk*, 269.

56. Hurewitz, *Diplomacy in the Near and Middle East*, 2:74–5.

57. Ibid., 2:75.

58. McCarthy, *The Ottoman Turks*, 378.

59. Ibid., 379.

60. Ibid., 381–2.

61. Ibid., 382.

62. Ibid., 383.

63. Ibid., 384.

64. Zürcher, *Turkey*, 155.

65. Mango, *Atatürk*, 344.

66. Hurewitz, *Diplomacy in the Near and Middle East*, 2:119–20.

67. Ibid.

68. Ibid.

69. Ibid., 2:122.

The Bosphorus. Courtesy of Rick and Susie Graetz.

Topkapi Palace. Courtesy of Rick and Susie Graetz.

The inner section of Topkapi Palace.
Courtesy of Rick and Susie Graetz.

Sultan Ahmed Mosque (Blue Mosque).
Courtesy of Rick and Susie Graetz.

Dolmabahçe Palace. Courtesy of Rick and Susie Graetz.

The ancient walls of Constantinople. Courtesy of Rick and Susie Graetz.

Hagia Sophia/Aya Sofya. Courtesy of Rick and Susie Graetz.

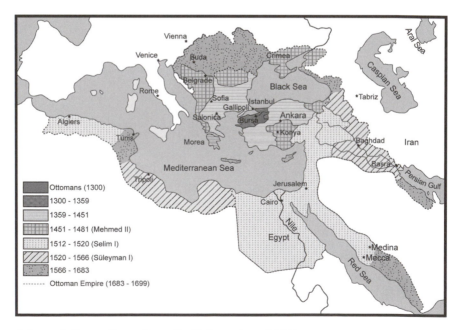

Adapted from Encyclopedia Britannica, 1997.

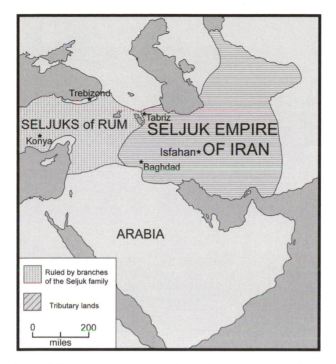

Adapted from Justin McCarthy, *The Ottoman Turks: An Introductory History to 1923* (London, New York: Wesley Longman Limited, 1997).

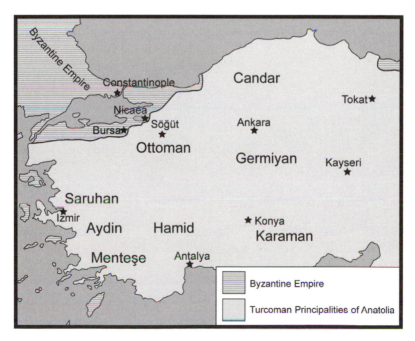

Adapted from Justin McCarthy, *The Ottoman Turks: An Introductory History to 1923* (London, New York: Wesley Longman Limited, 1997).

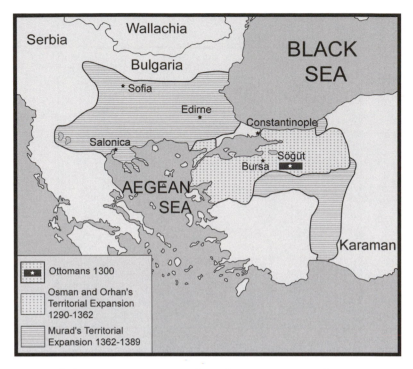

Adapted from Justin McCarthy, *The Ottoman Turks: An Introductory History to 1923* (London, New York: Wesley Longman Limited, 1997).

Adapted from Justin McCarthy, *The Ottoman Turks: An Introductory History to 1923* (London, New York: Wesley Longman Limited, 1997).

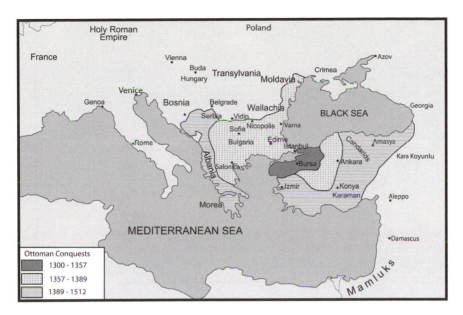

Adapted from Kemal Cicek, ed. *The Great Ottoman Turkish Civilization*, 4 vols. (Ankara: Yeni Türkiye, 2000).

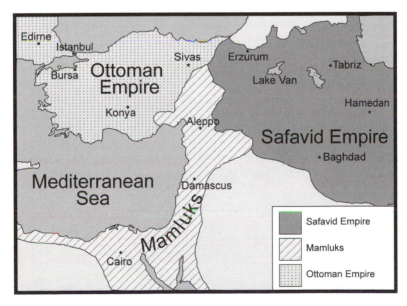

Adapted from Justin McCarthy, *The Ottoman Turks: An Introductory History to 1923* (London, New York: Wesley Longman Limited, 1997).

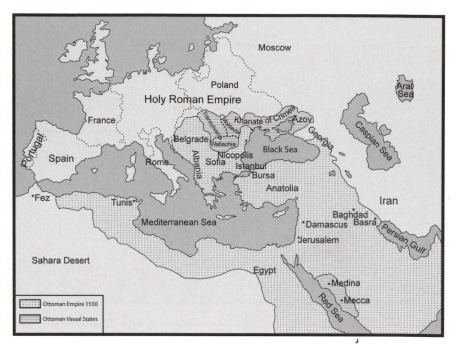

Adapted from Kemal Cicek, ed. *The Great Ottoman Turkish Civiliza-tion*, 4 vols. (Ankara: Yeni Türkiye, 2000).

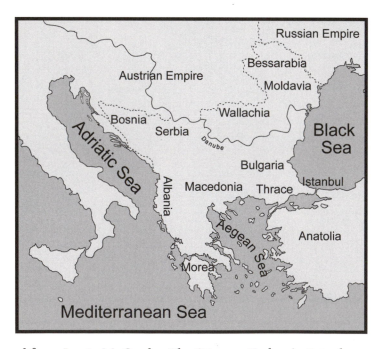

Adapted from Justin McCarthy, *The Ottoman Turks: An Introductory His-tory to 1923* (London, New York: Wesley Longman Limited, 1997).

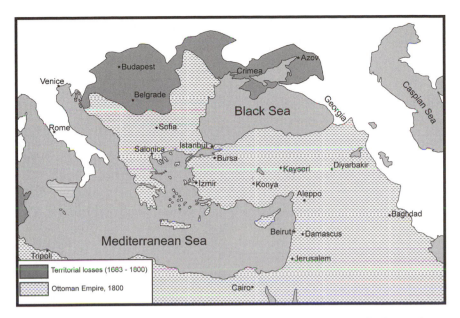

Adapted from Kemal Cicek, ed. *The Great Ottoman Turkish Civilization*, 4 vols. (Ankara: Yeni Türkiye, 2000).

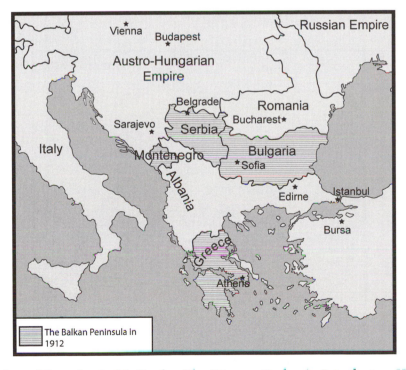

Adapted from Justin McCarthy, *The Ottoman Turks: An Introductory History to 1923* (London, New York: Wesley Longman Limited, 1997).

Adapted from http://www.turkeytravelplanner.com, 2004.

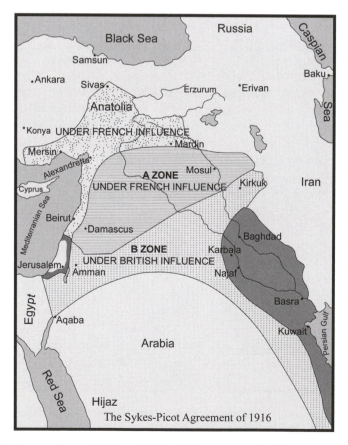

Adapted from the website of the Palestinian Academic Society for the Study of International Affairs.

BIOGRAPHIES

Abdülhamid II (1842–1918)

The last autocratic Ottoman sultan, who ruled from 1876 to 1909, Abdülhamid began his reign by supporting the establishment of a constitution and the creation of a parliamentary system of government led by the charismatic and ambitious Midhat Paşa. Soon, however, the new sultan disbanded the parliament and dismissed Midhat, seizing the reins of power and establishing an autocratic system where power derived solely from the sultan and the palace. Despite his growing autocratic tendencies, Abdülhamid built on the reforms that had been introduced during the *Tanzimat* period. He implemented a number of important educational, social, and economic reforms that left a profound impact on Ottoman society. He also tried to preserve the territorial integrity of the Ottoman state by using highly repressive measures, suppressing nationalistic movements, particularly among the Armenians, creating a secret police force, and imposing censorship. The sultan advocated Pan-Islamism or the unity of all Muslims under his leadership as a means of countering the Russian promotion of Pan-Slavism (the unity of Slavic people under the leadership of Russia), while at the same time reminding the British and the French that their Muslim subjects in the newly acquired colonies in India and North Africa viewed him as their spiritual leader. Despite his best efforts to modernize Ottoman society under an Islamic ideology, Abdülhamid failed to win the support of the newly emerging intelligentsia and army officers who supported the opposition as represented by Committee of Union and Progress (CUP). In July 1908, a group of young army officers staged a revolt and forced Abdülhamid to restore the 1876 constitution. Despite its victory, the CUP did not depose the sultan. In April 1909, however, after a counterrevolution forced CUP out of power, the army intervened and suppressed the rebellion. Shortly after, the sultan was deposed and removed to Salonica. In 1912, he was allowed to return to Istanbul. He died on February 10, 1918.

Evliye Çelebi (1611–1682)

Evliye Çelebi was the Ottoman traveler who left palace service and made traveling his sole purpose in life after seeing the Prophet Muhammad in a dream. Initially, he traveled in various provinces of the Ottoman Empire by attaching himself to various government officials and army commanders. Later, he traveled on his own and left the Ottoman territory for other countries. He visited Sudan, Iran, Russia, Poland, Austria, the German lands, the Netherlands, and Sweden. During his trips, Evliye Çelebi recorded his observations on a wide variety of topics, from the natural topography to the state of local administration and the names and achievements of prominent scholars, poets, artists, and architects. He also recorded folk tales, religious traditions, and customs, as well as popular songs and legends. His *Siyâhatname* ("Travel book") is, therefore, one of the most valuable sources for the study of the Ottoman Empire, Iran, the Caucasus, the Balkans, and Central Europe during the seventeenth century.

Ibrahim Şinasi (1826–1871)

Journalist, author, and critic, Ibrahim Şinasi began his career in the Ottoman government. With the support and encouragement from his patron, Mustafa Reşid Paşa, Şinasi studied in Paris from 1849 to 1854, where he came under the influence of modern European ideas. In 1860, Şinasi became the editor of a newspaper, *Tercümân-i Ahvâl* (Interpreter of Situations). In 1862, Şinasi left *Tercümân-i Ahvâl* and started a new newspaper, *Tasvir-i Efkâr* (Illustration of Opinions). As a member of a new generation of young Ottoman intellectuals, the patriotic and liberal-minded Şinasi criticized the despotic and highly bureaucratic policies of the leaders of the *Tanzimat* and their appeasing attitude toward European states. Fearing government retaliation, Şinasi left Istanbul for Paris in 1865 and left the editorship and the management of the newspaper to Namik Kemal. Aside from his articles, Şinasi also translated the poetry of Racine, La Fontaine, and Lamartine from French into Turkish. He also wrote plays, including the comedy *Şâir Evlenmesi* (Marriage of a Poet), which was published in 1859.

Kemal Atatürk (Mustafa Kemal Paşa) (1881–1938)

Founder of the Republic of Turkey, Atatürk was born in Salonica. He attended military school at Monastir and later in Istanbul. He joined the young officers who opposed Abdülhamid II and participated in suppressing the counterrevolutionary forces who tried to overthrow the government dominated by the Committee of Union and Progress (CUP) in 1909. In 1911, when Italy invaded and occupied Libya, he went to the North African province to fight the Italian forces. During the First World War, he fought at Gallipoli in 1915–16 and emerged as the hero when the Ottomans defeated the Allied forces. After the end of the war, he was sent by the sultan to eastern Anatolia to disarm the remaining Ottoman divisions in the region. Instead of obeying his orders, Atatürk joined the army units that had refused to disband and emerged as the leader of the national resistance movement, which organized the Turkish National Assembly in April 1920. The nationalist movement defeated the Armenians in the east and the Greeks in the west and established a Turkish republic in Anatolia and eastern Thrace. Atatürk abolished the institutions of *sultanate* and *caliphate*, sending the last Ottoman caliph into exile in 1924. He also embarked on an ambitious program of reforms, building a new economic infrastructure for the newly created country. He also reformed the educational system, changed the alphabet, and emancipated women.

Mahmud II (1784/85–1839)

The son of Sultan Abdülhamid I and a cousin of Selim III, Mahmud ascended the Ottoman throne in 1808 after the powerful *ayan*, Bayrakdâr Mustafa Paşa, overthrew the reigning sultan, Mustafa IV. The long reign of Mahmud was characterized by nationalist revolts in Serbia and Greece and the growing power and intervention of Russia in the Balkans. Mahmud tried to impose the authority of the central government over provinces by attacking the powerful *ayans* who had established themselves as autonomous rulers. His attack on Ali Paşa of Janina allowed the Greek nationalists to revolt and gain independence with support from Russia, France, and Great Britain. In 1826, the sultan dissolved the *janissary* corps. The conflict between Mahmud and the governor of Egypt, Muhammad Ali (Mehmed Ali), resulted into a series of military campaigns that ended with the defeat of Ottoman forces in 1833. The Egyptian victory forced Mahmud to seek the support of the Russian government by signing the Treaty of Hünkâr

İskelesi, which greatly increased the power and influence of the Russian state over the Ottoman Empire. Despite the military defeats and territorial losses, Mahmud remained committed to the implementation of important political, military, economic, and educational reforms until his death in 1839.

Mehmed II (1432–1481)

Mehmed ascended the Ottoman throne in 1444 at the age of twelve after his father Murad II abdicated in his favor. As a young sultan, Mehmed was under the influence of his advisers, Zaganos Paşa and Şihâbeddin, who advocated an immediate invasion of Constantinople. In 1446, his father returned to the throne and assumed leadership of the Ottoman government. After Murad died in 1451, Mehmed ascended the Ottoman throne for a second time. The young sultan was determined to fulfill the old dream of conquering the capital of the Byzantine state. In May 1453, Ottoman forces stormed and captured Constantinople, and Mehmed (now called "The Conqueror") proclaimed the city his capital. Mehmed dreamed of completing his conquest of Serbia by capturing Belgrade, but Ottoman forces failed to capture the city in 1456. Despite this failure, much of Serbia was incorporated into the Ottoman state in 1459. In 1463, Mehmed pushed westward and captured Bosnia-Herzegovina. Three years later, the Ottomans established a foothold in Albania. To the east, Mehmed conquered the kingdom of Trebizond in 1461 and defeated the armies of Uzun Hasan, the chief of the Ak Koyunlu (White Sheep) Turcomans who had established an empire in Iran. The defeat of Ak Koyunlu allowed Mehmed to incorporate the Turcoman principality of Karaman into his empire. Having neutralized the threat to his empire in the east, Mehmed shifted his focus to the west and attacked Venice. The Morea was thus brought under direct Ottoman rule. To the north, Mehmed established Ottoman suzerainty over Crimean Tatars in 1478. The alliance with the Crimean Tatars allowed Mehmed to impose Ottoman hegemony over the northern shores of the Black Sea. By the time Mehmed died in 1481, the Ottomans had established a foothold on the Italian peninsula with the goal of attacking Rome. During his reign, Mehmed sponsored the construction of many mosques and palaces, the most important being the Topkapi Palace in Istanbul, which remained the official residence of Ottoman sultans until the mid-nineteenth century.

Mustafa Reşid Paşa (1800–1858)

The Ottoman reformer, diplomat, and statesman Mustafa Reşid Paşa was born in 1800 and received a traditional *medrese* education.

He joined the scribal institution and in 1821 participated in the Ottoman campaign to crush the nationalist uprising in Greece. In 1828, Reşid served in the war against Russia. In the peace negotiations at Edirne in 1829, he was a member of the Ottoman delegation. In 1830, Reşid joined the delegation sent by Mahmud II to Egypt to negotiate with Muhammad Ali Paşa. In the military campaigns against Greek nationalists and Russia, he had witnessed the embarrassing performance of the Ottoman army. During his visit to Egypt, he saw first-hand the reforms of Muhammad Ali. When Muhammad Ali invaded Anatolia and defeated Ottoman forces near Konya, Reşid was sent to negotiate with Muhammad Ali's son, Ibrahim Paşa. Reşid went to Paris in 1834 to negotiate with the French government about the withdrawal of French forces from Algeria. In 1835, Reşid was appointed Ottoman ambassador to Paris. A year later, the sultan sent him to London as his ambassador. During his tenure as the Ottoman ambassador in London, Reşid developed a close relationship with influential British officials. In the summer of 1837, he returned to Istanbul and was appointed minister of foreign affairs. In 1838, he was sent to London to convince the British government to sign a treaty against Egypt. Instead, he signed a commercial treaty with the British government, which opened the Ottoman market to British goods and investment. After the death of Mahmud II in the summer of 1839, Reşid Paşa played an important role in writing the Noble Edict of *Gülhane*, which inaugurated the era of *Tanzimat*. During the reign of Sultan Abdülmecid (1839–1861), he served as the grand vezir six times and attempted to introduce administrative, social, economic, and educational reforms using advanced European countries as his model. In the crisis that led to the Crimean War (1853–1856), he used the British and the French to isolate and eventually defeat Russia and secure the inclusion of the Ottoman state in the Concert of Europe.

Namik Kemal (1840–1888)

Poet, journalist, playwright, novelist, critic, and a member of the group that came to be known as Young Ottomans, Namik Kemal was one of the most important literary and intellectual figures of the Ottoman Empire during the second half of the nineteenth century. Born into an old and prominent Turkish family, which traced its ancestry to an Ottoman grand vezir in the eighteenth century, Kemal was raised and educated by his grandfather, who was a high government official and a member of the *Mevlevi* mystical (*sufi*) order, where he learned *sama* (mystical chants) and Persian. Kemal began his government career as a secretary at *Bab-i Ali* or Sublime Porte in 1857. He then joined the Translation Office of the Ottoman Ministry of Foreign Affairs. When Ibrahim Şinasi published *Tasvir-i Efkâr*, Namik Kemal contributed articles to the newspaper. When Şinasi fled to Paris, Namik Kemal took over the newspaper, writing articles and criticizing the leaders of the *Tanzimat* for their authoritarianism and corruption. In collaboration with several other intellectuals, including Ziya, Namik Kemal founded the Young Ottoman movement. He and Ziya were, however, forced to leave Istanbul first for Paris and then London where they published *Hürriyet* (Liberty), which advocated a constitutional system of government. After his return from exile, Namik Kemal began to publish the newspaper *Ibret* (Admonition) in 1872. His most controversial work, however, was the patriotic play, *Vatan Yahud Silistre* ("Fatherland or *Silistria*"), which led the government to imprison him on the island of Cyprus. After the 1876 coup, which deposed Sultan Abdülaziz, Namik Kemal returned to Istanbul and played an important role in drafting the constitution that was introduced by Midhat Paşa. After the dismissal of Midhat by the new sultan, Abdülhamid II, Namik Kemal was detained and sent into exile in 1877. Namik Kemal believed in the introduction of a constitutional government. He also advocated the preservation of the Islamic identity of the Ottoman Empire. Thus, in his writings, he sought to reconcile the establishment of a modern political system based on individual liberties with Islamic beliefs and traditions, arguing that far from undermining Islam, the creation of a constitutional form of government could be viewed as a return to the original teachings of Islam.

Osman (1258/59–1326)

Osman, the founder of the Ottoman state, began his career as a frontier commander (*bey*) and a *gâzi* or a holy warrior, fighting against infidels. He first captured the important town of Eskişehir and, using it as his base, attacked and occupied Yenişehir. In July 1302, Osman defeated a Byzantine army outside Nicomedia (Izmit). The victory brought recognition and prestige for Osman and allowed the *beys* fighting under his command to push toward the Sea of Marmara and the Aegean. His son Orhan built on his father's conquests and took the important Byzantine city of Bursa in 1326.

Selim I (1470–1520)

After ascending the throne, Selim, also known as Yavuz (the Terrible), killed all his brothers, nephews, and most probably poisoned his ailing father. During Selim's short reign, the Ottoman Empire emerged as the supreme power in eastern Anatolia and the Arab world. Before confronting the threat posed by the Safavid dynasty in Iran, Selim massacred 40,000 people in Anatolia for their alleged pro-Shia/pro-Safavid sympathies. In 1514, at the Battle of Châldiran, Ottoman forces defeated the armies of Shah Ismail, who had emerged as the ruler of Iran and the founder of the Safavid dynasty in 1501. Selim annexed the Emirate of Dulkadir, which served as a buffer state between the Ottoman Empire and the Mamluks. Between 1516 and 1517, Ottoman forces attacked the Mamluks, who were defeated at the battle of Marc Dâbik/Marj Dâbiq (1516). The Mamluk sultan, Qansu al-Ghawri, was killed on the battlefield. The Ottoman forces inflicted another defeat on the Mamluk forces at Raydaniyya near Cairo. Syria and Egypt were thus brought under Ottoman rule. Western Arabia, including the two holy cities of Mecca and Medina, also accepted Ottoman suzerainty. With this conquest, the Ottoman sultan could claim the title of the protector of the two holiest sites in Islam.

Selim III (1761–1808)

The son of Mustafa III, Selim became fascinated with European culture and established a close relationship with Louis XVI. He introduced a reform program, *Nizam-i Cedid*, intended to establish central government control over the provinces that were becoming increasingly dominated by local notables or the *ayans*. The most important component of his reforms was a new army, which was opposed by the *janissaries* and other traditional-minded elements within the Ottoman ruling elite, such as the *ulema*. In addition, he could not secure a stable financial base for his military and administrative reforms without debasing the Ottoman currency and increasing taxes. The unpopularity of the sultan's reforms and the opposition of the *ulema* and the *janissaries* ignited a revolt, which deposed Selim from the throne. He was subsequently killed by order of his successor, Mustafa IV, in 1808.

Sinan (1489/90–1588)

Sinan was the chief imperial architect during the reign of Süleyman the Magnificent (1520–1566). Born into a Greek Christian family, Sinan was recruited into government service through the *devşirme* during the reign of Selim I (1512–1520). He served in the

Ottoman army during the reign of Süleyman the Magnificent, building bridges and citadels during the sultan's campaigns in Europe and Asia. He was greatly influenced by Byzantine architecture as well as by the Iranian architect, Acemi Ali, who had been brought back by Süleyman from Tabriz. The design and construction of some 477 buildings have been attributed to Sinan. The three largest and most important buildings he built are the *Şehzâde* (son of the shah) mosque (1543–1548) in Istanbul, which he built for Süleyman the Magnificent as a mausoleum for his son, Mehmed; the *Süleymâniyye* mosque complex (1550–1557), which included a mosque and fourteen buildings; and *Selimiyye*, which dominates the city of Edirne and is considered the masterpiece of this brilliant Ottoman architect.

Süleyman the Magnificent (1494/95–1566)

Süleyman, the son of Selim I, ruled from 1520 to 1566. During his reign, the Ottoman Empire reached the zenith of its power, capturing Belgrade in 1521 and using it as a territorial base to invade and conquer Hungary. At the battle of Mohács in 1526, the Ottomans inflicted a devastating defeat on the Hungarians, killing their king on the battlefield and putting an end to the Hungarian kingdom. Süleyman's victory signaled the beginning of the intense rivalry between the Habsburgs and the Ottomans. In 1529, the Ottoman forces laid siege to Vienna, but after a few weeks they withdrew. Having established a close alliance with France, Süleyman forced the Habsburgs to accept Ottoman rule over Hungary. To the east, Süleyman waged several military campaigns against Iran, capturing the cities of Baghdad in Iraq and Tabriz in Azerbaijan. Ottoman forces also seized parts of the southern Caucasus, including Georgia. Süleyman's foreign policy was based on an alliance with France, which would pressure and isolate the Habsburgs. In the east, the Ottomans enjoyed a close alliance with the Uzbeks in Central Asia, who carried out devastating raids against Iran's northeastern provinces. During Süleyman's reign, the Ottomans established their naval superiority in the Mediterranean under the command of Hayreddin Paşa, also known as Barbarossa or Barbaros, who was appointed *Kapudan-i derya* or grand admiral. Süleyman also intended to invade and conquer India by attacking the Portuguese navy and establishing Ottoman hegemony over the Persian Gulf. His long wars with the Habsburgs in Europe and the Safavids in Iran, as well as long distances and the enormous cost of such an undertaking, prevented him from realizing this project.

Yusuf Akçura (1876–1935)

Yusuf Akçura, also known as Akçuraoglu Yusuf, was a Kazan Tatar from Simbirsk on the river Volga. As a student in the War Academy in Istanbul, he joined the Young Turks and was exiled to Libya. He escaped from North Africa to France. In Paris, he studied at Ecole des Sciences Politiques. He returned to his homeland in 1904, where he wrote his most influential work, *Üç Tarz-i Siyaset* (Three Types of Policy). After the victory of the Young Turk Revolution, Akçura returned to Istanbul and in 1911 founded the journal *Türk Yurdu*. During the war of independence, Akçura joined the nationalist forces, and after the establishment of the Turkish Republic he was elected to the Grand National Assembly. He also served as the president of the Turkish Historical Society and taught history at Ankara University. In *Üç Tarz-i Siyaset*, Akçura presented Ottomanism, Pan-Islamism, and Pan-Turkism as the three dominant ideological trends of his time. He rejected Ottomanism, which called for the unification of all national groups living in the Ottoman Empire in a single Ottoman nation. He also dismissed Pan-Islamism as an ideology that could not generate sufficient unity and solidarity among the Muslims both inside and outside the boundaries of the Ottoman Empire. Instead, he called for Pan-Turkism, or the union of all Turkic peoples of the world. Akçura believed that Pan-Turkism could mobilize and unify the Turkic people around a common ethnicity and language.

Ziya Gökalp (1876–1924)

One of the most influential Turkish intellectuals of the twentieth century, Ziya Gökalp was a thinker, writer, teacher, and scholar, who devoted much of his life and writings to the study of the impact of Western civilization on Islam and Turkish national identity. He was born in Diyarbakir in southeastern Anatolia into a mixed Turkish and Kurdish family. As a student in Istanbul, he joined the Committee of Union and Progress (CUP), but he was arrested and sent back to Diyarbakir. When CUP seized power in 1908, Gökalp emerged as one of its ideological leaders and was elected to parliament in 1912. He also began to teach sociology at the *Dârülfünun* (The House of Sciences/ University) and published the newspaper *Peyman* (Agreement) and several intellectual journals. The majority of his works written between 1911 and 1918 and 1922 and 1924 were greatly influenced by the historical conditions of the late Ottoman period and the early stages of the nationalist movement. He witnessed the decline and the disintegration of the empire and the rise of a secular nationalist republic under Atatürk. Distinguishing culture from civilization, he asserted that culture incorporated the national characteristics of a nation, whereas civilization belonged to humanity and was therefore an international phenomenon. He advocated the idea of Turks abandoning Eastern civilization and adopting Western civilization while preserving their Turkish national identity and culture. He believed in secularism, democracy, Westernism, women's emancipation, and political as well as economic independence, the very principles adopted as the ideological foundation for the reforms implemented by the founder of modern Turkey, Mustafa Kemal Atatürk.

PRIMARY DOCUMENTS

Document 1: Love Poem (*Ghazal*) by Sultan Süleyman I, "the Magnificent," for Hürrem Sultan

My intimate companion, my prosperity, my beloved, my shining moon

My lover, my joy, my abundance, my sultan, the shah of beauties.

My life, my everything, my lifetime, my Kawthar, the paradisical river of wine

My spring, my laughter, my sun, my beauty, my smiling rose

My joy, my revelry, my rendezvous, my oil lamp, my light, my candlewick

My Seville orange, my pomegranate, my sweet orange, my taper burning in the bedchamber

My flower, my sweet, my hidden treasure, my serenity in the world

My precious, my Joseph, my riches, my heart, my khan of Egypt

My Stamboul, my Karaman, my sovereign realm of ancient Rome

My Badakhshan and Kipchak and Baghdad, my Khorasan

Mine of serpentine locks, arched brows, eyes full of mischief and languishing

You are to blame if I die, come to my aid, O you unbeliever!

Heavy of heart, my eyes wetted with tears, I am Muhibbi the fortunate

Seeing that I am your eulogist, I will forever sing your praises at your threshold.

Sources: "Sulayman the Magnificent and Khurrem Sultan: An Empyreal Love Story," *P Art and Culture Magazine: The International Magazine of Art and Culture* (Istanbul, Turkey), 7 (Winter 2003), 108–9. Translation from the Ottoman Turkish by Dr. Joyce Hedda Matthews.

Document 2: Treaty of Küçük Kaynarca, 1774

The Treaty of Küçük Kaynarca was signed on July 21, 1774, in Küçük Kaynarca (present-day Bulgaria) between the Russian Empire and the Ottoman Empire after the Ottomans were defeated in the Russo-Turkish War of 1768–1774.

I. From the present time all the hostilities and enmities which have hitherto prevailed shall cease for ever, and all hostile acts and enterprises committed on either side, whether by force of arms or in any other manner, shall be buried in an eternal oblivion, without vengeance being taken for them in any way whatever; but, on the contrary, there shall always be a perpetual, constant, and inviolable peace, as well by sea as by land.* * *

III. All the Tartar peoples—those of the Crimea, of the Budjiac, of the Kuban, the Edissans, Geambouiluks and Editshkuls—shall, without any exceptions, be acknowledged by the two Empires as free nations, and entirely independent of every foreign Power, governed by their own Sovereign, of the race of Ghenghis Khan, elected and raised to the throne by all the Tartar peoples; which Sovereign shall govern them according to their ancient laws and usages, being responsible to no foreign Power whatsoever; for which reason, neither the Court of Russia nor the Ottoman Porte shall interfere, under any pretext whatever, with the election of the said Khan, or in the domestic, political, civil and internal affairs of the same; but, on the contrary, they shall acknowledge and consider the said Tartar nation, in its political and civil state, upon the same footing as the other Powers who are governed by themselves, and are dependent upon God alone. As to the ceremonies of religion, as the Tartars profess the same faith as the Mahometans [Muslims], they shall regulate themselves, with respect to His Highness, in his capacity of Grand Caliph of Mahometanism [Islam], according to the precepts prescribed to them by their law, without compromising, nevertheless, the stability of their political and civil liberty.* * *

VII. The Sublime Porte promises to protect constantly the Christian religion and its churches, and it also allows the Ministers of the Imperial Court of Russia to make, upon all occasions, representations, as well in favour of the new church at Constantinople, of which mention will be made in Article XIV, as on behalf of its officiating ministers, promising to take such representations into due consideration, as being made by a confidential functionary of a neighbouring and sincerely friendly Power.* * *

XI. For the convenience and advantage of the two Empires, there shall be a free and unimpeded navigation for the merchant ships belonging to the two Contracting Powers, in all seas which wash their shores . . .* * *

Source: J.C. Hurewitz. *Diplomacy in the Near and Middle East: A Documentary Record: 1535–1914*, 2 vols. (Princeton, NJ: D. Van Nostrand Company, 1956), 1:54–61.

Document 3: The *Gülhane* Proclamation, 1839

The *Hatt-i Şerif* of *Gülhane* (The Noble Edict of the Rose Garden) was a 1839 proclamation by Ottoman Sultan Abdülmecid that launched the *Tanzimat* period of reforms and reorganization.

All the world knows that in the first days of the Ottoman monarchy, the glorious precepts of the Koran and the laws of the empire were always honored.

The empire in consequence increased in strength and greatness, and all its subjects, without exception, had risen in the highest degree to ease and prosperity. In the last one hundred and fifty years a succession of accidents and diverse causes have arisen which have brought about a disregard for the sacred code of laws and the regulations flowing therefrom, and the former strength and prosperity have changed into weakness and poverty; an empire in fact loses all its stability so soon as it ceases to observes its laws.

These considerations are ever present to our mind, and ever since the day of our advent to the throne the thought of the public wealth of the improvement of the state of the provinces, and of relief to the [subject] peoples, has not ceased to engage it. If, therefore, the geographical position of the Ottoman provinces, the fertility of the soil, the aptitude and intelligence of the inhabitants, are considered, the conviction will remain that by striving to find efficacious means, the result, which by the help of God we hope to attain, can be obtained within a few years. Full of confidence, therefore, in the help of the Most High, and certain of the support of our Prophet, we deem it right to seek by new institutions to give to the provinces composing the Ottoman Empire the benefit of a good administration.

These institutions must be principally carried out under three heads, which are:

1. The guarantees insuring to our subjects perfect security for life, honor, and fortune.
2. A regular system of assessing and levying taxes.
3. An equally regular system for the levy of troops and the duration of their service.

And, in fact, are not life and honor the most precious gifts to mankind? What man, however much his character may be against violence, can prevent himself from having recourse to it, and thereby injure the government and the country, if his life and honor are endangered? If, on the contrary, he enjoys in that respect perfect security, he will not depart from the ways of loyalty, and all his actions will contribute to the good of the government and of his brothers.

If there is an absence of security as to one's fortune, everyone remains insensible to the voice of the Prince and the country; no one interests himself in the progress of public good, absorbed as he is in his own troubles. If, on the contrary, the citizen keeps possession in all confidence of all his goods, then, full of ardor in his affairs, which he seeks to enlarge in order to increase his comforts, he feels daily growing and doubling in his heart not only his love for the Prince and country, but also his devotion to his native land.

These feelings become in him the source of the most praiseworthy actions.

As to the regular and fixed assessment of the taxes, it is very important that it be regulated; for the state which is forced to incur many expenses for the defense of its territory cannot obtain the money necessary for its armies and other services except by means of contributions levied on its subjects. Although, thanks be to God, our empire has for some time past been delivered from the scourge of monopolies, falsely considered in times of war as a source of revenue, a fatal custom still exists, although it can only have disastrous consequences; it is that of venal concessions, known under the name of "Iltizam."

Under that name the civil and financial administration of a locality is delivered over to the passions of a single man; that is to say, sometimes to the iron grasp of the most violent and avaricious passions, for if that contractor is not a good man, he will only look to his own advantage.

It is therefore necessary that henceforth each member of Ottoman society should be taxed for a quota of a fixed tax according to his fortune and means, and that it should be impossible that anything more could be exacted from him. It is also necessary that special laws should fix and limit the expenses of our land and sea forces.

Although, as we have said, the defense of the country is an important matter, and that it is the duty of all the inhabitants to furnish soldiers for that object, it has become necessary to establish laws to regulate the contingent to be furnished by each locality according to the necessity of the time, and to reduce the term of military service to four or five years. For it is at the same time doing an injustice and giving a mortal blow to agriculture and to industry to take, without consideration to the respective population of the localities, in the one more, in the other less, men than they can furnish; it is also reducing the soldiers to despair and contributing to the depopulation of the country by keeping them all their lives in service.

In short, without the several laws, the necessity for which has just been described, there can be neither strength, nor riches, nor happiness, nor tranquility for the empire; it must, on the contrary, look for them in the existence of these new laws.

From henceforth, therefore, the cause of every accused person shall be publicly judged, as the divine law requires, after inquiry and examination, and so long as a regular judgment shall not have been pronounced, no one can secretly or publicly put another to death by poison or in any other manner.

No one shall be allowed to attack the honor of any other person whatever.

Each one shall possess his property of every kind, and shall dispose of it in all freedom, without let or hindrance from any person whatever; thus, for example, the innocent heirs of a criminal shall not be deprived of their legal rights, and the property of the criminal shall not be confiscated. These imperial concessions shall extend to all our subjects, of whatever religion or sect they may be; they shall enjoy them without exception. We therefore grant perfect security to the inhabitants of our empire in their lives, their honor, and their fortunes, as they are secured to them by the sacred text of the law.

As for the other points, as they must be settled with the assistance of enlightened opinions, our council of justice (increased by new members as shall be found necessary), to whom shall be joined, on certain days which we shall determine, our ministers and the notabilities of the empire, shall assemble in order to frame laws regulating the security of life and fortune and the assessment of the taxes. Each one in those assemblies shall freely express his ideas and give his advice.

The laws regulating the military service shall be discussed by a military council holding its sittings at the palace of Seraskia. As soon as a law shall be passed, in order to be forever valid, it shall be presented to us; we shall give it our approval, which we will write with our imperial sign-manual.

As the object of these institutions is solely to revivify religion, government, the nation, and the empire, we engage not to do anything which is contrary thereto.

In testimony of our promise we will, after having deposited these presents in the hall containing the glorious mantle of the prophet, in the presence of all the ulemas and the grandees of the empire, make oath thereto in the name of God, and shall afterwards cause the oath to be taken by the ulemas and the grandees of the empire.

After that, those from among the ulemas or the grandees of the empire, or any other persons whatsoever who shall infringe these institutions, shall undergo, without respect of rank, position, and influence, the punishment corresponding to his crime, after having been well authenticated.

A penal code shall be compiled to that effect. As all the public servants of the empire receive a suitable salary, and as the salaries of those whose duties have not up to the present time been sufficiently remunerated are to be fixed, a rigorous law shall be passed against the traffic of favoritism and bribery (*richvet*), which the Divine law reprobates, and which is one of the principal causes of the decay of the empire.

The above dispositions being a thorough alteration and renewal of ancient customs this imperial rescript shall be published at Constantinople and in all places of our empire, and shall be officially communicated to all the ambassadors of the friendly powers resident at Constantinople, that they may be witnesses to the granting of these institutions, which, should it please God, shall last forever. Wherein may the Most High have us in His holy keeping. May those who commit an act contrary to the present regulations be object of Divine malediction, and be deprived forever of every kind of [protection] happiness.

Source: J.C. Hurewitz. *Diplomacy in the Near and Middle East: A Documentary Record: 1535–1914*, 2 vols. (Princeton, NJ: D. Van Nostrand Company, 1956), 1:113–16.

Document 4: The McMahon–Husayn Correspondence: July 14, 1915 to March 10, 1916

The Husayn-McMahon Correspondence refers to ten letters between Sir Henry McMahon, British High Commissioner of Egypt, and Husayn bin Ali, Sharif of Mecca. In return for an Arab revolt against the Ottoman government, the British promised Sharif Husayn an independent Arab state after the end of the First World War.

1. From Sharif Husayn, 14 July 1915

Whereas the whole of the Arab nation without any exception have decided in these last years to live, and to accomplish their freedom, and grasp the reins of their administration both in theory and practice; and whereas they have found and felt that it is to the interest of the Government of Great Britain to support them and aid them to the attainment of their firm and lawful intentions (which are based upon the maintenance of the honour and dignity of their life) without any ulterior motives whatsoever unconnected with this object;

And whereas it is to their (the Arabs') interest also to prefer the assistance of the Government of Great Britain in consideration of their geographical position and economic interests, and also of the attitude of the above-mentioned Government, which is known to both nations and therefore need not be emphasized;

For these reasons the Arab nation see fit to limit themselves, as time is short, to asking the Government of Great Britain, if it should think fit, for the approval, through her deputy or representative, of the following fundamental propositions, leaving out all things considered secondary in comparison with these, so that it may prepare all means necessary for attaining this noble purpose, until such time as it finds occasion for making the actual negotiations:-

Firstly.- England to acknowledge the independence of the Arab countries, bounded on the north by Mersina and Adana up to the 37° of latitude, on which degree fall Birijik, Urfa, Mardin, Midiat, Jezirat (Ibn 'Umar), Amadia, up to the border of Persia; on the east by the borders of Persia up to the Gulf of Basra; on the south by the Indian Ocean, with the exception of the position of Aden to remain as it is; on the west by the Red Sea, the Mediterranean Sea up to Mersina. England to approve of the proclamation of an Arab Khalifate of Islam.

Secondly.- The Arab Government of the Sherif to acknowledge that England shall have the preference in all economic enterprises in the Arab countries whenever conditions of enterprises are otherwise equal.

Thirdly.- For the security of this Arab independence and the certainty of such preference of economic enterprises, both high contracting parties to offer mutual assistance, to the best ability of their military and naval forces, to face any foreign Power which may attack either party. Peace not to be decided without agreement of both parties.

Fourthly.- If one of the parties enters upon an aggressive conflict, the other party to assume a neutral attitude, and in case of such party wishing the other to join forces, both to meet and discuss the conditions.

Fifthly.- England to acknowledge the abolition of foreign privileges in the Arab countries, and to assist the Government of the Sherif in an International Convention for confirming such abolition.

Sixthly.- Articles 3 and 4 of this treaty to remain in vigour for fifteen years, and, if either wishes it to be renewed, one year's notice before lapse of treaty to be given.

Consequently, and as the whole of the Arab nation have (praise be to God) agreed and united for the attainment, at all costs and finally, of this noble object, they beg the Government of Great Britain to answer them positively or negatively in a period of thirty days after receiving this intimation; and if this period should lapse before they receive an answer, they reserve to themselves complete freedom of action. Moreover, we (the Sherif's family) will consider ourselves free in word and deed from the bonds of our previous declaration which we made through Ali Effendi.

2. From Sir Henry McMahon, 24 October 1915

I have received your letter of the 29th Shawal, 1333, with much pleasure and your expressions of friendliness and sincerity have given me the greatest satisfaction.

I regret that you should have received from my last letter the impression that I regarded the question of the limits and boundaries with coldness and hesitation; such was not the case, but it appeared to me that the time had not yet come when that question could be discussed in a conclusive manner.

I have realised, however, from your last letter that you regard this question as one of vital and urgent importance. I have, therefore, lost no time in informing the Government of Great Britain of the contents of your letter, and it is with great pleasure that I communicate to you on their behalf the following statement, which I am confident you will receive with satisfaction:-

The two districts of Mersina and Alexandretta and portions of Syria lying to the west of the districts of Damascus, Homs, Hama and Aleppo cannot be said to be purely Arab, and should be excluded from the limits demanded.

With the above modification, and without prejudice of our existing treaties with Arab chiefs, we accept those limits.

As for those regions lying within those frontiers wherein Great Britain is free to act without detriment to the interest of her ally, France, I am empowered in the name of the Government of Great Britain to give the following assurances and make the following reply to your letter:-

(1) Subject to the above modifications, Great Britain is prepared to recognize and support the independence of the Arabs in all the regions within the limits demanded by the Sherif of Mecca.

(2) Great Britain will guarantee the Holy Places against all external aggression and will recognise their inviolability.

(3) When the situation admits, Great Britain will give to the Arabs her advice and will assist them to establish what may appear to be the most suitable forms of government in those various territories.

(4) On the other hand, it is understood that the Arabs have decided to seek the advice and guidance of Great Britain only, and that such European advisers and officials as may be required for the formation of a sound form of administration will be British.

(5) With regard to the *vilayets* of Bagdad and Basra, the Arabs will recognise that the established position and interests of

Great Britain necessitate special administrative arrangements in order to secure these territories from foreign aggression, to promote the welfare of the local populations and to safeguard our mutual economic interests.

I am convinced that this declaration will assure you beyond all possible doubt of the sympathy of Great Britain towards the aspirations of her friends the Arabs and will result in a firm and lasting alliance, the immediate results of which will be the expulsion of the Turks from the Arab countries and the freeing of the Arab peoples from the Turkish yoke, which for so many years has pressed heavily upon them.

I have confined myself in this letter to the more vital and important questions, and if there are any other matters dealt with in your letter which I have omitted to mention, we may discuss them at some convenient date in the future.

It was with very great relief and satisfaction that I heard of the safe arrival of the Holy Carpet and the accompanying offerings which, thanks to the clearness of your directions and the excellence of your arrangements, were landed without trouble or mishap in spite of the dangers and difficulties occasioned by the present sad war. May God soon bring a lasting peace and freedom to all peoples!

I am sending this letter by the hand of your trusted and excellent messenger, Sheikh Mohammed Ibn Arif Ibn Uraifan, and he will inform you of the various matters of interest, but of less vital importance, which I have not mentioned in this letter.

3. From Sharif Husayn, 1 January 1916

We received from the bearer your letter, dated the 9th Safar (the 14th December, 1915), with great respect and honour, and I have understood its contents, which caused me the greatest pleasure and satisfaction, as it removed that which had made me uneasy.

Your honour will have realised, after the arrival of Mohammed (Faroki) Sherif and his interview with you, that all our procedure up to the present was of no personal inclination or the like, which would have been wholly unintelligible, but that everything was the result of the decisions and desires of our peoples, and that we are but transmitters and executants of such decisions and desires in the position they (our people) have pressed upon us.

These truths are, in my opinion, very important and deserve your honour's special attention and consideration.

With regard to what had been stated in your honoured communication concerning El Iraq as to the matter of compensation for the period of occupation, we, in order to strengthen the confidence of Great Britain in our attitude and in our words and actions, really and veritably, and in order to give her evidence of our certainty and assurance in trusting her glorious Government, leave the determination of the amount to the perception of her wisdom and justice.

As regards the northern parts and their coasts, we have already stated in our previous letter what were the utmost possible modifications, and all this was only done so to fulfill those aspirations whose attainment is desired by the will of the Blessed and Supreme God. It is this same feeling and desire which impelled us to avoid what may possibly injure the alliance of Great Britain and France and the agreement made between them during the present wars and calamities; yet we find it our duty that the eminent minister should be sure that, at the first opportunity after this war is finished, we shall ask you (what we avert our eyes from to-day) for what we now leave to France in Beirut and its coasts.

I do not find it necessary to draw your attention to the fact that our plan is of greater security to the interests and protection of the rights of Great Britain than it is to us, and will necessarily be so whatever may happen, so that Great Britain may finally see her friends in that contentment and advancement which she is endeavouring to establish for them now, especially as her Allies being neighbours to us will be the germ of difficulties and discussion with which there will be no peaceful conditions. In addition to which the citizens of Beirut will decidedly never accept such dismemberment, and they may oblige us to undertake new measures which may exercise Great Britain, certainly not less than her present troubles, because of our belief and certainty in the reciprocity and indeed the identity of our interests, which is the only cause that caused us never to care to negotiate with any other Power but you. Consequently, it is impossible to allow any derogation that gives France, or any other Power, a span of land in those regions.

I declare this, and I have a strong belief, which the living will inherit from the dead, in the declarations which you give in the conclusion of your honoured letter. Therefore, the honourable and eminent Minister should believe and be sure, together with Great Britain, that we still remain firm to our resolution which Storrs learnt from us two years ago, for which we await the opportunity suitable to our situation, especially in view of that action the time of which has now come near and which destiny drives towards us with great haste and clearness, so that we and those who are of our opinion may have reasons for such action against any criticisms or responsibilities imposed upon us in future.

Your expression "we do not want to push you to any hasty action which might jeopardise the success of your aim" does not need any more explanation except what we may ask for, when necessary, such as arms, ammunition, &c.

I deem this sufficient, as I have occupied much of your Honour's time. I beg to offer you my great veneration and respect.

4. From Sir Henry McMahon, 25 January 1916

We have received with great pleasure and satisfaction your letter of the 25th Safar (the 1st January) at the hands of your trusty messenger, who has also transmitted to us your verbal messages.

We fully realise and entirely appreciate the motives which guide you in this important question, and we know well that you are acting entirely in the interests of the Arab peoples and with no thought beyond their welfare.

We take note of your remarks concerning the *vilayet* of Bagdad and will take the question into careful consideration when the enemy has been defeated and the time for peaceful settlement arrives.

As regards the northern parts, we note with satisfaction your desire to avoid anything which might possibly injure the alliance of Great Britain and France. It is, as you know, our fixed determination that nothing shall be permitted to interfere in the slightest degree with our united prosecution of this war to a victorious conclusion. Moreover, when the victory has been won, the friendship of Great Britain and France will become yet more firm and enduring, cemented by the blood of Englishmen and Frenchmen who have died side by side fighting for the cause of right and liberty.

In this great cause Arabia is now associated, and God grant that the result of our mutual efforts and co-operation will bind us in a lasting friendship to the mutual welfare and happiness of us all.

We are greatly pleased to hear of the action you are taking to win all the Arabs over to our joint cause, and to dissuade them from giving any assistance to our enemies, and we leave it to your discretion to seize the most favourable moment for further and more decided measures.

You will doubtless inform us by the bearer of this letter of any manner in which we can assist you and your requests will always receive our immediate consideration.

You will have heard how El Sayed Ahmed el Sherif el Senussi has been beguiled by evil advice into hostile action, and it will be a great grief to you to know that he has been so far forgetful of the interests of the Arabs as to throw in his lot with our enemies. Misfortune has now overtaken him, and we trust that this will show him his error and lead him to peace for the sake of his poor misguided followers.

We are sending this letter by the hand of your good messenger, who will also bring to you all our news.

Source: J.C. Hurewitz, *Diplomacy in the Near and Middle East: A Documentary Record: 1914–1956*. (Princeton: D. Van Nostrand Company, 1956), 2:13–7.

Document 5: The Sykes-Picot Agreement of 1916

In negotiations between Sir Mark Sykes, who represented the British government, and his French counterpart, Charles François Geoerge Picot, France and Great Britain defined their respective spheres of influence and control in the Arab Middle East after the downfall of the Ottoman Empire. The agreement contradicted some of the promises made by the British in the Husayn–McMahon correspondence.

It is accordingly understood between the French and British Governments-

1. That France and Great Britain are prepared to recognize and protect an independent Arab States or a Confederation of Arab States in the areas (A) and (B) marked on the annexed map, under the suzerainty of an Arab chief. That in area (A) France, and in area (B) Great Britain, shall have priority of right of enterprise and local loans. That in area (A) France, and in area (B) Great Britain, shall alone supply advisers or foreign functionaries at the request of the Arab State or Confederation of Arab States.

2. That in the blue area France, and in the red area Great Britain, shall be allowed to establish such direct or indirect administration or control as they desire and as they may think fit to arrange with the Arab State or Confederation of Arab States.

3. That in the brown area there shall be established an international administration, the form of which is to be decided upon after consultation with Russia, and subsequently in consultation with the other Allies, and the representatives of the Shereef of Mecca.

4. That Great Britain be accorded (1) the ports of Haifa and Acre, (2) guarantee of a given supply of water from the Tigris and Euphrates in area (A) for area (B). His Majesty's Government, on their part, undertake that they will at no time enter into negotiations for the cession of Cyprus to any third Power without the previous consent of the French Government.

5. That Alexandretta shall be a free port as regards the trade of the British Empire, and that there shall be no discrimination in port charges or facilities as regards British shipping and British goods; that there shall be freedom of transit for British goods through Alexandretta and by railway through the blue area, whether those goods are intended for or originate in the red area, or (B) area, or area (A); and there shall be no discrimination, direct or indirect, against British goods

on any railway or against British goods or ships at any port serving the areas mentioned.

That Haifa shall be a free port as regards the trade of France, her dominions and protectorates, and there shall be no discrimination in port charges or facilities as regards French shipping and French goods. There shall be freedom of transit for French goods through Haifa and by the British railway through the brown area, whether those goods are intended for or originate in the blue area, area (A), or area (B), and there shall be no discrimination, direct or indirect, against French goods on any railway, or against French goods or ships at any port serving the areas mentioned.

6. That in area (A) the Bagdad Railway shall not be extended southwards beyond Mosul, and in area (B) northwards beyond Samarra, until a railway connecting Bagdad with Aleppo via the Euphrates Valley has been completed, and then only with the concurrence of the two Governments.

7. That Great Britain has the right to build, administer, and be sole owner of a railway connecting Haifa with area (B), and shall have a perpetual right to transport troops along such a line at all times.

It is to be understood by both Governments that this railway is to facilitate the connexion of Bagdad with Haifa by rail, and it is further understood that, if the engineering difficulties and expense entailed by keeping this connecting line in the brown area only make the project unfeasible, that the French Government shall be prepared to consider that the line in question may also traverse the polygon Banias-Keis Marib-Salkhad Tell Otsda-Mesmie before reaching area (B).

8. For a period of twenty years the existing Turkish customs tariff shall remain in force throughout the whole of the blue and red areas, as well as in areas (A) and (B), and no increase in the rates of duty or conversions from *ad valorem* to specific rates shall be made except by agreement between the two powers.

There shall be no interior customs barriers between any of the above-mentioned areas. The customs duties leviable on goods destined for the interior shall be collected at the port of entry and handed over to the administration of the area of destination.

9. It shall be agreed that the French Government will at no time enter into any negotiations for the cession of their rights and will not cede such rights in the blue area to any third Power, except the Arab State or Confederation of Arab States, without the previous agreement of His Majesty's Government, who, on their part, will give a similar undertaking to the French Government regarding the red area.

10. The British and French Governments, as the protectors of the Arab State, shall agree that they will not themselves acquire

and will not consent to a third Power acquiring territorial possessions in the Arabian peninsula, nor consent to a third Power installing a naval base either on the east coast, or on the islands, of the Red Sea. This, however, shall not prevent such adjustment of the Aden frontier as may be necessary in consequence of recent Turkish aggression.

11. The negotiations with the Arabs as to the boundaries of the Arab State or Confederation of Arab States shall be continued through the same channel as heretofore on behalf of the two Powers.

12. It is agreed that measures to control the importation of arms into the Arab territories will be considered by the two Governments.

I have further the honour to state that, in order to make the agreement complete, His Majesty's Government are proposing to the Russian Government to exchange notes analogous to those exchanged by the latter and your Excellency's Government on the 26th April last. Copies of these notes will be communicated to your Excellency as soon as exchanged.* * *

Source: J.C. Hurewitz, *Diplomacy in the Near and Middle East: A Documentary Record 1535–1956*, 2 vols. (Princeton, NJ: D. Van Nostrand Company, Inc., 1956), 2:18–22.

Document 6: The Balfour Declaration of 1917

The Balfour Declaration of 1917 was an official letter sent by Britain's Foreign Secretary, Arthur James Balfour, to Lord Rothschild, head of the British Zionist Federation, stating that the British government viewed with favor the establishment of a Jewish national home in Palestine.

Foreign Office

November 2, 1917

Dear Lord Rothschild,

I have much pleasure in conveying to you, on behalf of His Majesty's Government, the following declaration of sympathy with Jewish Zionist aspirations which has been submitted to, and approved by, the Cabinet.

His Majesty's Government view with favour the establishment in Palestine of a national home for the Jewish people, and will use their best endeavours to facilitate the achievement of this object, it being clearly understood that nothing shall be done which may prejudice the civil and religious rights of existing non-Jewish communities in Palestine, or the rights and political status enjoyed by Jews in any other country.

I should be grateful if you would bring this declaration to the knowledge of the Zionist Federation.

Yours sincerely,

ARTHUR JAMES BALFOUR

Sources: Ian J. Bickerton and Carla L. Klausner, *A Concise History of the Arab-Israeli Conflict*, 4th ed. (Upper Saddle River: Prentice Hall, 2002), 59–60. Walter Z. Laqueur and Barry Rubin, eds. *The Israel-Arab Reader: A Documentary History of The Middle East Conflict*, 4th ed. (New York: Penguin Books, 1984), 18. J.C. Hurewitz, *Diplomacy in the Near and Middle East: A Documentary Record 1535–1956*, 2 vols. (Princeton, NJ: D. Van Nostrand Company, Inc., 1956), 2:25–6.

Glossary of Selected Terms

acemi oğlan Young Christian boys recruited through *devşirme* for service in the palace.

ağa/agha Master, chief, head.

ağa of janissaries The commander or chief officer of the *janissary* corps.

akin Raid.

akinci A raider.

askeri Military, Ottoman ruling class.

ayans Local notables, autonomous local leaders, especially in the Ottoman Balkans.

Bab-i Ali Sublime Porte.

bey Honorary title, prince or ruler in Anatolia in pre-Ottoman and early Ottoman times, governor.

beylerbey *Bey* of the *beys* or governor-general in early Ottoman times.

beylerbeyilik Greater province governed by a *beylerbey*.

beylik Principality, region of Anatolia ruled by a *bey*.

birun The outer section of the palace.

cami Mosque.

capitulations Agreements with European states that offered privileges such as reduction in customs duties.

caravansaray Hostel created to protect merchant caravans.

celâlis Anatolian rebels against the central government in the sixteenth century.

cizye Poll tax paid by non-Muslims (*zimmis*).

çelebi A title of honor and respect for individuals from the elite classes. Also, the title for the head of a religious or mystical order.

çohâdâr ağa The royal valet.

dârülfünun The house of sciences, modern university first conceived in 1845.

defterdâr Treasurer, minister of finance.

derebey Autonomous local leader, especially in Ottoman Anatolia.

derviş Member of a mystic fraternity.

devşirme Slaves of the sultans, recruited through the child levy, who became Ottoman administrators and soldiers.

divan Council of state.

divan-i hümâyun Imperial council, chief deliberative body of government.

emir/amir Prince, chief.

enderun The inner section of the palace.

esnaf Craftsmen, shopkeepers, small traders organized in guilds.

eyâlet A province.

fermân An imperial edict.

fetva Decision by *şeyhülislâm* or a *mufti* declaring the legality of an action under Islamic law.

gazâ/ghaza Holy war in the name of Islam.

gâzi Fighter who fights infidels in the name of Islam.

grand vezir The chief minister.

hajj Pilgrimage to the holy city of Mecca.

hammam Turkish bath.

khan/han Ruler, especially among the early Turks.

harem The secluded quarter where women's apartments are located.

hatt-i hümâyun Decree of the sultan, imperial edict.

hazine The treasury.

Hüdâvendigar Lord or emperor.

hütbe The Friday sermon in which the sultan's name was mentioned.

iç oğlan Young slave of the sultan who received his education at the palace.

iqta/ikta Land held in exchange for military service under Seljuks.

Imam In Shia Islam, a leader descended from Ali who acts as the leader of the community.

janissary The sultan's infantry corps recruited from young Christian boys who had been selected through *devşirme*.

jihad Holy war to defend or expand the rule of Islam.

kâdi Muslim judge.

kâzasker/kâdiasker The chief Islamic judge.

kafes The cage or the apartment in the imperial palace where a prince was secluded.

kânun Imperial/secular/administrative law.

kânunname Code of laws.

kapi Gate or Porte, a reference to the Ottoman government.

Kapi kullari Slaves of the Porte or sultan, who served as soldiers and administrators.

kapudan Captain at sea.

kapudan-i derya Grand admiral.

kizilbaş Literally "Red Heads," a reference to Shia Muslim tribal groups who supported the Safavid dynasty in Iran.

kul Slave.

madhhab One of the legal schools in Islam.

mamluk Military slave, especially in Egypt, and the name of the dynasty that ruled Egypt and Syria from 1257 to 1517.

medrese Islamic school.

millet A state-recognized religious community.

milli misak National pact.

miri Lands owned by the sultan and the Ottoman government.

mufti A Muslim jurist and theologian who gave legal decisions and interpreted the Islamic law.

mülk Private property.

nişânci The official in the imperial council who controlled the *tuğra*, or the official seal of the Ottoman state, and drew up and certified all official letters and decrees.

Nizam-i Cedid New Order or modern European-style reforms, including a new army introduced by Selim II.

Osmanli Ottoman.

padişah Sovereign, ruler, king, emperor.

paşa The highest title in the Ottoman governmental and military hierarchy.

pir The spiritual head and leader of a mystical or *derviş* order.

reâyâ Literally, flock, the sultan's tax paying subjects.

Rum Rome or Roman (Byzantine), Greek.

sancak Province in early Ottoman times, later a sub-province.

sancak bey Governor of a *sancak*.

segbans/sekbans "Keepers of hounds," or salaried soldiers trained in using firearms and serving an Ottoman governor.

Shia/Shiite Muslims who believe in following the guidance of divinely-chosen *imams*; the minority in Islam.

Silahdâr ağa Guardian of the sultan's arms.

sipâhi Cavalryman.

sir kâtibi Sultan's personal secretary.

sufi Mystic.

sultan Ruler, emperor.

Sunnah The practice of the Prophet Muhammad, taken as a religious and legal model.

Sunni Muslims who believe in following the consensus (*ijma*) of the community of believers as expressed by the *ulema*; the majority in Islam.

Şeriat Islamic law (Arabic: *Sharia*).

şeyh Elder, leader, and spiritual guide of a mystical fraternity.

şeyhülislâm Chief Mufti of the Ottoman Empire, head of the religious establishment.

Tanzimat "Reorganization." The period of reform in the Ottoman Empire, which began in 1839.

tekke A *derviş* lodge.

timar *Miri* land held in exchange for military service.

tuğra Monogram used by Ottoman sultans to confirm the legality of a document.

ulema Muslim theologians/jurists who act as the experts and doctors of the Islamic law.

vakif A tax-exempt pious foundation.

vâlide sultan Mother of the reigning sultan.

vezir Minister of state.

vilâyet A province in later Ottoman times.

yeni çeri *Janissary.*

zâviye A hospice run and managed by *dervişes* for travelers.

zimmi/dhimmi Christians and Jews.

ANNOTATED BIBLIOGRAPHY

Historical Surveys

Akşin, Sina. 2007. *Turkey from Empire to Revolutionary Republic: The Emergence of the Turkish Nation from 1789 to the Present.* Translated by Dexter H. Mursaloğlu. New York: New York University Press. A comprehensive survey of Ottoman and Turkish history from the rise of pre-Ottoman Turks to the political challenges facing the Republic of Turkey in the new century.

Finkel, Caroline. 2005. *Osman's Dream: The History of the Ottoman Empire.* New York: Basic Books. A detailed account of the Ottoman Empire from the formation of the state by Osman to its collapse in 1923.

Inalcik, Halil and Gunsel Renda, eds. 2002. *Ottoman Civilization*, 2 vols. Ankara: Ministry of Culture. A two-volume set covering Ottoman history, culture, and civilization.

McCarthy, Justin. 1997. *The Ottoman Turks: An Introductory History to 1923.* London, New York: Wesley Longman Limited. A history of the Ottoman Empire from the establishment of the state to its downfall that also contains valuable information about Ottoman society, culture, and civilization.

Shaw, Stanford J. 1976. *History of the Ottoman Empire and Modern Turkey, Volumes I and II.* Cambridge: Cambridge University Press. A highly detailed historical account of the Ottoman Empire and modern Turkey based on Ottoman archives and primary Ottoman and modern Turkish sources.

Origins of the Ottoman Empire

Cahen, Claude. 2001. *The Formation of Turkey: The Seljukid Sultanate of Rum: Eleventh to Fourteenth Century.* Translated and edited by P. M.

Holt. Longman Publishing Group. A historical analysis of the arrival of Turcoman tribes in Asia Minor, the rise and fall of the Seljuk sultanate of Rum, and the Turkification and Islamization of Anatolia.

Kafadar, Cemal. 1995. *Between Two Worlds: The Construction of the Ottoman State*. Berkeley: University of California Press. An important study of the early Ottoman state demonstrating how ethnic, tribal, linguistic, religious, and political affiliations were at play in the struggle for power in Anatolia and the Balkans.

Köprülü, M. Fuad. 1992. *The Origins of the Ottoman Empire*. Translated and edited by Gary Leiser. Albany: State University of New York Press. A seminal work by a brilliant Turkish scholar and historian who critiqued the traditional European theories on the origins of the Ottoman Empire.

Lowry, Heath W. 2003. *The Nature of the Early Ottoman State*. Albany: State University of New York Press. A critique of Paul Wittek's theory and an attempt to offer a new explanation on the origins and nature of the early Ottoman state.

Wittek, Paul. 1938. *The Rise of the Ottoman Empire*. London: The Royal Asiatic Society. An attempt to identify the origins of the Ottoman Empire in the religious zeal of the Turkish *gazis* to convert the Christian population of western Anatolia and the Balkans.

Ottoman History and Society in the "Classical" Era

Cook, M.A., ed. 1976. *A History of the Ottoman Empire to 1730*. Cambridge: Cambridge University Press. A useful account of the reigns of Bayezid II, Selim I, Süleyman the Magnificent, and Murad IV as well as the retreat of the Ottomans from Europe in the eighteenth century written by J.S. Bromely, Halil Inalcik, A.N. Kurat, and V.J. Parry.

Gibbons, Herbert Adams. 1916. *The Foundations of the Ottoman Empire: A History of the Osmanlis up to the Death of Bayezid I, 1300–1403*. New York: The Century Co. This book provides a detailed study tracing the life and career of Osman and his descendants, Orhan, Murad, and Bayezid, who laid the foundations of the Ottoman Empire.

Imber, Colin. 2002. *The Ottoman Empire, 1300–1650: The Structure of Power*. New York: Palgrave Macmillan. A brief and comprehensive survey of the Ottoman history followed by an analysis of the internal structure of the Ottoman system that includes an in-depth discussion of the succession process, the palace, the provinces, the legal system, and the military organization of the empire.

Inalcik, Halil. 1973. *The Ottoman Empire: The Classical Age 1300–1600*. Translated by Norman Itzkowitz and Colin Imber. New York: Praeger

Publishers. An analysis of the history of the Ottoman Empire from 1300 to 1600 that includes a discussion of the institutions that were responsible for the strength and cohesion of the Ottoman administrative system.

Kunt, Metin and Christine Woodhead, eds. 1995. *Süleyman the Magnificent and His Age*. London: Longman House. A collection of essays about the administration, politics, and socio-economic transformation of the Ottoman Empire in the sixteenth century.

Lybyer, Howe Albert. 1913. *The Government of the Ottoman Empire in the Time of Suleiman the Magnificent*. Cambridge: Harvard University Press. This book focuses on the governmental institutions of the Ottoman Empire during the reign of Süleyman the Magnificent.

Naima, Mustafa (Mustafa Naim). 1973. *Annals of the Turkish Empire from 1591 to 1659 of the Christian Era*. Translated by Charles Fraser. London: Arno Press. A history of the most important events that transpired in the Ottoman Empire from 1591 to 1659 by a well-known Ottoman historian and annalist.

Sugar, Peter. 1977. *Southeastern Europe under Ottoman Rule, 1354–1805*. Seattle: University of Washington Press. A comprehensive portrait of the Balkans under Ottoman rule, describing the religious, political, and economic features of the Ottoman state.

Tursun Beg. 1978. *The History of Mehmed the Conqueror*. Translated by Halil Inalcik and Murphey Rhoads. Minneapolis: Bibliotheca Islamica. A history of the life and accomplishments of Mehmed II, conqueror of Istanbul.

Uğur, Ahmet. 1985. *The Reign of Sultan Selim I in the Light of the Selim-Name Literature*. Berlin: Klaus Schwarz Verlag. A study of the reign of Selim I based on the historical works, which focus on his life and achievements.

Ottoman Institutions and Governmental Reforms

Davison, Roderic H. 1973. *Reform in the Ottoman Empire, 1856–1876*. New York: Gordian Press. An analytical study of the reforms implemented by the Ottoman government from 1856 to 1876.

Findley, Carter V. 1980. *Bureaucratic Reform in the Ottoman Empire: The Sublime Porte, 1789–1922*. Princeton: Princeton University Press. A comprehensive study of the rise of the modern bureaucracy in the Ottoman Empire with a particular emphasis on the reforms implemented from the reign of Selim III to the end of the Young Turk period.

Goodwin, Godfrey. 1994. *The Janissaries*. London: Saqi Books. Explores the origins, the rise and the decline of the *janissaries*, the elite troops of the Ottoman Empire until they were dissolved by Mahmud II in 1826.

Inalcik, Halil. 1976. *Application of the Tanzimat and Its Social Effects*. Lisse: Peter de Ridder. This work studies the impact of the reforms implemented during the era of *Tanzimat* in various provinces of the empire.

Karpat, Kemal H. and Robert W. Zens. 2003. *Ottoman Borderlands: Issues, Personalities and Political Change*. Madison: University of Wisconsin Press. A collection of essays on a variety of issues such as the status of central government authority on the Ottoman frontiers, the administrative structures of the Danubian Principalities, the tribal principalities, and the provincial administration in eastern and southeastern Europe, Anatolia, as well as the nature of the Safavid-Ottoman frontier and the Ottoman borderlands in Yemen, Albania, and north Caucasus.

Shaw, Stanford J. 1971. *Between Old and New: The Ottoman Empire under Sultan Selim III 1789–1807*. Cambridge: Harvard University Press. An excellent account of the decline of the Ottoman Empire, the military defeats suffered at the hands of Russia and the Habsburgs, and the reforms introduced during the reign of Selim III (1789–1807).

Ottoman History and Society in the "Modern" Era

Ahmad, Feroz. 1969. *The Young Turks: The Committee of Union and Progress in Turkish Politics*. Oxford: Clarendon Press. A political history of the Young Turks, with a particular emphasis on the events that led to the revolution of 1908 and the opposition that emerged against the Young Turks and forced them to consolidate power through military means.

Hanioglu, M. Şukru. 2001. *Preparation for a Revolution: The Young Turks, 1902–1908*. New York: Oxford University Press, 2001. A historical analysis of the Young Turk movement based on Ottoman archives and other primary sources.

Jelavich, Charles and Barbara. 1977. *The Establishment of the Balkan National States, 1804–1920*. Seattle: University of Washington Press. A historical account of the emergence of modern nation states in the Balkans during the nineteenth and twentieth centuries.

Jelavich, Barbara. 1983. *History of the Balkans: Eighteenth and Nineteenth Centuries, Volume I*. Cambridge: Cambridge University Press. A comprehensive history of the Balkans and the process through which the modern nation states of southeastern Europe emerged from the disintegration of the Ottoman Empire.

Kansu, Aykut. 1997. *The Revolution of 1908 in Turkey*. Leiden: E.J. Brill. An analytical study of the events that led to the victory of the Young Turk revolution and its immediate aftermath.

Kushner, David. 1977. *The Rise of Turkish Nationalism, 1876–1908*. London: Frank Cass. A comprehensive study of the origins of cultural nationalism among the Turks from the introduction of the first Otto-man constitution in 1876 to the Young Turk revolution of 1908.

Lewis, Bernard. 1961. *The Emergence of Modern Turkey.* London: Oxford University Press. A classic that traces the impact of European ideas and institutions on the Ottoman Empire.

Quataert, Donald. 2000. *The Ottoman Empire 1700–1922.* Cambridge: Cambridge University Press. An examination of the major political, social, and economic trends during the last two centuries of Ottoman rule that pays special attention to important topics such as gender, population, transportation, and agricultural production.

Zürcher, Erik-Jan. 2004. *Turkey: A Modern History.* London: I. B. Tauris. An excellent history of the Ottoman Empire and Turkey that extends from the end of the eighteenth century to the present.

Intellectual and Cultural History of the Ottoman Empire

Berkes, Niyazi. 1964. *The Development of Secularism in Turkey.* Montreal: McGill University Press. An important study of the intellectual history of the Ottoman Empire and Turkey during the last two centuries.

Braude, Benjamin and Bernard Lewis, eds. 1982. *Christians and Jews in the Ottoman Empire,* 2 vols. New York: Holmes and Meier. An examination of the role of the *millet* system as well as the status of Jews and Christians in the Ottoman Empire.

Edib, Halidé. 2004. *Memoirs of Halidé Edib.* New York: Gorgias Press. The memoirs of Halidé Edib Adivar (1882–1964), one of the most prolific Turkish women writers and politicians in the twentieth century.

Faroqhi, Suraiya. 2004. *The Ottoman Empire and the World around It.* London: I. B. Tauris. A study based on original sources that explores the long-established network of diplomatic, financial, and cultural connections between the Ottoman Empire and the rest of the world.

Faroqhi, Suraiya. 2000. *Subjects of the Sultan: Culture and Daily Life in the Otto-man Empire.* London: I.B. Tauris. A fascinating exploration of the daily life and the most basic activities of the people who lived under Ottoman rule.

Gökalp, Ziya. 1959. *Turkish Nationalism and Western Civilization: Selected essays of Ziya Gökalp.* Translated and edited by Niyazi Berkes. New York: Columbia University Press. Selected essays on Turkish national-ism and its relationship to Islam and western civilization.

Mardin, Şerif. 1963. *The Genesis of Young Ottoman Thought: A Study in the Modernization of Turkish Political Ideas.* Princeton: Princeton

University Press. A classic, which provides an in-depth analysis of the ideology and politics of the Young Ottoman movement.

Peirce, Leslie P. 1993. *The Imperial Harem: Women and Sovereignty in the Ottoman Empire.* New York: Oxford University Press. Winner of the M. Fuad Köprülü Book Prize, this book examines the sources of the power of the women of the imperial *harem* as they played a crucial role in the politics and culture of the Ottoman Empire.

Social and Economic History of the Ottoman Empire

Inalcik, Halil. 1994. *An Economic and Social History of the Ottoman Empire: 1300–1914.* Cambridge: Cambridge University Press. A detailed and analytical account of the social and economic history of the Ottoman Empire from the end of the sixteenth century to the beginning of the First World War.

Inalcik, Halil. 1995. *From Empire to Republic, Essays on Ottoman and Turkish Social History.* Istanbul: Isis Press. A collection of essays on a range of subjects such as Ottoman historiography, social structure of the Ottoman Empire, and the status of Jews under Ottoman system.

Inalcik, Halil. 1993. *The Middle East and the Balkans under the Ottoman Empire: Essays on Economy and Society.* Bloomington: Indiana University Turkish Studies. A collection of essays that examine the state, society, economy, and politics of the Ottoman Empire.

Issawi, Charles. 1980. *The Economic History of Turkey, 1800–1914.* Chicago: University of Chicago Press. A collection of primary texts and documents focusing on the economic transformation of the Ottoman Empire in the nineteenth and the first decade of the twentieth century.

Kasaba, Reşat. 1988. *The Ottoman Empire and the World Economy: The Nineteenth Century.* Albany: State University of New York Press. A study of the Ottoman economic transformation with a focus on the status and impact of the Christian capitalist class in the empire.

Owen, Roger. 1982. *The Middle East in the World Economy, 1800–1914.* New York: Meethuen. An economic history of the Middle East and the Ottoman Empire with a particular focus on the nineteenth and the first decade of the twentieth century.

Ottoman Rulers, Statesmen, and Scholars

Aksan, Virginia H. 1995. *An Ottoman Statesman in War and Peace: Ahmed Resmi Efendi, 1700–1783.* Leiden: E.J. Brill. A fascinating analysis of the Ottoman history and society during the eighteenth century through a discussion of the life and career of Ahmed Resmi Efendi who rose as a scribe (*katib*) to a high level official and an ambassador in the Ottoman central administration.

Alderson, AD. 1956. *Structure of the Ottoman Dynasty.* Oxford: Clarendon Press. This book discusses the genealogy of the Ottoman royal family and identifies the customs, rules, and the principles that regulated the relations among its members.

Çelebi, Evliya. 1991. *The Intimate Life of an Ottoman Statesman: Melek Ahmad Pasha, 1588–1662.* Translated by Robert Dankoff. Albany: State University of New York Press. A selection of passages from Evliya Celebi's Travels (*Siyahatname/ Seyahatnamesi*) that focus on the life of Celebi's patron, Melek Ahmed Paşa, who was an influential government official and military leader.

Djemal Pasha. 1973. *Memories of a Turkish Statesman, 1913–1919.* New York: Arno Press. The recollections of an important and controversial Young Turk leader who played a crucial role in Ottoman politics from 1913 to the end of the First World War.

Fleischer, Cornell H. 1996. *Bureaucrat and Intellectual in the Ottoman Empire: The historian Mustafa Âli (1541–1600).* Princeton: Princeton University Press. A fascinating study of the making of a sixteenth century Ottoman statesman, scholar, historian, and poet.

Reference Works

Bayerle, Gustav. 1997. *Pashas, Begs and Effendis: A Historical Dictionary of Titles and Terms in the Ottoman Empire.* Istanbul: Isis Press. A useful compilation and glossary of Ottoman historical terms.

Cicek, Kemal, ed. 2000. *The Great Ottoman Turkish Civilization,* 4 vols. Ankara: Yeni Turkiye. A four-volume study of the Ottoman Empire and its history, politics, culture and economy by a group of Turkish and non-Turkish scholars.

Hurewitz, J.C. 1956. *Diplomacy in the Near and Middle East: A Documentary Record: 1535–1914,* 2 vols. Princeton, NJ: D. Van Nostrand Company, Inc. A valuable collection of treaties and agreements in English translation that relate to the political and military developments in the Ottoman Empire and the rest of the Middle East from 1535 to 1956.

Somel, Selcuk Aksin. 2003. *Historical Dictionary of the Ottoman Empire.* Lanham, MD: Scarecrow Press. This book contains a detailed chronology of Ottoman history as well as entries on the sultans, influential statesmen, thinkers, intellectuals, events, and institutions that shaped the Ottoman Empire.

INDEX

About the Author

MEHRDAD KIA is Professor of Central and Southwest Asian History at the University of Montana.